lmes,
ective
ns

HOMAS

Published by
Devyn Press, Inc.
Louisville, KY 40241

Sherlock Holmes, Bridge Detective Returns

As indicated by the title, this is the sequel to "Sherlock Holmes, Bridge Detective" heralded as the "fun" bridge book of the year 1974.

Again the reader escapes into the wonderful world of Baker Street as the mighty Holmes continues to dazzle the kibitzers and his opponents in the "Challenge Match", the world's first, big, head-to-head bridge competition. But the Challenge Match, pitting Holmes and the good Doctor Watson against the social Betty Castle and politician Harry Skurry, does not occupy all of Holmes' time. He also solves six baffling mysteries, all comparable to "The Adventure of the Panamanian Girls" from the original, which was selected as one of the thirteen great bridge stories of all time.

In addition, the super sleuth bridge player wins "The London Cup" and engages in the first International Match of the world of bridge, all the while inventing bridge conventions. Any bridge player must have wondered from time to time from where the sophisticated style of the experts evolved. Finally we have the answer. It was Holmes, with his shrewd analytic mind, realizing the needs and filling them.

Walk back through the curtain of time and become a Holmes type detective a bridge detective, that is.

Note:

"Sherlock Holmes Bridge Detective Returns" comes to print, as did its predecessor, via the services of the sinister "Santa Monica Printers," an organization composed solely of descendents of Professor Moriarty's infamous ring. Their assistance was secured under duress and only by the author's threat of exposing unknown and heinous crimes of the late Professor. You think I jest? Let me reveal that Moriarty was evolving the short club just prior to meeting his doom in the hands of Sherlock Holmes at the falls of Reichenbach.

Computerized type provided by "Heath and Associates." Detailed research reveals that this group evolved from the crime syndicate of the Old Baron Dowson, dealt with sternly by Holmes in "The Case of the Mysterious Imprint." How singular that Holmes should return via the descendents of his sworn enemies.

However, the friends of Mr. Sherlock Holmes will be glad to know that he is alive and well and joins the author in wishing them good reading and good bridge.

Illustrations by Debbie Wilson

In rallying to the flag the original team that forged the first Sherlock Holmes Bridge Book, it was natural that we call once more on the talents of Debbie Wilson for illustrations. As readers of the original know, Miss Wilson is a youthful phenomenon. While in her mid-teens Debbie was turning out commercial art and shortly thereafter was an assistant animator on the full-length cartoon film, "Shinbone Alley", based on the Don Marquis stories. The position of staff artist for radio station KRLA followed along with freelance exploitation art and covers for various Hollywood Record Companies. On special assignment, she became the official portrait artist for the Pasadena Jr. Chamber of Commerce. All this before she was twenty of course.

To widen her horizons, Miss Wilson served as communications director for "Action Industries," in Dallas and returning to California she became Production Artist for Welsh Graphics. As a side-line, Debbie makes signs for industrial firms and restaurants, sandblasting and carving them. The final result is a Wilson product from start to finish.

There must be something to be said for heredity since John Wilson, noted animator and president of "Fine Arts Films," is Daddy.

Though not a bridge player, Debbie is a Holmes fancier being more than a little partial to the brilliant Irene Adler of "A Scandal in Bohemia" fame.

About the Author
an Interview

QUESTION: Mr. Thomas, you were formerly of the entertainment profession?

ANSWER: Yes, I started on the New York stage. Very young I might add. One of my first plays was "Thunder on the Left" adapted from the Christopher Morley novel. Mr. Morley was one of the founders of The Baker Street Irregulars. It was through him that I became interested in Mr. Sherlock Holmes.

QUESTION: But you continued as an actor?

ANSWER: Yes. In those days they wrote awfully good parts for children. I was starred in 12 Broadway shows. R.K.O. bought the picture rights to one of them. "Wednesday's Child," which was the greatest boy part ever written. The movie version was my first motion picture.

QUESTION: How many movies did you make?

ANSWER: Over thirty major studio productions. Then came the war. That involved me for five years.

QUESTION: Did you return to pictures?

ANSWER: No. They weren't the same afterwards. I did over five thousand radio programs from New York and pioneered in live television.

QUESTION: Ah yes, you were "Tom Corbett, Space Cadet" for how many years?

ANSWER: Five years on national TV. I guess if I added all the TV shows up they would total over a thousand. Of course, I was writing at this time as well. Tom Corbett, True Story, NBC-T.V., Theatre Five, ABC.

QUESTION: Then what happened?

ANSWER: I retired. The Broadway stage had changed. The Major Picture Studios were gone. TV had become midget movies. I decided I had lived through part of the golden age and had been far more lucky than most.

QUESTION: How did you come to bridge?

ANSWER: I started playing when I was eight. Teaching just happened. There I was retired . . . playing golf, tournament bridge and chasing girls. It was great. Suddenly, I was teaching the Buffum and Robinson Store chains simultaneously with around 18,000 students a year.

QUESTION: Do you still do this?

ANSWER: Not as much. I teach at Hinshaws Arcadia and the Virginia Country Club and private classes. Eight a week on an average. The magazine takes a lot of time.

QUESTION: What magazine?

ANSWER: "The Quarterly." I've been the Editor and Publisher since 1969. Then, there are the books.

QUESTION: How many books have you written?

ANSWER: Three bridge books. Lots of articles and stories, of course.

QUESTION: How about the golf and . . . err . . . other things?

ANSWER: No time.

QUESTION: You gave all that up? Why?

ANSWER: Two things. The look is one. It's that look you see in a student's eyes when you know that they know. It's a thrill. Then there's my traveling.

QUESTION: You travel around the country a lot?

ANSWER: No. I travel in time. I live in Hollywood in a California skyscraper. On a clear night I can see as far as Long Beach. I do a lot of time traveling then. I find I'm doing it a lot in the day now too.

QUESTION: You travel *in time*? *Where*?

ANSWER: To London, of course. To gas lit streets, hansom cabs and Holmes, fresh on the scent of a wrong doing. At first it seems a little primitive but it gets to you after awhile. Nowdays, we have everything. However, people don't seem to be happy. But they are back there. Mrs. Hudson, bless her heart, works awfully hard. So does Billy the Page Boy and Lestrade and Gregson. But somehow they all seem happy and contented. They don't have too much you know, by our standards. But they have peace of mind. The World of Baker Street is a wondrous place.

QUESTION: I see.

ANSWER: I don't think you do, really. You sort of have to experience it. Do you have any more questions?

QUESTION: Just one! Where are you going now?

ANSWER: Back to Baker Street. So long.

DEDICATION

This book is dedicated, in friendship, to
he who was there at the very beginning.
GEORGE GOODEN, of course.
Still the greatest bridge teacher of them all.

TABLE OF CONTENTS

INTRODUCTION

As was revealed in "Sherlock Holmes, Bridge Detective;" the famous dispatch box which had rested so long in the vaults of Cox's Bank at Charing Cross was finally opened according to the will of John H. Watson, M.D. Among the memorabilia dealing with that most unusual of men, Mr. Sherlock Holmes, was Watson's detailed "Diary of the Challenge Match" which proved that Holmes was a bridge player.

It was the feeling of your author that this unrevealed facet in the life of the master sleuth would be astonishing news to both bridge players and followers of the incomparable Holmes.

Let us be completely frank. No one was even surprised!

Bridge experts, social players and aficionados of the great detective's career were universal in their feeling of "What else?"

Victor Mollo; great British bridge expert, journalist and author expressed the consensus succinctly: "How obvious that Holmes, master of inference and deduction, should have been attracted to bridge."

Ira Corn, Jr., creator and captain of the twice world champion "Aces" team stated in his syndicated column: "This refreshing new book deals with a series of interesting hands from the challenge match played by Holmes and Watson. This excellent work is a 'fun' book designed to instruct the reader regarding bridge reasoning."

The nonpareil B. Jay Becker, bridge editor for King Features Syndicate commented: "It would seem that Arthur Conan Doyle has somehow or other been brought back to life with this fascinating collection of hands."

Note that none of these gentlemen of world renown expressed the slightest amazement that Holmes was intrigued by the greatest of games. After due consideration, your author must agree. Show me a talented bridge player of either sex or any nationality or coloration and you reveal a person who must, perforce, think like a detective.

A number of questions from readers influenced this publication of a second book dealing with adventures of Sherlock Holmes relative to bridge and other things. The most common point of interest was the unknown cases of Holmes brought to light by the "Diary."

Within these pages are six Holmes novelettes previously unpublished because of their association with bridge or due to other considerations which will become glaringly obvious.

In the original Holmes bridge book, hands were selected for their individual interest. In this sequel, I have attempted to group hands dealing with certain innovations which Holmes introduced to the bridge world of his day. Many references to the seeming omnipotence of the great sleuth regarding the trends which modern bridge would follow prompted this method of presentation. While Holmes played in the dawn of modern bridge, his methods were certainly not antediluvian.

One other point should be made. The volume of Watson's words regarding the exploits of Holmes was simply amazing. His diligence in recording matters dealing with the Challenge Match and bridge in general was equal to his carefully compiled case histories of the detective. In the study of his output, your author was greatly assisted by The American Bridge Teachers' Association, a completely non-profit organization devoted to the promotion of better bridge teaching throughout the world. I must cite certain members in particular who were especially helpful: Catherine Jourdan, Betty Lind and William Casey Kozak. Also Nicholas Barouk who is now playing in a bigger game.

If following the bridge career of the super sleuth turns you into a bridge playing detective, you will play the better for it. But bridge is a game and games are created to be enjoyed.

My sincerest hope is that you will enjoy yourself as you follow the adventures of Holmes at the bridge table and elsewhere.

Frank Thomas
1975

A telegram from Shaw.

THE MYSTERY OF THE TWO CLUBS

We return to the historic Challenge Match fairly late of a Friday afternoon. The weather was mild outside the Grosvenor Square Bridge Club considering the time of year. Despite this fact, and the upcoming week-end, the main card room of the club was jammed with kibitzers intent on the progress of the first head-to-head match in the history of modern bridge. Originally, the experienced team of Betty Castle and Harry Skurry had been established as heavy favorites at six to one. However, the dark horse emergence of Sherlock Holmes, as a master player and theorist, had whittled down the odds which now stood with the bookmakers at six to five, take your pick. The very social Betty and her pudgy politician partner knew they were involved in the fight of their life. The air at the sedate bridge club was charged, daily, with the excitement one might expect at the start of the running for the Wessex Cup.

Considering the hour and the fact that neither side was vulnerable, it was mutually agreed that when either side scored a game it would signal the conclusion of the day's play. Then this interesting hand was dealt.

TO BE OR NOT TO BE

```
                      WATSON
                      ♠ 8 5 3
                      ♡ J 8
                      ◇ A 10 9
                      ♣ A Q J 10 6

SKURRY                                    CASTLE
♠ 9 7 6                                   ♠ A 4
♡ K Q 10 3                                ♡ A 7 5 4 2
◇ 8 5 2                                   ◇ J 7 6 4 3
♣ 7 3 2                                   ♣ 9

                      HOLMES (Dealer)
                      ♠ K Q J 10 2
                      ♡ 9 6
                      ◇ K Q
                      ♣ K 8 5 4
```

CHALLENGE MATCH BIDDING: (neither side vulnerable)

Holmes	Skurry	Watson	Castle
1S	pass	2C	pass
3C	pass	3S	pass
4S	pass	pass	pass

Holmes evaluated his opening bid as slightly better than minimum because of the excellent texture of his suit. Watson's two club response was based on ample values. Now Holmes chose to raise his partner's suit as a forward-going action. Watson tested Holmes' spades by offering a belated raise and the great detective went to game.

Harry Skurry led the heart king. Study Betty Castle's hand and plan your defense.

THE PLAY

As Skurry's heart king hit the table and dummy's ominous club suit was revealed, Betty's lips tightened slightly and her busy mind conceived a prize bit of opponent-frustration. Holmes played the heart eight from dummy and Betty rose with her heart ace, taking the trick. Now she returned her club nine. Holmes, well-knowing Betty's capabilities, immediately realized that she must hold the trump ace and was setting up a ruffing trick in clubs. Holmes captured the club nine with dummy's queen. He now played the diamond nine from dummy to his queen of the suit. Next came the diamond king which Holmes overtook with dummy's ace as there was a series of quick glances among the onlookers. Now the sleuth played the diamond ten from dummy. When Betty covered with her jack, Holmes discarded his heart nine.

With two tricks in her possession and one sure to come with the trump ace, Betty returned a low heart to Skurry's known queen. But Holmes had cut this communication line and trumped low so Harry's queen was not played after all. Now the detective finally went to work on trumps, leading the spade king. Betty took the trick and returned a diamond and Holmes trumped. Two rounds of spades extracted the outstanding cards in the suit and Holmes claimed the remainder of the tricks via his overpowering club holding.

"The best laid plans," said Betty Castle with a moue.

"Your plan was splendid, partner," said Skurry. "When I saw your overtake on the first trick and the club return, I thought we had Holmes for sure. A spade lead puts you in again and a heart to my queen allows me to lead the second club for the ruff that sets the contract."

"Fortunately, my partner's vision was excellent as well," said Watson immediately.

Sherlock Holmes had a question. "Then you would have preferred to be declarer on this holding, Harry?"

"The score I am entering in your favor indicates that I would have." Skurry's voice was somewhat tart.

"Well, since we are finished for the day, let us quickly replay this hand and give you your wish."

Holmes faced the cards upwards and recreated the hands but altered their position at the table.

```
                WATSON
                ♠ 9 7 6
                ♡ K Q 10 3
                ◇ 8 5 2
                ♣ 7 3 2
SKURRY                              CASTLE
♠ K Q J 10 2                        ♠ 8 5 3
♡ 9 6                               ♡ J 8
◇ K Q                               ◇ A 10 9
♣ K 8 5 4                           ♣ A Q J 10 6
                HOLMES
                ♠ A 4
                ♡ A 7 5 4 2
                ◇ J 7 6 4 3
                ♣ 9
```

"Now," said Holmes, "you are playing the hand at four spades and Watson leads the heart king. Following Betty's thoughtful defense, I overtake the trick with my ace and return a club."

Skurry's expression indicated that he intended to humor his temporarily eccentric opponent.

"I take the trick in dummy, lead a low diamond to my king" he said, "and return the queen of diamonds which I overtake with dummy's ace." He did so. "Now I lead the diamond 10 and when you cover with the jack, I discard my remaining heart card."

"Splendid," said Holmes. "I now return a diamond."

"Which I ruff with my ten of spades to prevent an overruff. Now I lead the spade king," said Skurry firmly.

"Which I take with my ace," responded Holmes, "and play my fifth diamond."

"I ruff with my spade jack, play the spade queen and . . . and . . ."

Skurry's voice dwindled to a halt and a sad expression enveloped his face.

"And Watson's spade nine proves to be the setting trick," concluded Holmes. "Now where would you rather be with this holding?"

"On defense," admitted the politician sheepishly.

"Let me contest your choice again," responded Holmes, with a twinkle in his eyes. "Against this line of defense, Watson and I go down one for fifty points. But observe that the declarer hand holds one hundred honors so the deal still results in a fifty point profit."

The day's play ended in a roar of laughter in which Skurry had the good grace to join.

Departing from the club, Holmes had a comment for his partner which proved prophetic.

"When the defense holds a control card in the opponents' trump suit, it is frequently possible to wreak havoc with a reasonable contract."

The truth of Holmes' idea was particularly apparent when he and Watson become involved in the first international match, as we shall learn anon.

It was still daylight when Holmes and Watson descended from the hansom cab which had brought them from the Grosvenor Square Bridge Club to 221B Baker Street. Neither had a chance to use his key as the door to the famous domicile, owned by that most patient and loyal Mrs. Hudson, burst open revealing Billy. The Page Boy had evidently been watching for their arrival from within. His face mirrored concern as he extended a telegram towards the great detective.

"Mr. 'Olmes — I'm that put out."

"About a telegram, Billy? We receive lots of those, goodness knows." Holmes' voice was soothing.

"And send a few as well," thought Watson to himself.

"But, sir, I don't know when this 'ere missive came." By now, Billy was closing the door behind Holmes and Watson. "Mrs. 'Udson didn't 'ear the bell bein' in back cleanin' the 'ole bleedin' afternoon and I was not on ta premises." Billy fancied words like "missive" and "premises" which he had acquired from Baker Street's two most famous residents.

The concerned page boy now picked up a bulky package from the hall table.

"Then, just 'afore you come, this package arrived. The bloke wot brought it said it 'ad been sent by train from Shaw wiv instructions to be delivered by special messenger on arrival."

"Perhaps the telegram will explain the package," said Holmes, mounting the stairs. "Best come up with us, Billy, as fast action may be called for."

Within the famous suite of rooms shared by Holmes and Watson the great detective opened the telegram which his eyes devoured rapidly.

"No mystery here," he said. "Billy, have a hansom downstairs in fifteen minutes. Then hustle over to the telegraph office and send a message to Constable Bennett, Police Station, Shaw. Leaving five-thirty from Paddington. Holmes." The detective looked at Billy keenly. "You can remember that, I'm sure."

Billy tapped his head with a forefinger. "Word for word, Mr. 'Olmes. I'm on me way." Billy took what he called "the detectin' business" seriously.

As the door closed behind the page boy, Holmes turned to Watson.

"Can you throw some things in a bag quickly, ol' boy? I have had some previous dealings with one John Bennett who is the constable in Shaw. It is a little country town in Herefordshire. Bennett is experiencing considerable difficulties relative to the Trewlaney matter and requests assistance."

Watson needed no urging. His army experience with the Northumberland Fusiliers had made him a prompt traveler. It was but a short time later that both Watson and Holmes were aboard the five-thirty at Paddington. Holmes, with his long, gray traveling-cloak and cloth cap, disposed of a small valise and placed the bulky package, which had just made the same trip in reverse, alongside him on the seat. Watson put a somewhat larger bag in the luggage rack and they both settled down for their trip to Herefordshire.

As the train pulled out, Watson lit up a cigar. Soon they were traveling westward at fifty miles an hour and far removed from their familiar surroundings.

"Perhaps you will explain the Trewlaney matter to me," suggested the doctor, "as well as that package evidently sent to us in some haste."

"Fortunately, I have a grip of the essential facts of the Trewlaney case," replied Holmes. "This parcel contains the recent papers from the area which we can study on the way down. The London press made very brief reference to the affair. I can tell you that Martin Trewlaney, a banker by trade, was murdered while alone in his house in Shaw. The cause of death was a severe blow by a blunt weapon on the back of his head. As I understand it, an adopted son, Charles Trewlaney, is in custody now on suspicion of murder. Bennett's telegram made reference to the Silver Blaze affair but did not explain the connection. Since we are fortunate in having this carriage to ourselves, I suggest we go through these country journals and see what additional facts we can uncover. In the bucolic surroundings of Herefordshire, a murder is bound to capture a major portion of the newsprint."

And so Watson and Holmes buried themselves in the contents of the package sent by Constable Bennett for their perusal on their lengthy trip. Watson read steadily, searching for some unusual fact which might excite an idea in Holmes' mind. Holmes read at intervals, interrupted by pauses for reflection, as though arranging the facts. They were long past Reading when Watson broke the silence.

"Here's something that might be of interest, Holmes. A complete coverage of Charles Trewlaney's testimony before the Coroner's Court of Inquiry."

"I've already read another account but let us see what your paper has to offer," said Holmes.

As Holmes pored over the newspaper Watson handed him, the doctor leaned back for a moment to relax. Darkness had long since fallen. The train was steaming through the Stroud Valley and approaching the Severn river when Watson's head jerked upwards with a start and he realized that he had dozed off. Holmes was gazing out the window at the passing darkness. There was little to see outside the speeding train and what there was Holmes was not conscious of. His eyes had that deep, introspective look which signified that his mercurial brain was flitting over pieces of the puzzle and fitting them into a mosaic of the mind.

Sensing Watson's awakening, the master sleuth turned towards his friend and companion of so many adventures with a slow smile. "Some sleep may prove of future benefit," be said. "We may very well have busy times ahead of us."

Watson indicated the newspapers scattered over the compartment. "Has anything suggested itself to you, Holmes?"

"At the moment I'm suffering from a plethora of surmise, conjecture, and hypothesis. Let us see what we have been able to discover up to this time."

The great detective leaned back in his seat, his eyes on the ceiling and his words wandered over the facts at their disposal.

"Martin Trewlaney was a widower who lived with his adopted son, Charles. There had been indications of a recent strain in their relations, a point which the coroner's inquest did not pursue to any appreciable depth. It was the banker's habit to sit before the fire in his study of an evening reading the works of Thackeray. Death was definitely established as occurring between the hours of eight and ten. Constable Bennett evidently was able to secure a forensic medicine expert promptly. The body was discovered at eleven in the evening by Charles Trewlaney who stated that he had just returned from Hereford where he had been on business. According to his testimony, his adopted father was seated in his customary chair, his head slumped forward from the fatal blow. The windows of the room were closed but not locked. Now, Charles Trewlaney contended that he had just arrived on the ten forty-five from Hereford. However, in counter-testimony, the station master at Shaw states that he definitely saw him arrive previously on the six o'clock special. It was the testimony of the station master and some other evidence that resulted in Charles Trewlaney's receiving a verdict of "suspicion of murder" at the inquest. Pending further investigation, the case is to go before the magistrates in Hereford."

"What 'other evidence' do you refer to, Holmes?"

"Possibly, the papers you read stated there were two occupants in the Trewlaney household. The cook and maid were not in residence and left, as was their custom, at seven. This fact was proven by definite evidence. However, one of the papers, the 'Ross Inquirer', I believe, was more complete and noted the presence of a third occupant."

From Paddington to Shaw.

Watson registered amazement. "How could this fact go unrecorded elsewhere?"

"Martin Trewlaney had a dog, Lama by name. The animal and the banker were inseparable. The old gentleman even took him to his bank office with him. Now I understand Constable Bennett's reference to the Silver Blaze affair."

"Of course, said Watson, with a flood of understanding. "The dog that didn't bark in the night."

Holmes registered ennui. "Dear me, Watson, that was but a trivial example of observation and inference. By the time you finished making our racehorse adventure public, you had it sounding like a veritable triumph of deductive reasoning."

Watson was on firm ground. While he knew that Holmes consistently contended that he, Watson, tended to over-dramatize the detective's superb reasoning powers, he also knew that Holmes secretly was delighted at having his *métier* appreciated and applauded.

"May I remind you, my dear Holmes, that no one else drew the inference which you did from the dog's behavior? Had you not, the great Silver Blaze might never have been found. But to return to the Trewlaney affair, I see the similarity now. Since the dog, Lama, and his master were constantly together, no doubt the canine was in the murder room."

16

"He was," agreed Holmes. "You will recall that the banker was seated and struck from behind. The outer doors to the house were not locked. Anyone might have entered and the elderly gentleman could well have been dozing in his chair. But the prosecution will contend that had a stranger entered the house, the dog would have certainly alerted his master to the fact. However, Charles Trewlaney was no stranger. Hence, it is the dog that may weave the rope that hangs him for murder."

Watson had a puzzled expression. "My dear Holmes, instead of enjoying a quiet dinner we have two middle-aged men flying westward on what seems to be an open and shut case." ."

"Ah, but there is always a little more than meets the eye. I deduce this partially from lightly-touched items in the news accounts and also from the fact that Constable Bennett sent a plea for assistance. John Bennett, though buried in a backwater village, has carefully schooled himself in the latest methods of crime detection. I have carried on an intermittent correspondence with him for some time. The constable is alert and efficient. If he feels there are doubts and unresolved elements relative to this homicide, I am prepared to 'go along with him' is, I believe, the popular expression. Also, it would seem that the peaceful hamlet of Shaw was, in times gone by, the scene of deep-seated enmities and bloodshed. But these facets will be polished for us by the good constable upon our arrival."

When the train halted at the small station of Shaw, Holmes and Watson were the only travelers to alight. A tall individual in a square-cut uniform coat with hat, who had been pacing the station platform, hurried to their side.

"Mr. Holmes," he said, "it is certainly a pleasure."

"It has been a while, Bennett," stated Holmes. "This is my associate, Doctor Watson."

As Watson shook hands with the Constable, he wondered under what circumstances this country policeman and Holmes had met previously, but no mention of this incident from the past was made.

"I have rooms for you at 'The Queens Arms' which is our only inn hereabouts.

It is but a short distance from here. The proprietor's wife is laying out a cold supper for you. Considering your time of departure from London, I would imagine you could both do with a bite."

As Holmes and Watson admitted to this fact, Bennett took the larger suitcase from Watson and led them down the street. It was but a short time later that they were in a pleasant room in the inn enjoying some excellent cold roast beef and a very tasty game pie.

Constable Bennett joined Holmes and Watson in a yard of stout and lit a cigar. As he ignited it and drew a first puff, he snatched the cigar from his mouth with an exclamation of surprise.

"How strange that I should decide to smoke this at such a time since it was a gift from the murdered man!"

"An Indian cigar," commented Holmes, "of the type rolled in Amsterdam."

The antecedents of the cigar were of no interest to Watson but he did note that it was a particularly strong one even though he was a smoker himself.

"As to the murder, gentlemen," said Bennett, "I trust the journals I sent provided some information."

"In outline form," was Holmes' response. "I was immediately intrigued by the fact that you were able to establish the time of death as between eight and ten on the fatal night."

"Fortunate happenstance," replied the Constable. "At eleven, young Charles Trewlaney came bolting out of his adopted father's house and almost ran into my arms. I was making a final round of the night just to make sure things were in order. I had just seen Doctor Devon Almont right here in the Queens Arms in the pub."

"Almont?" asked Watson, with considerable surprise.

"He retired two years ago and came to live here," explained Bennett.

"I didn't know that. Naturally, I've read his articles in 'The Lancet' with great interest."

"You were indeed fortunate, Bennett," stated Holmes, "to have one of the foremost pathologists in the world at your beck and call."

"I certainly beckoned," replied Bennett. "When young Charles told me that he had found Martin Trewlaney with his skull crushed, I hightailed it over here and got Doctor Almont. Then the three of us returned to the Trewlany house. Shaw is a small community and we were in the murder room within a short time. Doctor Almont checked the coagulation of blood on the back of the murdered man's head and tested the rigidity of the body and delivered the opinion that the deed had been done between eight and ten."

"Almont's opinion would be accepted by any jury. In conjunction with Alexandre Lacassagne of France, he has made giant contributions to the advancement of forensic medicine." Holmes thought for a moment. "If young Trewlaney had just arrived from Hereford, he is in the clear, but I understand the station master contested this."

Bennett nodded. "Pierce is a friend of young Charles who is well-liked by one and all. He saw the boy get off the last carriage of the six o'clock. It meant nothing to him at the time but at the inquest he had to tell what he had seen."

"Unwillingly," said Holmes. "That lends all the more credence to his words. Perhaps you had better relate what occurred, Bennett."

The constable's eyes narrowed in thought as though not wishing to overlook a single fact.

"Charles was in a state of semi-shock, but after discovering the body, he had the presence of mind to close the door to the study before leaving the house. As I mentioned, the three of us returned there promptly. Upon opening the study door, we found everything as Charles had hastily related to me. Martin Trewlaney was slumped in his chair in front of the fireplace. The right side of his skull was a sight indeed."

"The back of the skull, according to the newspapers," mentioned Holmes.

"That is correct."

"And the dog, Lama? He was still in the room?"

This point seemed of special interest to Holmes.

"Yes, sir, responded Bennet. "When Charles closed the door behind him, how could the little fellow get out?"

"That is my point, or, at least, a point of puzzlement." The detective chewed reflectively on a piece of beef. "Charles Trewlaney testified that when he returned to his home, he found the door to the study closed. For his own sake, he might much better have said that the door was open. Had this been the case, the possibility could have existed that the dog was in some other part of the house when the fatal blow was struck."

"That bothered me also," replied the Constable.

"Another thought," continued Holmes. "From your description and that in the papers, Trewlaney's skull had been shattered from behind and very severely. Would not a blow of such strength have driven the body from the chair?"

"Not necessarily." It was Watson who responded to this idea. "It was mentioned that the corpse was well beyond the three score and ten. At that age, bones tend to become more fragile. The blow need not have been delivered with great strength."

"A good point, my dear Watson."

Bennett continued. "Whatever the weapon was, we did not find it. After inspecting the wound in greater detail, Doctor Almont delivered the opinion that it was caused by a club or stave perhaps but definitely of wood. Lama was very nervous and whining but Charles was able to quiet him. A book was on the floor, open, as though it had fallen from Martin's hands."

"Which it probably had," reflected Holmes.

"There was a half-consumed cigar in a tray by the chair. I believe that it was in the tray and lit when Martin was killed. It looked like it had gone out of its own volition."

"Now that is interesting," said Holmes. "I should have guessed the victim was a smoker since he made you a gift of a cigar."

"Twas the same type that I'm smoking right now," replied Bennett. "Martin had them sent to him from Amsterdam, as you divined, Mr. Holmes."

"What else can you tell us, Bennett?" asked Holmes.

"Well, sir, the maid and cook had left at seven and a number of people saw them crossing the town square at that time. They both have families who testified that they returned home at their regular time and stayed there the entire night."

"So," said the great detective, "the murdered man was alone and someone, anyone, could have entered the house."

"For a fact," agreed Bennett. "We don't lock doors in Shaw since crime, as such, really doesn't exist. Oh, occasionally a couple of sheep are missing but they always turn up. After paydays, a few of our local cut-ups drain the bottle a mite too deep and I have to make motions like a policeman but that's about the whole of it. Until now," he added.

"But it was not always thus," prompted Holmes.

"Well, sir, now we go back a ways, long before my time. It was in the days of Monks Holes and the religious wars and this was not the peaceful countryside it is now. Martin Trewlaney was childless and adopted Charles who was a foundling. There is another resident, Horace Ledbetter, who has a farm on the outskirts. He is the last of his family as well. He has a niece, Agnes Bisbee, who lives with him but she is the daughter of his dead wife's sister and no blood kin. The local feed and grain store belongs to Vincent Staley who never did marry. 'Tis said he has some relatives in Lancashire but I don't know that for a fact. But it is a fact that at one time all three of the families were large ones and owned a lot of the land in these parts. It is hard to put a finger on what started it all. Some say that one of the Staleys was a wild lad with a taste for liquor and an eye for lassies. He was supposed to have been riding through the countryside and came upon one of the Ledbetter girls and had his way with her. The next thing was the Staley estate was attacked in force by the Ledbetters and it was a pitching battle with a lot of bodies that never rose again. How the Trewlaneys got into it is also a mite vague due to the passage of time. One story is that the oldest Trewlaney tried to make peace between the two families and was cut down by mistake. Whatever the reasons, the three families went after each other with a vengeance. 'Twas like one of those Scottish feuds one hears of that went on so long that the original cause is unknown."

To Holmes' complete surprise, Watson advanced an opinion regarding this.

"Possibly, you are referring to the Sutherland-MacKaye Feud which continued for seven hundred years. However, the cause is known. The two clans went to war due to an argument as to which one had been appointed by the king to defend the north against the Dane. This local bloodletting sounds more like the Hatfield-McCoy affair which occurred in the southern United States. Or, perhaps, the Lincoln County War which was in the American west." As both Bennett and Holmes stared at him, Watson amended his last statement. "No, the Lincoln County Cattle War was of far shorter duration than the conflict you describe. However, it did produce William Bonney, known as "Billy the Kid.' "

Holmes' eyes were almost glazed. "Watson, I never dreamed you were such a fount of wisdom regarding feuds and family strife."

"Well . . . I . . "Watson searched for words. "It just happened to be a subject that interested me at one time."

"Obviously," commented Constable Bennett. "In any case, the Trewlaneys and the Ledbetters and the Staleys had a real go at it and the war continued from father to son. When law finally came, it was not a case of their drawing swords on sight but there were a lot of disappearances and unusual deaths. Finally, they whittled each other down so much there was not enough left to fight. But it is a fact that Martin Trewlaney, Horace Ledbetter, and Vincent Staley hated each other from childhood and their feeling did not mellow with the coming of age.'

"What a strange saga," commented Watson.

"But definitely connected with the death of Martin Trewlaney. It gives us two potential suspects with more motive for murder than most assassins might have," was Holmes' comment.

Holmes seemed content with the preliminary review of facts. Now he rose to his feet restlessly. Gone was the quiet thinker and logician of Baker Street and, instead, there was the great detective intent on the chase. His eyes shone with a steely glitter and his whole whipcord body seemed to cry for action.

"The hour is late," said Holmes, "but is it possible for us to examine the Trewlaney house now?"

"I was in hopes you would suggest it," stated Constable Bennett. "Being a bachelor, it was with no effort that I have been staying there to make sure that sensation-seekers don't disturb the premises."

By the simple process of leaving "The Queens Arms" and crossing the town square, Bennett and the Baker Street twosome found themselves at the door of a large victorian mansion set well back from the tree-shrouded street. No lights were visible in the small village and the silence was broken only by the sound of night crickets and the infrequent hoot of a distant owl. The residents of Shaw were obviously of an "early to bed" philosophy. However, as the trio approached the house, their arrival was signalled by a series of excited barks.

"Lama," said Constable Bennett. "The maid keeps the place in trim till there is a disposition of the estate and together we try and take care of the little tyke."

As he unlocked and opened the outer portal, a small terrier with a long, heavy coat rushed around them with diligent barks. Bennett was a familiar story and the little dog sniffed at Holmes' and Watson's boots to learn what he could. Evidently he detected nothing of a suspicious nature and preceded them within. As Bennett led Watson through the large hall towards a side door, Holmes paused to let the dog smell his hand and then took the liberty of stroking the long hair, a gesture of familiarity which found no resentment from the terrier. Allowing Lama to show him the way, Holmes joined his friends in the room where Martin Trewlaney had breathed his last.

The study, like the house itself, was of considerable age and Holmes admired the beautiful wood paneling on the walls which must have dated back to the time of Cromwell or before. Bennett carefully explained that nothing had been moved though the maid had insisted on opening the windows and airing out the area. Even so, Watson could still detect, faintly, the acrid odor of the Indian cigars which the deceased was evidently addicted to. It was a man's room with some trophies of the chase on the walls. An ancient suit of armor was standing in one corner.

Holmes inspected the chair in which Trewlaney had been sitting, noted the attendent ashtray and, finally, seated himself in the chair. An unusual affinity seemed to have sprung up between Lama and the great detective. After some small urging and a couple of suggestive pats on his knee, Holmes was able to coax the creature to hop up onto his lap where the little fellow made himself quite comfortable and appeared to go to sleep. Holmes remained immobile so as not to disturb the dog as he offered a suggestion.

"I am given to understand that at London's Globe Theatre and similar places where melodrama is a staple part of the diet, the investigator is forever re-creating the crime. Let us attempt the same procedures, casting you, Watson, in the sinister role of assailant unknown."

"As you wish, Holmes," replied the doctor, well knowing that the little games which his friend chose to play frequently climaxed in amazing revelations. "What actions are called for in your manuscript?"

"You approach me from the door — stealthily, of course." Watson did so. "Now, I am sitting here, as Trewlaney naturally, with a lighted cigar. I take a puff and place the cigar in the ashtray, of necessity with my right hand so, presumably, my left hand is holding a book."

"The fallen book was on the left side of the chair," interjected Bennett.

Holmes continued his fantasy. "Watson, you have a wooden weapon in your hand and you deliver a resounding whack to the back of my head." In dumb show, Watson followed directions. "Now," continued Holmes, "I presume that the path of the blow which you just delivered would bash me on the right side somewhat even though you are directly behind me since you happen to be right-handed."

"You are correct, Holmes," agreed his medical confrere.

A keen glance from Holmes prompted Bennett to produce a pocket notebook which he riffled quickly and then read from.

"The right occipital and parietal bones of the victim's skull were shattered by a blow from a heavy weapon." He flipped his notebook shut. "That was the statement of Doctor Devon Almont," he continued.

There was a sardonic smile on the detective's face. "And, my dear Bennett, whilst you made reference to the Silver Blaze incident, I rather fancy that you considered another matter with which I was once occupied. May I hazard the guess that young Charles Trewlaney is left-handed."

The constable nodded, with a gleam of admiration in his eyes.

"I did not wish to muddle your thought process with my own ideas, but you have arrived, unerringly, at the point that has bothered me."

"I'm delighted that you are both in agreement," said Watson, with a touch of asperity in his voice. "Would someone explain this to me?"

"Black Jack of Ballarat," quoted Holmes. "Come now, Watson, if you were left-handed would you have delivered the same blow which you just did in dumb show?"

"Of course not," said Watson. "How stupid of me." His mind flashed back to another time and a baffling mystery which had also taken place in rural surroundings. "But wait just a minute," he continued, prompted by another thought. "If Charles is ruled out as the murderer, we are left with Horace Ledbetter and Vincent Staley as suspects. Would the dog now dozing in your lap, Holmes, have allowed either of them to enter the house, much less this room, without raising a row?" The doctor turned to Constable Bennett. "What breed of canine is Lama anyway? I don't recall ever seeing one like him before."

"Mostly terrier, I would imagine," was Bennett's answer. "A mixed breed."

"Let me disagree on that point," stated Holmes.

Suddenly, while gently stroking the subject under discussion, Holmes' lips pursed and he emitted a shrill whistle. The dog lay undisturbed on his lap.

"Good heavens, Holmes," stammered Watson, "what was that for?"

"Merely an experiment, ol' boy." Holmes' glance returned to Bennett. "As to Lama's ancestry, let me assure you that he is a pure bred and blue blood indeed. As Watson well knows, following the incident at Reichenback Fall, I placed myself in voluntary exile for several years since two most vindictive enemies of mine, who were part of Professor Moriarty's gang, were still at liberty. During that period I traveled to Tibet and visited Lhassa to confer with the head lama. Sitting in my lap, gentlemen, is a Lhasa-Apso, also known as a Tibetan terrier. They are bred in that country as watchdogs. During my travels, I suggested that the breed might be introduced to England, but others, more knowledgeable on the subject, felt that our lowlands might not prove suitable to the strain. Anywhere in England is the lowlands to Lama here, since his native habitat is at sixteen thousand feet above sea level. However, our comparatively heavy atmosphere doesn't seem to have bothered this little chap so perhaps my original thought was not without merit."

"This is all very interesting, Holmes," said Watson, "but you still haven't answered my question."

"The Lhasa-Apso is peculiar in that it is the only dog, to my knowledge, which frequently has blue eyes. Oh, occasionally a Dalmatian may have one blue eye but not two. Consider for a moment, both of you, how many blue-eyed dogs either of you have seen."

Watson and Bennett exchanged a glance and then a shrug. "I don't usually make note of the color of a dog's eyes," said the Constable, "but I daresay you are right, Mr. Holmes."

"Both of Lama's eyes are blue," stated Holmes, as though this brought the matter to an end.

"For the life of me," persisted Watson, "I fail to see what the little fellow's eye coloration has to do with this case."

"Blue-eyed dogs are very subject to congenital defects, Watson. The most common one is deafness. Lama is as deaf as a post."

"But he barked his head off when we arrived," said Watson.

"His sense of smell, dear boy, more acute in a canine than his sense of hearing. On the night of the murder, I picture Lama peacefully asleep at his master's feet in his soundless world. You noted, of course, that my shrill whistle of a moment ago did not even make him flinch. Trewlaney was smoking one of his Indian cigars, the odor of which Lama has become unwillingly accustomed to through the passage of time. But the cigar smell effectively smothered the dog's ability to raise a scent. The acrid smoke anesthetized Lama's olfactory sense. Through no fault of his own, the poor dog was completely incapable of performing the task which he was bred to do. Namely, to be a good watchdog."

"That does it," snapped Bennett. "I knew young Charles couldn't have been the culprit."

"So," mused Watson, "we are back to Horace Ledbetter and Vincent Staley, both of whom suffer from congenital defects themselves. Namely, a blind hatred of each other and of Martin Trewlaney."

"Very well put, Watson," said Holmes, with approval. "However, the hatred had existed for decades. What fanned the spark into flame at this particular time?"

"I can give you one theory, Mr. Holmes," said the Constable. "In a village like Shaw, little happens that isn't public knowledge promptly. Feed and grain is not the business it once was in these parts. Vincent Staley owed the bank a considerable amount. He had asked for an extension which, due to Martin Trewlaney, was denied. Staley is on the brink of ruin."

"Excellent, Bennett," said the great detective. "Now you give us a motive of the moment, a tool to force a man over that precipice called 'desperate action'." The sleuth of Baker Street was thoughtful for a quiet time. "But we are still in the tender area of circumstantial evidence. How about Horace Ledbetter, the other prime suspect?"

"Just prior to the inquest, I rode out to his farm. His niece, Agnes Bisbee, said that the day of the murder she had had a personal conversation with Ledbetter which had thrown him into a rage and that he had ridden off to Marley. The Ledbetter property is midway between Shaw, here, and Marley. I haven't had the chance to catch up with him since that time."

The Constable concluded his statement with a hesitant air. Holmes' eyes were regarding him searchingly as though reaching within the recesses of his brain. "There is something else, obviously," commented the detective.

Bennett nodded. "It didn't come out at the inquest since it seemed to have no bearing at the time, but young Charles and Agnes Bisbee have been keeping company, if that is the correct way of putting it. They've had to be pretty sly about it, too, considering the circumstances."

"Montague and Capulet," Holmes' eyes had a faraway look. "But, you see, it does explain a great deal. Charles Trewlaney states that he returned to Shaw at ten-forty-five and the station master says he was on the six o'clock train. The young lover was silent because Romeo was with Juliet. Agnes Bisbee had a discussion with her uncle which threw him into a rage. About her intention to marry the stepson of his hereditary enemy, no doubt. The recent strain in the relations between Martin Trewlaney and his stepson can be laid at the same doorstep of the star-crossed lovers."

Gently lifting the dog from his lap and placing him on the floor, Holmes rose to his feet.

"The hour is late but the time spent has been profitable. I doubt if Charles Trewlaney need appear before the magistrates nor, indeed, the assizes."

"But there is a strong possibility of Vincent Staley doing both those things." Bennett's voice was grim. "Let me walk you back to the inn, gentlemen. You have, indeed earned a mite of rest in what is left of the night."

While Watson had enjoyed a lengthy nap on the train trip to Shaw, the country air acted like a soporific upon him. It was late the following morning when he forced his eyes open to find Holmes, fully dressed, standing beside the bed of his room and smiling at him. Watson grabbed at the watch, formerly the property of his departed brother of sad memory, which was on the bedstand beside him. One look provoked a groan.

"Great Scott, Holmes, you have allowed me to sleep away the morning!"

"No matter, dear fellow. My expedition proved a simple one and required no assistance."

"Expedition, indeed," said Watson climbing from his bed and dressing as rapidly as possible. "Where to, may I ask?"

"Marley, of course," replied Holmes. "You will recall that on the day of the murder, Agnes Bisbee said her uncle had ridden off to Marley in a rage. But Bennett stated that Ledbetter's farm was equadistant between Marley and Shaw. It occurred to me that Ledbetter might well have said he was riding to Marley but actually have directed his horse here."

"Placing him on the scene of the crime," commented the doctor, pulling up his trousers. "And what, pray tell, did you learn in this adjacent hamlet?"

"Much more than I anticipated. Obviously, Agnes had informed her uncle of her love for Charles Trewlaney. The news was such a shock to the old fellow that he rode into Marley like Rob Roy on the run. Leaving a foam-flecked horse, he promptly made for the only public house available and spent what was left of the evening disposing of a complete bottle of very old Irish whiskey. This induced a certain truculence in his general attitude and the local constable was summoned. This protector of the peace, Farquhar by name, placed Horace Ledbetter with some difficulty in what our American cousins call: 'the local pokey'. Ledbetter spent the entire night in a cell in the Marley jail."

"Good heavens," said Watson, adjusting his waistcoat. "This gives Ledbetter an alibi.

"The very best I can think of since it is supplied by the authorities themselves."

As Holmes helped Watson into his coat, there was a loud knocking on the door.

"Do come in," said Holmes, and the door opened revealing an agitated Constable Bennett.

"Forgive me, gentlemen," said Bennett, entering rapidly. "Things have taken a sudden turn."

"So Holmes has just told me," remarked Watson.

The constable shot an inquisitive glance at the detective. "They said downstairs you had hired a four-wheeler early this morning. I was looking around town for you before coming here. Have you chanced upon something?"

" 'Twill wait," said Holmes, with an airy gesture of one hand. "What have you learned, Bennett?"

"As you know, I have been staying at the Trewlaney house to protect the evidence. This morning, I dropped by my digs and found an envelope under my door." Bennett extracted a piece of cheap paper from his pocket. "Let me read you the contents: 'Young Charles did not arrive at Trewlaney's till just before eleven. Why don't you follow the finger of guilt which points directly to Horace Ledbetter?'

"It's signed: 'one who knows',," concluded Bennett.

"Your anonymous correspondent might just as well have affixed his name," said Holmes.

"My thought exactly, Mr. Holmes. Vincent Staley trying to implicate his enemy. I came here at once but they said that you had already departed. Therfore, I went to Staley's home. There was no response to my knock but I noticed the door ajar. Something prompted me to look inside and it's a good thing I did, gentlemen. I found Vincent Staley in his bedroom with his head bashed in."

"Good heavens!" exclaimed a startled Watson.

"Hmmm!" added Holmes. "A turn of events which I certainly did not foresee."

Bennett looked harassed. "I haven't made the fact known as yet."

"Just as well," was the detective's comment.

"I thought you gentlemen would accompany me to Ledbetter's farm. He is a tough old coot and I may need assistance in placing him under arrest."

Watson looked dazed. "But he has an alibi."

Holmes explained the situation to Bennett. "Constable Farquhar of Marley assured me that Horace Ledbetter was under lock and key in the Marley jail the entire night of the murder of Trewlaney."

Now it was the constable's turn to look dazed.

'Farquhar, eh? A good man. Bit of a local celebrity since he is our best dancer in these parts. Considered the master of 'The English Quick Step.' "

Watson looked like he had just bitten into a lemon

"Well, he has quick-stepped our only suspect right out of the picture."

"Not necessarily, my dear Watson."

"Half a moment, Holmes. Young Charles is innocent, being a left-handed man, and incapable of delivering the death blow to his stepfather in the manner in which it was done. Staley has been murdered himself and Horace Ledbetter has an ironclad alibi. Surely you cannot make anything sensible out of this hopeless tangle? Unless another suspect appears in a *"Deus ex Machina'* manner, we are at a hopeless dead end."

Holmes' eyes had narrowed thoughtfully. "The only way of arriving at what can be true is the careful elimination of what cannot be true. And there is a glimmer of light relative to this complex affair. Our solution lies in following your thought, Bennett, and departing immediately for the Ledbetter farm."

Using the same four-wheeler that Holmes had secured for his trip to Marley, the trio were soon heading down a country road with Holmes at the reins. He set the horses at a good pace and it was not long before they pulled up in front of the substantial farm house that was their destination. They were met at the door by Agnes Bisbee, a comely girl with the cream-like complexion native to the locale. Her eyes were red from weeping.

At the Ledbetter Farm.

"Agnes, we wish a word with your uncle," stated Bennett.

"He is in the barn," said the woebegone girl. "Though I don't know in what condition. The past few days have been a nightmare. He was gone all of one night and he's been drinking steadily and up at all sorts of hours."

The recounting of recent events proved too much and she began to sob.

"Now, now," said Holmes, with as close to a fatherly tone as he could come. "Things may not be quite as bad as they seem. Charles Trewlaney will shortly be released from custody and his name cleared of any complicity in the heinous murder of his stepfather."

The girl's tears ceased at this news and Holmes indicated the barn.

"Now, if you will excuse us, I believe we can arrive at the end of this most regrettable chain of events," he said.

Bennett followed by Holmes and Watson marched purposefully to the barn but found the door locked. He knocked authoritatively.

"Lee' me in peace," said a slurred voice from within.

"It is Bennett, Ledbetter. Open this door in the name of the law."

There was a silence for half a minute and then the sound of a bar being removed. Half of the large barn door slid open revealing a gnarled man of six feet in height with a weatherbeaten face topped by a shock of white hair. He was dressed in work clothes. His calloused hands and wide frame bespoke of strength and that durable power produced by hard manual labor.

"I'm glad there are three of us," thought Watson. "He looks like he could be a bit of a handful."

The farmer indicated with a vague gesture for his visitors to enter and turned inside and made his way to an anvil on which rested a depleted bottle and a tin tankard. He poured himself a considerable amount of whiskey and downed it in a gulp.

" 'Tis about Staley that I'm here," said Constable Bennett.

"Aye! I've been expectin' ya." The farmer's eyes were bleary and his speech thick but his brain appeared to be working. Watson later advanced the theory that he had drunk himself sober, a physical peculiarity which has been known to happen.

"I'll no beat the bushes abaht it. 'Twas yesterday of an evening hour. I came out here in search of some bottles that I had hid away from Agnes' eyes. When I opened the door, there was Staley, curse his black heart! He was by the door with a club in his hand. I'd surprised him all right and he rushed at me. 'Twas all so fast. I grabbed this here fence rail what I had been workin' on." The farmer indicated a stout piece of oak on the floor of the barn. 'Wi' it, I blocked his first blow and swung. 'Twas a lucky hit or I would not be talkin' to ya now. Caught him full in the forehead, I did, and he was dead afore he hit the ground. What went through my poor addled pate then I canna' tell ya. Somehow I were plagued with the idea of gettin' his carcass out of here so I saddled my mare. She was skitterish I'tell ya for she smelled Staley's blood, but I got him hoisted over her withers and into the saddle meself. Then I rode into Shaw and put the body in his house. I had the idea that if his corpse be found in Shaw, I would not be involved, but 'twont work. I been livin' wi' the deed and that fierce moment for these hours past and it will nay do. I killed him."

With a groan, Ledbetter sank onto a bale of hay and buried his face in his hands.

"There seems to be ample grounds for a plea of self-defense," stated Holmes. "You said Staley had a club. Is it still here?"

Ledbetter just gestured towards a wall of the barn. Holmes crossed to the indicated spot and secured a stave of seasoned wood which he studied carefully.

"This, gentlemen," he continued, addressing Bennett and Watson, "will prove to be the murder weapon which did away with Martin Trewlaney. The series of events are now clear. Impelled by blind rage, Vincent Staley stole into the Trewlaney house and murdered his enemy. He felt that suspicion would fall on Ledbetter here. But when the authorities moved against young Charles, his plans went awry. Therefore, he left the anonymous message at your door, Bennett, where he knew you would find it and then came out here with the murder weapon. He was in the process of concealing the weapon in Ledbetter's barn where it could be found without too much difficulty. However, being surprised in the act, he sprang upon Ledbetter with intent to kill."

Holmes turned his attention to the farmer.

"The fact that you have made a clean breast of the matter will carry considerable weight in court, my good man. While you do have the death of another human being to weigh on your conscience, the fact remains that Vincent Staley would eventually have faced the same fate from the law though by different means."

Thus ended this strange tale of violence and death. Analysis of the club used by Staley definitely proved that it was the Trewlaney murder weapon. Horace Ledbetter was charged with murder with the defense entering the plea of self-defense. Evidently, his implication in the affair did weigh heavily on the old man for he passed away before the case went to the Assizes. This spelled finis to the blood feud that had been part of the history of the area for so long.

Charles Trewlaney married Agnes Bisbee. Not being inclined towards either farming or banking, Charles and his bride purchased the "Queens Arms Inn". But in recognition of the man who had cleared his name, Charles changed the name of the establishment. Should you visit the sleepy hamlet of Shaw, you will note that the only inn displays the sign of "The Ace of Sleuths". This rather unusual name elicits numerous questions which the proprietors do not choose to answer.

In his careful recounting of the affair, Watson was all for calling it, "The Case of the Blue-Eyed Dog". Holmes demurred, pointing out that the actual solution revolved around the presence of two death-dealing weapons. Therefore, Watson re-titled the affair: "The Mystery of the Two Clubs". In itself, this would seem of scant importance save for the fact that the name did connect with a great bridge innovation which Holmes conceived shortly afterwards.

ENTRY ASSASSINATION

```
                    WATSON (Dealer)
                    ♠ 7 5 3
                    ♡ void
                    ◇ 10 9 7 4 2
                    ♣ A K 10 6 3
     SKURRY                              CASTLE
     ♠ A K                              ♠ 9 8 4
     ♡ A Q J 8 5 2                      ♡ 7 4 3
     ◇ J 6                              ◇ A K 5 3
     ♣ Q J 4                            ♣ 8 7 5
                    HOLMES
                    ♠ Q J 10 6 2
                    ♡ K 10 9 6
                    ◇ Q 8
                    ♣ 9 2
```

CHALLENGE MATCH BIDDING: (Holmes-Watson vulnerable)

Skurry	Watson	Castle	Holmes
—	pass	pass	pass
4H	pass	pass	pass

On the particular day that this hand was dealt, Harry Skurry had not been too fortunate with cards or play. After three passes, he bid what he thought he could make in the hope of breaking his jinx.

Watson made the normal lead of the club king. Study Holmes' hand and see what kind of a defense you can come up with.

On his partner's club king, Holmes played the club nine. Watson continued the suit playing the ace with Holmes following with the club two. Watson continued with a low club on which Holmes played the diamond eight and Harry, much to his surprise, won the trick with his club queen. It was at this point that Jerome Jeckle, who was kibitzing the match tapped his temple with his forefinger indicating that, in his opinion, the great sleuth was completely barmy. No one paid him heed since Jeckle was considered a clod by one and all. Skurry shot a quick look at Watson suspecting him of holding the outstanding trump cards. However, the politician realized that if Watson held the four missing hearts, his contract was doomed anyway so he played a small diamond to dummy's ace. Holmes dropped his queen. Back came a heart from dummy and when Holmes played low, Harry finessed his trump jack which held as Watson showed out. Now the harsh light of truth came to Skurry's eyes. With a resigned air, he led another diamond to dummy's king and Holmes trumped the trick and returned his spade queen. Nothing could prevent the sleuth from capturing another heart trick to set the contract.

Skurry's disappointment in not making his contract was swallowed up by genuine admiration.

"Holmes, had you but trumped the third club, I could have reached dummy twice via the diamond suit and picked up your trumps with ease. Watson's ace and king of clubs and the club ruff would have been the only tricks for the defense."

"I was," replied Holmes, "rather intent on preventing you from reaching dummy more than once."

Jerome Jeckle, his face red, chose this moment to vacate his chair and leave the club.

Holmes evolves "Haltmon."

THE GREAT IDEA
SPOT CARDS

SKURRY
♠ Q 7 4 2
♡ 10 5 3
◇ 7 4
♣ 9 8 5 3

HOLMES (Dealer)
♠ A 10 6 5
♡ K 9
◇ A Q 10 5
♣ Q J 7

WATSON
♠ J 8 3
♡ A J 8 7
◇ K 8 2
♣ A K 4

CASTLE
♠ K 9
♡ Q 6 4 2
◇ J 9 6 3
♣ 10 6 2

CHALLENGE MATCH BIDDING: (neither side vulnerable)

Holmes	Skurry	Watson	Castle
1NT	pass	4NT	pass
6NT	pass	pass	pass

In modern times, the bidding might not have progressed in this fashion. However, this hand is of special interest since it served as the spark for one of Holmes' greatest ideas.

The detective's opening bid was reasonable. Watson, with sixteen high card points, bid four notrump which had nothing to do with the new Blackwood Convention of American origin. He was simply inviting Holmes to go to six notrump with more than minimum values for his opening bid. This was known as a"quantitative raise".

Holmes had a minimum opening notrump but he rather fancied his tens in the spade and diamond suits and felt that his heart nine might be of value. High spot cards pull their weight in notrump. Holmes and Watson had been having a splendid round on this particular day's play and it was the sleuth's feeling that when you were going good it paid to keep pushing. This theory is open to question but it seemed to serve Holmes well.

Skurry, faced with a choice of unappetizing leads, hoped to hoodwink Holmes. He selected the heart five. Holmes played the heart seven from dummy and after a moment of thought, Betty Castle played low. Holmes took the trick with the heart nine and knew that he was in trouble. Three heart tricks were now certain along with three club tricks. If he could bring home the diamond suit, his winning total would be ten tricks and the ace of spades would provide the eleventh. Holmes needed an extra winner which he might secure from the spade suit. But he also needed to play the diamond suit correctly.

The detective went after his money suit first and played the diamond ace to cater to a possible singleton jack. His opponents followed suit. Now Holmes played his diamond five to dummy's king and again Harry and Betty followed. The moment of truth was upon him as he played a diamond from dummy with Betty smoothly playing her nine. Holmes well knew that the odds favored a four-two split in the suit but he reasoned that he would undoubtedly lose a spade to Skurry and a diamond loser to the same hand spelled disaster. He went against the odds playing his diamond queen. Holmes had taken the wrong position but Harry, at this point, did the same thing. He signalled his partner with the spade seven. Now Holmes saw a possible way out. Can you envision what he had in mind?

Sherlock Holmes played a small club to dummy's ace. He then led the spade jack from the board which Betty covered with her king. Holmes took this trick with his spade ace and then played his spade ten. Harry rose with his spade queen but Betty's nine in the suit dropped. Now Holmes had three spade winners and his slam came home.

It was that evening at Baker Street after a leisurely dinner that an idea was discussed which had a great influence on the bidding technique of the day. Holmes, the fingers of his long hands steepled in characteristic fashion, was gazing into the hearth fire. Outside, a dark, turbid sky hung low over rooftops. A yellow fog had insinuated itself into Baker Street. Lights in adjacent windows seemed to float in the murk like channel beacons in Southampton Harbor. Watson was working on his Diary of the Challenge Match and the sound of his quill pen was interrupted occasionally by the snap and pop of exploding sap from oak logs that glowed with a ruddy hue. The welcome warmth pervading the room produced a drowsy lassitude which caused Watson's eyelids to grow heavy. But the mind of Holmes was immune to this siren song of Morpheus.

"Confound it, Watson," he said, suddenly. "We have been wallowing in a sea of indecision!"

"Eh?" asked Watson, his head coming erect. "Sea of India?"

"Indecision. Forgive me, old friend, I did suddenly burst forth like a verbal snapping turtle. But what can be more ignominious than suddenly to realize that one has been blithely ignoring the very obvious."

Watson was now completely alert. "What can have piqued you to such an extent, Holmes?"

"It was that six notrump contract this afternoon."

"You played it magnificently."

"In truth," said the great detective, "I overbid and then compounded that error by playing the diamond suit incorrectly. We were most fortunate to make the slam. However," he added, philosophically, "it is only reasonable that fortune smile on occasion. But that was not the point that has been bedevilling me." Holmes crossed to the desk taking a piece of foolscap on which he marked two hands. "I am reproducing my hand, Watson, and making some alterations in yours:"

HOLMES	WATSON
♠ A 10 6 5	♠ K Q 8 3
♡ K 9	♡ A 8 7
◇ A Q 10 5	◇ K 8 2
♣ Q J 7	♣ A 6 4

"Please note" continued Holmes," "that you still possess sixteen points. After my opening one notrump, your slam invitational four notrump bid, in accord with our present methods, would be reasonable."

"And six notrump could very well make," interjected Watson.

"Agreed. But note that six spades is an odds-on favorite to come in. After drawing three rounds of trumps, if a diamond loser exist, it can be trumped in dummy."

Watson's head was nodding. "I see your point."

"Actually, Watson, this opens up a whole new outlook. At present, our opening bids of one notrump deny posession of a five-card major suit. I can envision situations where this might prove impractical but let us hold to this thesis for the time. However, I might very well open one notrump with one four-card major suit or even two. Here, let me demonstrate further."

Holmes rapidly created two new hands.

HOLMES	WATSON
♠ K J 6	♠ Q 5 4 3
♡ A J 8 7	♡ K Q 9 4
◇ Q 7	◇ 8 2
♣ A J 10 8	♣ Q 7 4

Holmes indicated the hand he had given himself. "I could open one notrump with this holding. What would your response be?"

"Two notrump, of course," replied Watson. "I do have nine high card points."

"I would pass your bid," said Holmes. "Even that contract would be fraught with peril. If our opponents did not find their diamond suit on the opening lead, they certainly would after gaining the lead via the spade ace or possibly the club king. However, we have an excellent chance, with these same cards, of making four hearts."

Watson's eyes glowed. "Two diamond losers and a certain spade but if the club finesse is on you are, as I believe the Irish put it — 'in, like Flynn.' "

Holmes now indicated Watson's sample hand. "Please note that while you do possess nine high card points, your doubleton gives you an additional distributional point if the contract can be played in a trump contract."

"But my doubleton diamond is a wasted value, Holmes, since you also have two cards in the suit."

"That is neither here nor there," answered Holmes. His voice was slightly testy. "The theoretical point is that you might very well have an eight point hand in high cards or even seven but still possess enough distributional values to make game if we can locate a suitable holding in the majors."

"How do you propose to do that, Holmes?" queried Watson.

"By falling back on an oft-used device. Taking a bid which is of limited practical value and giving it a specialized meaning. Assuming you open the bidding with one notrump and the second hand passes, I propose that if I now bid two clubs, I am making a completely artificial bid. I am asking you if you hold a four-card major suit. Since my bid commits us to take more tricks, I must have a certain amount of strength. Eight or nine high card points, at least, or possibily seven with very favorable distribution. I also must have an interest in the major suits — namely, at least four cards in one, or perhaps both."

"What governs my responses?" asked Watson, who was becoming more excited by the moment.

"For one round, there are only three bids available to you. If you have four spade cards, you bid two spades. With four hearts you bid that suit. Not holding four cards in either major suit, you respond two diamonds."

"I see," said Watson. "My two diamond bid being as completely artificial as your club bid. But, Holmes, suppose I hold four cards in both major suits?"

"You bid two spades. At least, that is my thought at the moment. But if this idea has practical merit, we must start somewhere and the only true test is at the table."

"Agreed," said Watson. "But hold a moment, Holmes. Several questions come to mind. Suppose you have a long suit and a very weak hand?"

Holmes positively beamed with appreciation. "How very astute of you, old friend. This is exactly the situation where this device may prove amazingly valuable. Let us presume that I am holding this rather uninteresting collection." The quill pen moved rapidly.

HOLMES
♠ Q 9 7 6 4 3
♡ 7 2
♢ 6
♣ 9 7 4 2

"I hear you open one notrump and now bid two spades. Had I wished to explore the possibility of a game in spades, could I not have bid two clubs conventionally? Therefore, my two level response in either major suit, hearts, or diamonds can only mean that this is where I wish the hand to be played. Your most descriptive opening bid makes it fairly simple for me to decide where we should be."

Watson was surveying Holmes' latest diagram with shrewd eyes. "Reverse the black suits, ol' boy," he requested.

Holmes considered the thought with interest. "I see what you are getting at. But cannot I have my cake and eat it as well? I shall bid two clubs. If you respond two spades, I shall pass. We have found an eight card trump suit, at least. But should you bid two hearts or two diamonds, I will now bid three clubs expressing an extreme desire to be allowed to play at that contract."

Holmes resumed his seat by the fire with a satisfied expression. "As we test this theory, Watson, I am certain that other usages will suggest themselves. The possibilities are almost unlimited."

"Your last word brings one more thought to mind," said Watson. "This two club conventional bid should require a minimum of seven high card points for the sake of safety. Is there any upper limit for the bid?"

"I think not," responded Holmes. "The two club bidder might have a huge hand but, since the bid is absolutely forcing, he is certain to have a chance to describe his values."

Now it was Watson's turn to create a hypothetical hand. Rising from the desk he showed it to Holmes.

WATSON
♠ A Q 9 6 4 3
♡ 7
◇ 7 6 3
♣ Q 5 2

"Your previous hand suggests this. What is my action with these cards?"

"Four spades is your bid over my one notrump opening," Holmes' reply was immediate. "After all, you know that I possess at least two spade cards and you hold reasonable high card and distributional values to contract for game." As Watson nodded in agreement, Holmes continued somewhat dreamily. "I am sure other minds have been considering this approach, Watson, and equally certain that our discussion of this evening relative to this approach has been skeletal indeed. However, since you seem to approve, we shall put it to the test at the table and try and iron out problems as they occur."

It was the following day that Holmes and Watson explained the new device which they were incorporating into their bidding system to Harry Skurry and Betty Castle. Needless to say the kibitzers, especially the bridge journalists present, were all ears. Memory of other Holmes innovations had sharpened them to the possibility of another giant step forward in the bridge technique of the day.

Several hands involving Holmes' two club convention did come up on that very day. Other hands I have carefully selected from Doctor Watson's Diary of the Challenge Match in an attempt to show how Holmes' idea was developed and improved and even found a name.

"The Ace of Sleuths" Inn.

THE BAG JOB

SKURRY
♠ J 10 9
♡ 8 7
◇ 8 5 3
♣ A J 7 4 3

HOLMES (Dealer)
♠ A Q 5
♡ K Q 9 2
◇ K J 7 6
♣ Q 9

WATSON
♠ K 8 2
♡ A J 5 3
◇ Q 9 4 2
♣ 8 2

CASTLE
♠ 7 6 4 3
♡ 10 6 4
◇ A 10
♣ K 10 6 5

CHALLENGE MATCH BIDDING: (neither side vulnerable)

Holmes	Skurry	Watson	Castle
1NT	pass	2C	pass
2H	pass	4H	pass
pass	pass		

Harry Skurry later commented that Holmes and Watson could hardly have been dealt better values to use their new "toy". Harry's manner was seemingly jocular in his reference to toy but secretly he was touched by the green goddess of envy. When Holmes' idea had been first explained, Skurry was shrewd enough to realize that it had great merit and he was annoyed that the idea had not been his own. While his admiration for Holmes had proved something of a balm for the wound of being replaced as a leading light in the bridge world of the day, he was human.

When Watson bid two clubs in response to his partner's opening one notrump, Betty shot a quick glance of interrogation at the detective. Holmes nodded.

"I interpret Watson's bid as convention and artificial."

The bidding smoothly arrived at the heart game. Harry led the spade jack.

Holmes took the spade lead with dummy's king. He then played a low heart to his king and followed with his trump queen. He now returned to dummy with a low heart to the ace, extracting the last outstanding card in the suit. A low diamond off the board put Betty into a slight trance. She well knew her partner would not have led a spade away from the ace and his jack lead denied the queen. Betty shrewdly placed both cards in Holmes' hand. Therefore, she did not rise with her diamond ace to return partner's suit. However, the fact that the only other card she could play was the tenspot made life easier for Holmes. He covered the diamond ten with his jack which held the trick. Now Watson's diamond nine was a very comforting card to have. Holmes returned a low diamond to dummy's queen which Betty captured. Betty now made the obvious club shift. The defense collected their two club tricks but that was as far as they could go.

"Of course," said Skurry, "against three notrump I lead my club four and we collect five tricks right off the top. The contract is defeated two tricks." He shook his head with a wry smile. "It would seem, Betty, that we had better adopt Holmes' two club convention and immediately."

Ezra Maise of the Ace Feature Syndicate was seen to make notes at this point. Bertram Jabot Beckerié, the great French bridge journalist, who was among the kibitzers of the day was similarly occupied. This caused Holmes to make a general comment.

"Gentlemen, while I believe this thought may prove of assistance in bidding, it is a new concept. Since the possible card combinations are almost beyond comprehension, should we not wait further testing of the device?"

Holmes' sensible suggestion might have born fruit save for another hand which arose during the same session of play. Also, Betty Castle chose to disagree with him.

"You may think it needs testing, Mr. Holmes, but I am convinced. The three notrump contract was doomed while four hearts was in the bag all the time. A bag job," she concluded with a twinkle in her eyes.

Betty was referring to "The Mystery of the Rajah's Ruby", a case of Holmes' recorded in Watson's "Diary of the Challenge Match" which I hope to tell you about some day.

THE CLINCHER

SKURRY
♠ 7 3
♡ 8 7 4
◇ A 9 5
♣ Q J 10 7 6

HOLMES (Dealer)
♠ K J 10 4 2
♡ K 5
◇ J 6 4
♣ 8 5 3

WATSON
♠ A Q 6
♡ A Q 10 6
◇ K 8 3 2
♣ K 2

CASTLE
♠ 9 8 5
♡ J 9 3 2
◇ Q 10 7
♣ A 9 4

Skurry-Castle vulnerable.

The bidding of this hand was so inventive that it gave the bridge theorists of the day much to think of. Holmes and Skurry had obvious passes and made them. Watson opened one notrump but with misgivings. Had he possessed a five-card minor suit, he would have considered his hand really too strong for a notrump opening. It is interesting that many experts of our time would have been in complete agreement with the good doctor. After Betty Castle passed, Holmes' shrewd mind seized upon a means of describing his values with great accuracy. Do you see what he had in mind?

Holmes bid two clubs. Skurry was not certain that he wished a possible club lead from Betty so he did not double this artificial bid despite his excellent club holding. Watson now bid two hearts. After Betty passed again, Holmes bid two spades. Skurry's eyebrows elevated slightly. However, he did not ask for an interpretation but simply passed. Now Watson did some deep thinking. Had his partner held a long spade suit with scant values, he would simply have bid two spades over the opening notrump bid. Holding ten points and a spade suit of five cards or more, the detective might well have jumped to three spades. Yet, he had adopted neither of these lines of action. What was going on? Watson marshalled his thoughts. By bidding two clubs, Holmes had signified eight or nine points at least. Seven was a possibility but the absolute minimum. By inference, Watson's bid of two hearts denied four spade cards. Yet Holmes had then bid spades knowing his partner could hold no more than three. Now the doctor's thoughts bore fruit. His partner was promising five spades and seven or more points but not ten. Watson's hand was worth nineteen points with spades as trumps. He promptly went to four spades. Every eye in the room was riveted on this — for the time — exotic auction.

Harry Skurry led the club queen and Holmes followed small from dummy. Betty automatically dropped the club nine. Skurry had played bridge a long time and promptly played a low spade. Holmes took the trick with dummy's ace and led the club king. Betty ran up with her ace and, following Harry's defense, returned another spade, but it was too late! Holmes won the trick in hand and led his last club which he trumped with dummy's spade queen. He returned to his hand via the heart king. A top spade drew Betty's remaining trump and the detective led his low heart to dummy's ace. Hoping that the heart jack might drop, he played dummy's queen of the suit, discarding a diamond from his hand. Luck was not with him so Holmes took the only other line of play available. He played dummy's heart ten which Betty covered with her jack. Holmes trumped the trick and led a low diamond towards dummy's king. Skurry was on the spot and he knew it. He played his diamond ace and then returned a top club. But Holmes had a spade in reserve. He trumped the trick and led his last diamond to dummy's good king. Holmes had lost two clubs and a diamond but he had made his contract.

There was a burst of applause from the onlookers and Holmes and Watson's opponents joined in the enthusiasm.

"Mr. Holmes," said Betty, "I don't see how else you could have described your holding. Naturally, your two spade bid was not forcing."

"How true," replied Holmes. "Watson just happened to hold an absolute maximum for his bid. We might well have ended up in two spades had his hand been different. Or two nontrump if he had but a doubleton in spades."

The detective directed his gaze to Skurry. "Your shift to a trump on the second trick was a very well-conceived defensive move."

Harry Skurry was capable of smiling in the face of adversity. "Holmes, you are being gracious. You make no mention of the fact that had I made the opening lead of a spade, Betty and I could have defeated your ambitious contract.

You see, of course, what Harry was thinking of, with some regrets.

That evening, on Baker Street, Holmes made mention of the same hand. "You know, Watson, had you been the dealer and opened with one notrump and I held the same hand but the diamond ace instead of the jack, what would have been my bid?"

"Three spades, forcing to game," replied Watson, rapidly. "Is that not the way we have agreed to handle the situation?"

"For the moment," replied Holmes. His eyes had a faraway look.

FRUSTRATION

SKURRY
♠ Q J 10 9
♡ 7 6 2
◇ J 10 9 5
♣ 5 4

HOLMES
♠ A 5 3
♡ A Q J 10 9 4
◇ 8 2
♣ K 7

WATSON (Dealer)
♠ K 7 4
♡ K 3
◇ A Q 4
♣ A 10 9 8 3

CASTLE
♠ 8 6 2
♡ 8 5
◇ K 7 6 3
♣ Q J 6 2

The following was the bidding as it actually occurred. As Holmes explained later, he was not at all happy about it.

Holmes	Skurry	Watson	Castle
—	—	1NT	pass
3H	pass	3NT	pass
4NT	pass	5H	pass
6H	pass	pass	pass

Harry Skurry held two sequences and, reasonably, chose to lead the strongest one. He placed the spade queen in the center of the table. Concentrate on the hands of Holmes and Watson and plan your play.

It took but a moment for the detective to spot two possible losers and but a moment more to realize that he had two possibilities of disposing of one of them. Do you see the way his mind was working?

On the spade lead, Holmes played low from dummy and took the trick in his hand. He now played the heart ace. To the surprise of some onlookers, he now laid down the club king and continued the suit to dummy's ace. Back came the club ten which Betty covered with the jack. Holmes trumped with the heart nine and Skurry discarded the spade nine. Now Holmes led his heart four to dummy's king. The nine of clubs drew Betty's queen and Holmes trumped with his heart ten while Skurry discarded a low diamond. Holmes played his trump queen removing Skurry's final heart. He then played a low spade to dummy's king. On the club eight, Holmes discarded a diamond from his hand. He then played the ace of diamonds from dummy and followed it with the queen. Betty covered the trick with her king forcing Holmes to trump and concede a spade. Had Betty not covered dummy's queen, Holmes had planned to discard his losing spade, a move that could not cost him anything at all.

On this particular day's play, the previous hand signalled the end of the action. As Holmes and Watson departed from the Grosvenor Square Bridge Club, Watson noted a distinct preoccupation on the part of Holmes. At the door, they were approached by a complete stranger.

"My apologies, gentlemen," he said, "but would you give me the distinct pleasure of shaking you both by the hand." And he seized their hands in turn, pumping them with energy. "My name is Grover Gitley," continued the stranger, "and I am more in your debt than either of you will ever know."

Holmes, his mind having been elsewhere, was momentarily nonplussed. Something had to be said, and it was Watson who said it.

"You are a bridge funder, Mr. Gitley?"

"Heavens, no, and undoubtedly never will be," was the response. "Gitley and Company is the firm I own. We manufacture nail files. Mr. Holmes — Doctor Watson — since you both have made bridge so popular, our sales have been booming. People are taking much better care of their hands now that they are playing bridge. You have my undying gratitude."

And after this most unusual meeting, Grover Gitley departed with a beaming face.

Watson became convulsed with laughter.

"My dear Holmes," he gasped, " you do attract some of the strangest happenings!"

"A plural there, ol' boy," responded the detective. "After all, you taught me this fascinating game." His face sobered. "Regarding that last hand, Watson, I was most frustrated in the bidding. I think we should discuss it."

And they did in a hansom headed towards Baker Street.

"You will recall, Watson," said Holmes, as they jostled along, "that I advanced the thought originally that this bidding device could open up many avenues. We have just seen an indication of one of them. Your opening notrump found me with a most unusual hand. Fourteen high card points plus a six-card suit, the latter fact being the crux of the matter. My jump to three hearts was game-forcing but misleading. With six hearts plus a known doubleton or more in your hand, I wanted to play in a heart slam. After you denied my heart suit by re-bidding three notrump, I was placed in a most frustrating position. I embarked on a Blackwood sequence with a worthless doubleton in diamonds. Had you shown me but one ace I would have been in a pretty fix indeed."

"True," answered Watson thoughtfully. "I might well have held the black queens rather than the diamond ace and we could have lost two immediate tricks in that suit. Do you have a possible solution, Holmes?"

"Let us consider this," said the detective. "I hold a five-card spade suit plus game going values of ten points. Should you open one notrump, I wish to insist on game in my suit or notrump. I bid two clubs which is absolutely forcing for one round. Let us assume you respond two diamonds. Now I jump in my suit signifying my length and strength."

"It does seem like going round Robin Hood's barn a bit."

"Agreed," said Holmes. "However, it releases the immediate jump in a major suit to indicate six cards plus fourteen or fifteen points. The bid now is slam invitational."

Well, we can cetainly try it out," said Watson.

CONFIRMATION

SKURRY (Dealer)
♠ J 10 7 6
♡ J 7 5 3
◇ 10 9 4
♣ 10 7

HOLMES
♠ K Q 5
♡ A Q 9 6 2
◇ 8 5
♣ 6 5 2

WATSON
♠ A 8 4 2
♡ K 10
◇ A Q 7 3
♣ K J 8

CASTLE
♠ 9 3
♡ 8 4
◇ K J 6 2
♣ A Q 9 4 3

CHALLENGE MATCH BIDDING: (Castle-Skurry vulnerable)

Holmes	Skurry	Watson	Castle
—	pass	1NT	pass
2C	pass	2S	pass
3H	pass	3NT	pass
pass	pass		

A considerable amount of playing time elapsed before the Baker Street partnership were able to incorporate this newest approach of Holmes' into their bidding. Opening notrumps are specific bids and don't occur with the regularity we might wish them to. Also suitable responding hands are required. Finally, after Skurry dealt and passed, Watson found himself with a nice balanced hand of sufficient strength and bid one notrump. Holmes came forth with his artificial response of two clubs to which Watson dutifully replied two spades. Now Holmes went to three hearts, showing his five-card suit and game-going strength. Watson, with but two hearts, chose the final contract of three notrump and Holmes respected his wishes.

As Holmes pointed out later, this approach which gave the partnership such flexibility did not come without some cost. Betty Castle, on lead, could certainly pin-point Watson as holding exactly four spades and two hearts. However, this knowledge was of little value to her on this particular hand and she had no reason not to open her club four in hopes of developing this long suit and setting the contract.

On the club lead, Watson was assured of a trick in the suit regardless of how the missing honors were distributed. Three spades and the diamond ace were sure winners as well. Therefore, Watson needed but four heart winners to fulfill his contract. Of course, clubs could prove a problem but only if the good doctor allowed them to be. Betty's club lead fetched Skurry's ten, taken by Watson's jack. Betty promptly placed the club king in the declarer's hand. Now Watson showed his style by playing a low spade to dummy's king. Back came a low heart on which Watson played his ten, not really concerned whether it won or lost. His purpose, as is obvious, was to keep Betty in the lead. When the heart ten held the trick, it was just frosting on the cake. Watson quickly cashed his heart king and returned to dummy via the spade king. Now the astute doctor ran his hearts, discarding two diamonds and a spade from his hand. Now he led a low spade from dummy to his ace. During the play of the major suits, Betty had been forced to find four discards. She had dropped two diamonds and two clubs. Watson cashed his diamond ace and threw Betty on lead with his diamond queen. The lady was able to cash her club ace but had to give Watson 'his eleventh trick via the club king.

"A nice bit of avoidance, partner, ending up with an end play," was Holmes' approving comment.

Skurry had a grim look. "If I could have just gotten on lead with a heart or spade, we would have murdered this contract."

"How now, Skurry," said Holmes, with a twinkle in his eyes. "A detective cannot allow murder to occur and a doctor is also dedicated to the preservation of life."

"In this case, it would seem that Doctor Watson is also dedicated to the preservation of contracts," said Betty Castle.

This forced a grudging smile from Skurry. "Well, he's jolly good at it," admitted the politician.

DUCK SOUP

SKURRY
♠ A 4 2
♡ K 6 4 3
◊ 7 5 2
♣ K 10 3

HOLMES
♠ K J 8 7 6
♡ 10 5
◊ Q J
♣ J 8 6 5

WATSON
♠ Q 10 9 3
♡ 9
◊ A K 9 8 6
♣ Q 7 2

CASTLE (Dealer)
♠ 5
♡ A Q J 8 7 2
◊ 10 4 3
♣ A 9 4

CHALLENGE MATCH BIDDING: (both sides vulnerable)

Castle	Holmes	Skurry	Watson
1H	pass	2H	pass
3H	pass	4H	pass
pass	pass		

Betty Castle was quite surprised when she picked up her hand. Not because it presented any bidding problems, but because immediately prior to the deal, Holmes had mentioned what he chose to call "the variable hand". The great sleuth had expressed the thought that while the cards which come your way do not change, their value does as the bidding progresses. Betty opened her long suit realizing that her hand could vary from minimum to good dependent on whether her hearts found support from partner.

Harry's simple raise was not made promptly. He did have ten points and good ones at that. However, he considered the square shape of his hand as a defect. Skurry withstood the temptation to invent a club suit and contented himself with a single raise on maximum values. Now Betty's hand looked considerably better and she invited game by going to three hearts. Her invitation was promptly accepted. Holmes chose to lead the heart five.

It took Betty exactly two seconds to plan her play and it should not take you much longer. Being a fine player, and also having played a great deal against a detective, she spotted the obvious clues. You would certainly play the hand the same way she did. The important point is your speed of detection.

Taking the opening heart lead in her hand, Betty promptly played her low spade to dummy's ace. She now led a low spade from dummy which she trumped with her heart jack, a precaution which she could well afford with only one trump outstanding. A low heart to dummy's king disposed of Holmes' last trump card and Betty ruffed dummy's last spade and led a low diamond. Holmes took the trick with his jack and continued the suit. Watson overtook his partner's diamond queen with his king and cashed his diamond ace. However, Watson was now in an impossible situation. A spade lead gave declarer an obvious ruff and sluff opportunity as would a diamond continuation. Feeling that "the jig was up", Watson led his low club. Betty played low and captured Holmes' jack with dummy's king. Back came the club ten which Watson covered, promoting Betty's club nine to the game going trick.

Present on this day was a certain Winhaven Hyde who, though a bridge-fancier, had a most unsavory reputation. He was, in fact, later barred from the Grosvenor Square Bridge Club. With ill grace, he chose this moment to make a comment:

"The hand played itself," he stated, with a sneer. "It was duck soup!"

Holmes fastened him with a frosty look. "Sir," said he, "I very seldom forget a face, but in your case I shall be delighted to make an exception."

How coincidental that many years later the comic, Groucho Marx, used this very same line and, with his brothers, starred in a cinema production entitled: "Duck Soup"!

The Apple Vendor.

"THE HOAX"

A warm south wind had sprung up on the particular day in question causing the weather to mellow unusually considering the season of the year. Holmes and Watson had just vacated 221 B Baker Street and were walking towards the nearest corner in search of a hansom to transport them to the Grosvenor Square Bridge Club for the afternoon session of the Challenge Match.

As they strolled along, grateful for the warming sun, they were intercepted by a tall, unkempt man with a tray of apples and what attempted to pass for a winning smile.

"Happles, gentlemen?" he croaked indicating his tray. "Nyture's remedy and bonny for the 'ealth."

Replete from a substantial and late breakfast, Holmes attempted to wave him away. The smile remained fixed as the man extended one of his sales items towards the pair, but his message altered.

"Mr. 'Olmes, 'im as uses the sneesh sent me."

Holmes' pace slowed and then halted, as he apparently examined the sample apple. "Yes?" he responded, questioningly.

" 'E be saying to keep a lookout for a man with a patch." The street hawker shrugged his shoulders as if his sales attempt had failed and walked down the street.

Watson, who had watched this unusual exchange with puzzlement, resumed motion to keep up with Holmes' brisk stride.

"What was that all about?"

The great detective was smiling and extended a hand in a wide gesture as though indicating the weather.

"I believe, my dear Watson, that I have mentioned from time to time, that my brother, Mycroft, would have made a splendid detective. His powers of observation are phenomenal and his brain is the most orderly storehouse imaginable. Yet, I do believe he tends to be overly subtle."

"What has 'Mycroft to do with this apple-vendor?"

"He uses snuff on occasion. 'Sneesh' is a Scottish expression for snuff. We have just received a message."

"If we have, it must be in code."

"Not at all," replied Holmes. "Evidently, we will come in contact with a man with a patch — an eye patch, I imagine, since patches on clothes are too common to be an identification mark. I doubt if Mycroft meant his message as a warning. Surely, he would have been more explicit in that case. So we shall watch out for a man with an eyepatch but not be too obvious about it. With all this hocus-pocus, it would seem Mycroft is involved in another of his deep games."

The pair did find a hansom on the corner and their trip to the bridge club was without incident.

NULLIFY THE THREAT

WATSON
♠ A Q 9 8 2
♡ Q 7 6
♢ K J 9
♣ 5 3

SKURRY
♠ J 7
♡ A K J 9 5
♢ 5 4
♣ J 9 8 7

CASTLE
♠ K 10 5 4
♡ 10 8 4 3 2
♢ 7 3 2
♣ 10

HOLMES (Dealer)
♠ 6 3
♡ void
♢ A Q 10 8 6
♣ A K Q 6 4 2

CHALLENGE MATCH BIDDING: (Holmes-Watson vulnerable)

Holmes	Skurry	Watson	Castle
1C	1H	1S	4H
5D	pass	6D	pass
pass	pass		

Holmes' hand was so strong that he could afford to bid his minor suits in their natural order, longest first. Had he been 6-5 in clubs and diamonds but without the king of clubs, the great sleuth would have, no doubt, opened a diamond to facilitate later bidding. Skurry's one level overcall was reasonable as was Watson's spade bid. The good doctor sensed a game somewhere with his excellent holding. Betty now jammed the bidding by leaping to four hearts. Watson's bid had made her hand look better. She had five-card heart support and a singleton. Holmes, with an offensive-oriented holding, refused to be shut out and bid five diamonds. The detective and Watson treated this reverse type bid as a one-round force. Now Watson did some thinking after Harry Skurry passed. Harry's overcall undoubtedly promised five heart cards and Betty's pre-emptive leap promised the same number. Therefore, with his own three hearts, Holmes must have a void. Surely Holmes would not have come into the bidding at the five level without a five-card diamond suit, therefore he must have six clubs and two spades. Watson, able to picture his partner's distribution with absolute accuracy, bid six diamonds.

Harry Skurry led the heart king. How would you play the hand?

THE PLAY

Holmes ruffed the heart lead with his diamond queen, just as a matter of good playing procedure. He led a low diamond to the board. Now Holmes played dummy's club three, taking the trick with his ace. Another low diamond was led to Watson's hand and another club led from dummy. Betty Castle gratefully ruffed this trick on which Holmes played a low club. At this point, Betty's gratitude evaporated as she realized what had happened. She returned a heart, forcing Holmes to trump the suit before Harry played, thus destroying the value of dummy's heart queen. However, this did not help the defense. With the opposing trumps disposed of, Holmes ran four club tricks discarding four spades from dummy. Now a spade to dummy's ace, a heart ruff in the closed hand and a spade ruff on the board and the slam was home.

Betty was fretful. "If I just hadn't trumped that club."

"It would have made no difference," responded Holmes. "I would then have taken the trick and ruffed a club with Watson's last diamond, thus establishing the clubs. A heart ruff back to my hand would allow me to extract your last diamond and then cash out the club suit and give up a spade in the end."

Betty dimpled, "Well, defeat is somewhat more palatable if it is inevitable. That was a brilliant line of play, Mr. Holmes."

"It does seem a good procedure," stated Holmes, thoughtfully, "to try to establish a side suit first."

"It is also a good procedure to have your opponents ruffing losers rather than winners." Betty got in the last word but it was a good one.

A BIT OF GUILE

```
                    WATSON
                    ♠ J 10 3
                    ♡ 9 8 7
                    ◇ A Q J 7
                    ♣ K 7 2
SKURRY                              CASTLE
♠ 8 7 4                             ♠ A 9 5 2
♡ K J 5 3 2                         ♡ 10 6 4
◇ K 5 2                             ◇ 10 8 3
♣ 9 3                              ♣ A 6 5
                    HOLMES (Dealer)
                    ♠ K Q 6
                    ♡ A Q
                    ◇ 9 6 4
                    ♣ Q J 10 8 4
```

CHALLENGE MATCH BIDDING: (neither side vulnerable)

Holmes	Skurry	Watson	Castle
1C	pass	1D	pass
1NT	pass	2NT	pass
3NT	pass	pass	pass

Holmes' opening bid needs no comment, nor does Watson's diamond response. Holmes now rebid one notrump limiting his hand and confirming a reasonable club suit since he did not respond in a major. Watson, with 11 high card points and a fit with partner's clubs, invited game by raising to two notrump. Holmes, counting on his clubs to produce tricks, took the fling and went to the game.

Harry Skurry didn't like the position of his diamond king and, on the bidding, realized that Betty Castle should have some entry cards. He chose to practice a little deceit and led the heart two.

Holmes took time to study the situation. While the heart lead did give him two immediate tricks, it struck at a weak link. For all the thirteen honor cards in his hand and dummy, the great detective only had three immediate winners. To promote tricks, he had to lose the lead permitting a continuation of the heart attack. However, Skurry's lead looked like fourth best. Holmes rapidly saw that he could develop four tricks in clubs which, along with his certain two heart winners, gave him six tricks. Two spade winners plus the diamond ace would bring home the contract. Therefore, Holmes decided to disdain the diamond finesse. Setting up the clubs would cost his heart control and losing to the diamond king would set the contract.

With a slight nod of his noble head, Holmes moved to bring in the game. Taking the opening heart lead in his hand with the queen, he immediately led a low club to dummy's king. Betty took the trick with her ace and returned her heart six. This card puzzled Holmes somewhat as he won with his spade king. Betty took this trick as well and returned her heart four. Skurry happily cashed three heart tricks and the contract was down.

"Unfortunate, partner," said Watson.

"Chicanery," corrected Holmes, looking at Skurry with respect. "Deceit is dangerous unless practiced at just the right time. My congratulations, Skurry, you fooled me completely."

Since Watson had a puzzled expression, Holmes elaborated.

"My wily opponent chose to lead his heart two which convinced me that the outstanding hearts were divided four and four. Had the opening lead been the heart three, I probably would have played the hand completely differently and made it by the way. In fear of a five card heart suit on my left, I would have driven out Betty's club ace, as I did. When she returned a heart removing my last guard in the suit, I would have been forced to adopt the winning line of play. A diamond for a finesse of dummy's queen. Back to my hand with a club to repeat the successful finesse in diamonds. Dummy's ace would have dropped the diamond king and I would have run home with four clubs, four diamonds, and two hearts for game with an overtrick. My line of play seemed reasonable at the time but things were not quite what I thought them to be."

This phrase came back to Holmes at a later time and in connection with a very different matter.

At the end of the day's play, Holmes demurred as Watson made to hail an available hansom at the entrance to the Grosvenor Square Bridge Club.

"It is really quite balmy, my dear Watson. Let's stroll for a bit." As they fell in step and made their way down the street, Holmes added: "Besides, I noted that the hansom driver did not have an eye patch."

"I see," said Watson. "You feel we are more available as pedestrians."

"That was my thought," agreed the detective. After a moment, he stated: "Dear me, Watson, don't regard every passer-by as if in search of a long-lost friend. Let us just calmly allow this little saga to unfold."

The pair soon found themselves close to the Strand when Watson stiffened suddenly.

"I've spotted him!"

"I know," responded Holmes. "He made sure that you did. Let us just continue to the corner. Watson, old fellow, you resemble a bird dog waiting for a gun to go off."

A cadaverous individual with an eye patch had been standing on the opposite side of the street and he slowly turned and entered the Waldo Winn-Chichester book store. To an observer, it might well have seemed that Holmes and Watson were discussing bridge hands but such was not the case at all. They languidly crossed the street and, cued by an apparent sudden thought of Holmes, also entered the book establishment. Their quarry was immediately apparent at one end of the store devoted to the classics. Holmes directed his steps in an opposite direction to the games section. There he located a book by Ewald Flemson, the well-known English bridge theoretician, which he indicated to Watson as though making a point. Flemson's work, which had much to do with Holmes' development of the two club convention, held no fascination for Watson on this day.

"He is leaving the shop, Holmes," he muttered.

"Indeed he is," agreed Holmes. "Now Watson, I am going to engage in a discussion with the proprietor for a moment. Would you be kind enough to wander over to where our one-eyed friend was engrossed in that large volume of Shakespeare and appear to glance through it casually. It is quite possible you may find something of interest within."

Watson, poised to pursue the departed man, was caught short but did as his friend requested. First regarding several plays of Ibsen with counterfeit interest, he finally extracted the large omnibus volume of Shakespeare's plays from its resting place and skimmed through it. Approximately halfway through, he discovered a thin piece of paper which he managed to slip from the book and place in his ulster pocket. Replacing the volume of Shakespeare, Watson turned to find Holmes awaiting him near the door of the establishment. A warning glance from the great detective curbed Watson's natural exuberance and a discreet silence was preserved until they. were safe from prying eyes in their suite at 221 B Baker Street.

There, Holmes spread Watson's discovery on the desk, reading aloud:

"My dear S. Important you and Watson dine at the Grenadier tonight at seven. Please cancel any conflicting engagements. Sneesh."

Holmes regarded his intimate friend with a tight smile. "It appears that Mycroft is obsessed with using his code signature of Sneesh and yet . . ."

He lapsed into silence and a furrow appeared upon his brow.

"Obviously, he must be intent on secrecy," hazarded Watson.

"Yet he addresses the message to 'S' and refers to you directly by name. Also, the message is written in his own easily identifiable angular scrawl."

"Possibly to assure you the message is genuine?"

"We seem beset by possibilities, Watson, but they will undoubtedly be resolved in part or whole tonight. Whatever affair is on Mycroft's mind, I have little doubt that he considers it of national importance."

Watson could well agree with this. Early in his acquaintance with Holmes, he had been led to believe, by a casual remark of the detective, that Mycroft audited the books of some government departments. He also believed that Holmes' older brother lodged in rooms in Pall Mall. It was much later that he realized that Mycroft was a key figure in the British government and considered indispensible. Privately, Watson believed that Mycroft lodged at that unusual, nay almost sinister, Diogenes Club. Ostensibly, a men's club devoted to silence, it was Doctor Watson's opinion that this was just a blind and that the Diogenes Club was, in truth, the headquarters for an unacknowledged and unknown branch of the English Secret Service. Needless to say, it was a highly excited Watson who accompanied his detective friend to the Grenadier that evening.

Upon arrival, they were notified that a reservation had been made in the name of Sherlock Holmes and ushered to a private room on the second floor of this ancient and renowned tavern. Awaiting them at a table set for three was the corpulent figure of Mycroft Holmes. His peculiarly light, watery gray eyes had that faraway, introspective look that Watson only observed in Sherlocks' when he was exerting his full mental powers. Greetings were brief since a waiter appeared with the overture to an obviously pre-ordered meal. As soon as he departed, Mycroft wasted little time.

"As you both must have surmised, we are faced with a difficult situation. I could say 'I am' but use the plural since it is a government matter."

"Evidently," said Sherlock, "a situation in which you feel Watson and I can be of some help, judging by the elaborate means of effecting this meeting."

Watson was always grateful for his friend's mention of himself but harbored no illusions as to his personal contributions. It did cause him to wonder as to his inclusion, by request, in this obviously high level meeting. Mycroft's motives were frequently obscure but he had a most orderly and rational mind.

"Some background is needed to clarify the situation," said Holmes' brother. "With his increase in mechanical aptitude, man has been remarkably consistent in his pursuit of certain things. Power sources being one. Endlessly, the homo sapien has tried to harness the power of the tides or the heat of the sun. In the fields of destruction, he has been equally dedicated in his pursuit of the automatic weapon. In medieval times, the arbolast had the velocity to pierce armor but the English crossbow was faster as the French learned to their dismay at Agincourt. Then came gunpowder. It solved the force and speed of the projectile but was remarkably slow. That was why that military genius of the colonies, General George Washington, selected his best marksmen to shoot and detailed lesser talents in his army to load for them. While one expert shot firing the muzzle-loaders fed to him by others did confound our redcoats, he still was not capable of sufficient rapidity of fire. Then came the breech-loader and the self-contained cartridge and mankind was on the way. The fundamental idea being, as you can both see, to turn a soldier into a one-man army as regards firepower."

As both Holmes and Watson nodded, Mycroft amended his last remark.

"That sentence was somewhat overstated but you can realize the government's interest when you consider that England is really a small country though our commitments are wide-spread. We are hardly ever involved in a conflict without being outnumbered. With additional sophistication in weaponry, the discipline and valor of the British soldier will not be enough to repel vastly superior manpower.

"Now to present a clear picture, I must digress. The government makes it a practice to subsidize the experiments of various individuals who possess that rare ability to envision things which have previously either not been considered or have proved impractical. This is not a policy on which we hold a monopoly, by the way. The money is secured through secret funds and one of the recipients has been a Homer Wren. Wren is a typical high I.Q. University graduate with an obsession for experimentation confined to the field of explosives. He first caught our eye several years ago with a prototype of a bomb not activated by contact or impact but by a timing device quite similar to the common spring-winding clock. The idea offered obvious possibilities, especially in the field of sabotage. Three experiments were held, none of which were successful. Fortunately, these test runs did not result in any loss of life though on two occasions it was a near thing. However, the expenditure was not a complete loss. The timing device suggested something to an inventor called Mahler, of whom I sincerely hope neither of you have ever heard."

Sherlock Holmes shot a quick look at Watson who shook his head.

"The name is unknown to me," said the detective.

"And a good thing," continued Mycroft Holmes. "This is strictly secret, gentlemen, but Mahler has come up with an idea in a different field which we are keeping very much under wraps. He has developed the fool-proof safe based on a timing device."

Noting his brother's expression of incredulity, Mycroft continued with conviction. "It works, Sherlock. The safe has no lock or combination. The time for its being opened is set and the door is closed. It cannot be opened by anything short of explosives until the pre-set time has elapsed."

"Ingenious," admitted Sherlock. "The cracksman has nothing to work on save the timing device."

"Which is inside the safe," said his brother. "I mention this since Homer Wren took umbrage to the Mahler safe claiming that the invention was, in part, based on his own experiments. However, the devices were so dissimilar, the government did not agree. Since Wren's bomb project fizzled out because he could not solve his detonation problem, it was felt that his subsidy should be terminated. I took a different view, feeling that he could very well come up with something and was worth continued backing as a speculation.

"In the meantime, the march of the automatic weapon continued. A cluster of barrels, crank-operated and revolving through a central firing mechanism was evolved. It produced the effect of a rapid-fire cannon or shotgun, if you will, and was used with some success by the American army of the west against hostile Indians. However, it was a cumbersome weapon and its number of shots was limited. Now, of course, we are working on smaller cartridges of the rifle type fired by a single hammer which is belt-fed. It has the apt name of 'the machine gun.' "

"But, surely," interjected Watson, "this must be a devilishly effective weapon indeed."

"It is," answered Mycroft grimly. "However, it has drawbacks which is why it is still in the planning stage. For one thing, it is a heavy weapon, not easily mobile. It has a large number of parts making it susceptible to breakdown under battle conditions. It heats abnormally and this is a problem as yet unsolved. It requires a tripod and time to set up for action, plus at least two men to operate it. And it may be completely outdated if Wren's claims are true."

Sherlock's head was nodding. "I thought friend Wren would re-enter the picture."

"Wren *is* the picture," was Mycroft's dry response. "With your occupation in the field of crime, Sherlock, you and Doctor Watson may not realize that we are in a period of great unrest. The Sudanese now have rifles equal to English army issue. A vast Asiatic nation has long cast greedy eyes at India, which is a cauldron. Especially the Afghans with whom Watson, here, had an unfortunate experience. Meanwhile, Europe is rapidly becoming an armed camp. Franco-German relations are particularly strained."

"And you feel that Wren might have a solution, or at least a temporary one?" questioned Sherlock.

"Quite possibly. Wren claims to have constructed what may be the ultimate in automatic weapons. It consists of a rifle-sized gun weighing less than eight pounds. It has only forty-five working parts and will fire any nine millimeter ammunition. Somehow, if his statements prove true, he has developed a firing mechanism of unbelievable rapidity. The Wren Gun, as he calls it, is spring-fed and will fire 500 rounds a minute."

Watson's mouth dropped abruptly. "I am no ballistics expert," he stammered, "but that sounds impossible. With such a weapon there would never have been a first Afghan War, much less a second one."

Holmes had a comment. "You have several times referred to 'if Wrens statements are correct'. I presume the weapon has not been tested."

Mycroft nodded. "Now we return to Wren's resentment of the Mahler safe invention. He has shown portions of his drawings to our best men in the field. Enough to convince them of the distinct possibility that the Wren Gun will operate according to the inventor's claims. But he has refused to accept additional sums for its development. He has laid down the following demands: He will deliver personally the plans of the Wren Gun tomorrow — Friday — here in London. He absolutely refuses to part with the plans and is insisting on a bulk payment for the complete rights. Due to certain unavoidable governmental commitments, those authorities capable of approving the payment of such a large sum of money are not available until Monday. Wren provided a solution which, as he puts it, protects his interests as well as England's. He will arrive in London at Liverpool station and proceed to a certain office in the government buildings which contains the only Mahler safe now in existence. He will place his plans in the safe and see to it that the timing device is set to open at nine a.m. on Monday. At that time, he will be present along with the necessary ballastics expert who will study his plans, plus certain government officials. If the expert agrees that the Wren Gun is workable, he will be paid the sum he demands and the matter will be closed."

"That seems like a reasonable solution," said Holmes. "Over the weekend he certainly cannot open the safe nor can you."

"I rather imagine the price he is asking is a high one," said Watson.

51

Mycroft Holmes shuddered. "Very. But not exorbitant if the Wren Gun is what he says it is."

"And now the obvious question, my dear brother," said Sherlock. "Where do Watson and I figure in this intricate affair?"

"You would not, if I were a happy optimist and assumed that no knowledge of this unusual weapon existed elsewhere. But in regard to a matter of this importance, I am inclined to extreme pessimism. When Wren boards the train for London, there will be only one seat available for him in the carriage he is instructed to take. The remainder of the passengers will all be security agents. When he arrives in London, there will be a dray pulled by two horses, one especially selected because it is lame. This will allow the dray to approximate the speed of a walking man and it will be within sight of Wren during his entire trip from the station to his destination. In addition, a series of hansom cabs will be standing by. As one goes past Wren, keeping him in view, another will replace it. Wren's route is carefully understood by the man himself and he has agreed not to deviate from it. Every precaution that we could imagine will be taken. But there is one thing I fear. It is possible that somewhere there exists a man with a mind as intricate as yours, Sherlock. Between now and two p.m. tomorrow, I want you to picture yourself as an enemy agent intent on securing the plans for the Wren Gun. You have an added advantage inasmuch as I have given you a blueprint of our security measures. I will give you the route Wren will follow. What you and Watson do after that will be your decision."

Mycroft lapsed into silence as the waiter appeared with the main course. After his departure, a rare smile appeared on the face of the second most powerful man in England.

"I would have to be a fool indeed if I did not seek that one extra ace to have up my sleeve."

Needless, to say, Holmes assured his brother that he would devote his full energies to this matter of such national importance. Mycroft carefully traced the route the inventor would take on the following day. Holmes remained quite silent through the remainder of the meal following which the meeting broke up. Holmes and Watson left first. By what means Mycroft Holmes departed from the Grenadier Tavern, they did not know.

Back at 221B Baker Street, Watson preserved a discreet silence feeling that Holmes was carefully considering plans he might use were he, indeed, in the employ of a foreign power. But when the great detective crossed to the Persian slipper on the mantel to fill his pipe, Watson, who was so sensitive to his moods, felt that there had been an abandonment of deep thought.

"Your brother certainly took precautions to keep our meeting a secret. He must be highly concerned about this matter, and small wonder."

Holmes nodded as he lit his Meerschaum. "You will recall that it was Mycroft who was responsible for Wren's continued association with the British government. If this gun proves effective and practical, the whole event could well prove the high point in Mycroft's career." Then he shook his head in a puzzled manner. "As to his attempts at secrecy, they baffle me somewhat."

"How so, Holmes?" asked Watson, eagerly. "I recall your mention of hocus-pocus previously."

"Let me alter that colloquialism to 'flim-flammery'. Mycroft's bulk makes him a hard man to conceal and yet we meet in a public place."

"But in a private room," stated Watson.

"Which was reserved in the name of Sherlock Holmes," stated the detective. "Something to think about when you go to sleep, my dear Watson."

Early the next morning, with Watson in tow, Holmes did a strange thing. So as not to reveal Wren's route to a possible observer, he went to the vicinity of the destination first. Several blocks from the secret office which was to be the repository of the much-anticipated plans, he back-tracked at a leisurely rate by foot heading in the direction of Liverpool Station. But he never got close to the railroad station. It was in the middle of a block that he cautioned Watson.

"We've found what we're looking for, ol' boy."

Watson tried to appear nonchalant as he idly surveyed the scene of a bustling morning street but could find nothing revealing or, for that matter, different from the other blocks which they had traversed. His look at Holmes expressed puzzlement.

"On the opposite side of the street, a slight distance from that pub is a singular sign," explained Holmes. "It reads: 'Beware of Pickpockets.' "

"And a good idea, too," said Watson. "There's many a light-fingered gentleman plying a thriving trade these days."

"And those are the ones who frequently post such signs," replied Holmes. "I think we can now return to Baker Street, old friend. Our battle station has been selected for us."

"But Holmes, what did you mean about that sign?"

"Were you walking down the street and saw it, what would your automatic reaction be?" asked the great detective.

"Why, I would check my wallet, I suppose."

"Of course, you would, and a pickpocket watching you carefully would then know where it was."

"So that's how you think they will do it." Watson was entranced.

"A possibility," stated Holmes, but a shadow crossed his eyes. "Frankly, it is the why that is puzzling me at the moment."

In retrospect, Watson decided that his friend's cryptic remark was the most mystifying part of the entire affair.

By fortunate happenstance, Betty Castle had accepted an invitation to spend a long weekend with Lord and Lady Merrow so there was to be no "Challenge Match" play on this particular Friday, which held so much promise from the standpoint of adventure. Back at Baker Street Holmes went to his desk in the sitting room and was leafing through a particular book of clippings from his extensive files. Watson recognized the volume immediately. It contained information on very select happenings, mainly of a criminal nature, which were so unusual in their *modus operandi* that they were unique and unrepeated. Holmes frequently referred to them by way of mental stimulation, as he put it.

"I note you are studying your exotic file," commented Doctor Watson.

Holmes closed the Morocco-bound volume with a look of annoyance.

"Actually, I'm wasting my time," he said, as he rose to replace the book in its customary spot. "What has me bothered is not some elaborate and hitherto unknown scheme but the bland simplicity of this entire affair."

He then lapsed into an almost truculent silence which Watson wisely did not attempt to intrude upon.

Holmes toyed with his lunch, smoked incessantly, paced their quarters and gave every indication of extreme dissatisfaction. But his long-time companion, Watson, was an old hand at the game. Philosophically, he applied himself to his "Diary of the Challenge Match" and was making note of two hands played on the previous day. As his quill pen was crossing paper, reconstructing hands, bidding, and play, he sensed Holmes' presence behind him. Looking up, he was surprised to find that a triumphant smile had replaced Holmes' frowning concentration. The detective indicated Watson's work.

"That is an ingenious title you came upon, my dear Watson."

" 'A Bit of Guile?' " Concern touched Watson's features. "I hope you don't mind my recording that particular hand. Skurry did come up with an effective piece of deception."

"Hoodwinked me completely," agreed Holmes. "By all means, dear fellow, let us give him complete credit for a shrewd and well-timed opening lead." Holmes crossed to the window, gazing out thoughtfully. "A bit of guile," he repeated, as if savoring the words.

If Holmes had seemed at loose ends previously, his manner changed abruptly. Out came the chemical equipment and he was busy with retorts and his Bunsen burner and the variety of equipment which he used so often. The results of his almost frantic activity was a small vial of colorless liquid. He then rummaged through the drawers, locating a hypodermic needle which he carefully filled with the liquid of his creation. A small cork sealed the needle which Holmes now wrapped in a handkerchief which he placed in his coat pocket. Gazing at his fellow-lodger triumphantly, Holmes relaxed.

"We are now prepared, my dear Watson, for some guile of our own."

Much to Watson's surprise, Holmes exhibited no interest in Liverpool Station where Homer Wren was to arrive. Rather, he walked, with Watson, to that particular block along Wren's proposed route which had attracted his attention in the morning. Glancing at his watch, he said:

"Wren's train should be arriving about now so we shall suffer through that most difficult period in any case, waiting."

And wait they did, Watson, fretfully, and Holmes, calmly. But the doctor noted that Holmes checked to assure himself that the pickpocket sign was still in place, which it was. Fortunately, there was a *cul-de-sac,* containing several shops, on the opposite side of the street from the sign and the pub adjacent to it. It was here that Holmes and Watson were able to stand without appearing obvious.

Mycroft had shown both Holmes and Watson several pictures of Homer Wren and when he appeared on the opposite side of the street a block away, he was easy to identify. He was youngish and erect with premature white hair. He walked at a moderate rate of speed. Behind him was the dray making slow progress because of the lameness of one of the horses. All the signposts were there.

As Wren was almost opposite them, his eye caught the pickpocket sign. Watson saw his left hand automatically feel the right inside pocket of his coat. At this point, the entrance to the pub flew open abruptly and a man was ejected forcibly by a burly bartender. He bumped into Wren and the pair fell to the ground. Watson almost cried out and made to rush across the street but he was held firm by the steely arm of Holmes.

"Not yet, old friend," cautioned the detective.

From the same side of the street, a man suddenly appeared and ran across the thoroughfare.He helped Wren to his feet, brushing him off. Still, Holmes made no move, watching intently with his hawk-like eyes. At this point the man who had been propelled from the pub began to curse in a voice blurred from drink. He seemed disposed to blame the inventor, Wren, for the collision. The third member of the trio whose shoulder span was ominous, took the inebriated man firmly by the arm and walked him down the street with little difficulty. It was now that Holmes moved, crossing the street with Watson in tow. The inebriate was protesting, to no avail, as he was being removed from the scene, and Homer Wren suddenly found himself flanked by Holmes and Watson.

"I believe it would be expedient, Mr. Wren, if Doctor Watson and I accompanied you the rest of the way," said the detective in his most urbane manner. Recognition spilled over the inventors face.

"You are Sherlock Holmes," he said quietly. "Your brother mentioned that our paths might cross." Wren felt his inside pocket again and seemed reassured. "I shall be delighted to have your company, gentlemen."

Two large men who had been in the dray and had descended from it at the outburst of action, resumed their positions at a sharp glance from Holmes.

The rest of the trip was without incident.

It was in a nondescript office with the sign: "Asiatic Imports Dept." on the door that Mycroft Holmes awaited their arrival. Nodding to Wren, Mycroft fastened his brother with a questioning look.

"Something happened, didn't it?"

Holmes nodded. "Rather obvious, I thought, and not effective. At least, I don't think it was, but we shall soon know."

With Mycroft was an elderly man with thick glasses, who was introduced simply as Wells.

"Mr. Wells is an expert on safes. If you have any questions regarding the operation of the Mahler safe, he will answer them." Mycroft addressed this to Homer Wren.

It was Wells who opened the door leading from the ante-room in which they were standing, revealing a sizeable inner room. The dominant feature was a large safe set in the wall. Watson judged that the room was constructed of reinforced concrete.

As Mycroft and Wren entered the vault-like chamber, Holmes indicated for Wells to follow. With a moment of privacy available, he whispered to Watson, rapidly:

"When I take out my coat handerchief, Watson, I want you to pretend that you have a seizure of some sort. Your medical knowledge will make the doooit realistic, I know."

Watson gave Holmes a look of amazement as he followed the master sleuth into the inner room. Wells was opening the massive safe as Wren watched him intently. The inside of the safe door glistened with recessed bolts of steel. There was a small box-like arrangement within the now-revealed interior which the strong-box expert indicated.

"That is the timing device. We shall set it for sixty-six hours, it now being three p.m. on Friday. Once the door is closed, nothing short of the complete demolition of this room can open the safe."

Wren nodded with satisfaction. "If you will show me the mechanism, I'm satisfied. I have some knowledge of timing devices, as you may already know."

"One moment," said Sherlock Holmes. "Before these impressive security measures go into effect, had we not better check the contents of your pocket, Mr.

Wren?" As the inventor looked at him blankly, the detective continued: "Surely, you realize that an attempt was made to pick your pocket. Would it not be prudent to verify that your plans for the Wren Gun are still in your possession?"

The inventor removed a bulky envelope from his inside pocket and broke the seal.

"I recognize the envelope and seal, Mr. Holmes, but your caution cannot be denied."

Spreading the papers which he removed from the envelope on a flat table, he studied them carefully, with Holmes standing at his elbow. The detective chose this moment to remove his coat handkerchief. Watson suddenly staggered and produced a chilling groan. He would have fallen if Wren and Mycroft had not grabbed him. The Doctor's breath came in rapid gasps and his eyes fluttered. Wells rushed to join the others, but it was Holmes who assumed command.

"Stand back, gentlemen, please. My dear friend is subject to these attacks, especially during moments of stress."

Holmes waved smelling salts under Watson's nose.

"After-effects of his most unfortunate wound in the second Afghan War," he explained.

In a few moments, Watson was sufficiently recovered to stand. Homer Wren assured those present that his plans for the Wren Gun were intact and he and Wells placed them in the Mahler safe setting the time device and closing the door.

Mycroft regarded the apparently recovered Watson and his brother somewhat strangely.

Sherlock Holmes had a question. "At nine a.m. on Monday, the safe will open, as I understand it?"

"And not until then," said Wells, with finality.

"May I ask who, in addition to Mr. Wren, and I assume you, Mycroft, will be here?"

His brother shot a look of inquiry at Homer Wren.

"Since Mr. Sherlock Holmes may have prevented the theft of the plans, I see no reason for him not to be informed," said Wren.

"Lord Cantlemere and Lord Bellinger will both be here," stated Mycroft. "Also Connaught from the Ardsdale Armory. He is our best man on mobile weaponry. If Connaught, after inspecting the plans, agrees that the Wren Gun will deliver, Lords Cantlemere and Bellinger are authorized by Her Majesty's Government to transact the necessary business arrangements."

"The last two gentlemen I know quite well," said Sherlock. "If Mr. Wren has no objections, I would like to be present come Monday morning with Doctor Watson."

The face of the inventor creased into a smile.

"If Her Majesty's ministers have no objections, I certainly haven't. Monday morning I will receive a very large sum of money and the presence of the world's greatest detective will be welcome. In fact, Mr. Holmes, I am prepared to offer you a considerable fee if you and Doctor Watson would accompany me to the City and Suburban Bank at the conclusion of my business Monday."

"We can waive the question of fee," said Holmes. "I would just like to see this matter to its conclusion."

The matter stood at that. Watson spent a most restless weekend. As was his habit so frequently, Holmes was disinclined to discuss the case at all. Beyond saying that Watson portrayed a man with a sudden illness very convincingly indeed, he made no comment of his strange request to his friend. Sunday night, the good doctor found sleep almost impossible.

It was somewhat before nine a.m. that Holmes and Watson appeared at the office of the pseudo-Asiatic Imports Dept. Lord Cantlemere and Lord Bellinger were already there and greeted Holmes warmly. They both had good cause to welcome his presence. (Note: See "The Adventure of the Mazarin Stone" and "The Adventure of the Second Stain.")

Mycroft Holmes arrived shortly thereafter with Wells and the group was complete when a most confident Homer Wren appeared. With Wren was a small, wizened man who was introduced to Holmes and Watson as Connaught. There followed a few moments of waiting, during which Lord Bellinger nervously fidgeted with the seals of his watch-chain. Lord Cantlemere's hatchet face, with its mid-Victorian whiskers, twisted into the semblance of a smile.

"I do trust, Mr. Holmes, that today will not provide another example of your unusual sense of humor, which I have good reason for remembering, along with your amazing professional powers."

The comments of the aged peer were cut short by a distinct click which magnetized the attention of everyone in the room. Wells rose to his feet.

"The safe can now be opened," he said simply, and proceeded to perform that task.

Connaught followed him into the safe and took the plans from their resting place atop the timing device. With Homer Wren at his side, he opened the envelope, laying out the papers on the plain table available. Drawing up a chair, he buried himself in the diagrams. Wren secured a seat alongside him to answer any necessary questions. Save for the rustle of paper, the silence was complete. Watson noted that a sizeable dispatch case was close to the chair occupied by Lord Bellinger.

"The payment is evidently to be made in pounds sterling," he thought.

Suddenly, the paper sound increased as Connaught turned a page and then another and another as if searching for something. Then he reassembled the diagrams in order and began on the first page again. After ten minutes that seemed like ten hours, he looked up slowly at Homer Wren.

"Your spring load device is well-engineered. She'll need a rim fire bullet but that is nay ma problem. It's yurrr brrreech mechanism, mon. She'll fire all right but she'll no deliverrr 500 rrrounds a minute nor annythin' like it." Turning to Cantlemere and Bellinger, the aged Scot delivered his opinion. "Gentlemen, the gun will nay live up to her specifications."

With a hoarse cry, Wren snatched the diagrams from Connaught, leafing through them. A gnarled finger pinpointed one drawing for him.

"Check your recoil ejector mechanism, mon, and tell me 'twill wurrrk." Connaught's voice was grim.

Wren's eyes were flashing over complex drawings and his visage was white and strained. Suddenly, he lifted his face and there was a murderous look about him as he surveyed the others in the room.

"Your weaponry expert is correct. These plans aren't worth the paper they are written on." With a wild gesture, he swept the diagrams onto the floor. "And they aren't my plans."

The room erupted into sound. Wren sprang towards Wells but was intercepted by the considerable figure of Mycroft Holmes. Cantlemere and Bellinger were firing questions at Connaught. Only Holmes seemed calm as he retrieved the diagrams from the floor.

"Gentlemen, please," he said. While his voice was low, its steely quality brought all other sound to a halt. "We have a group of specialists here — an inventor, a weaponry expert, a master locksmith — three public servants with long and loyal careers, and a medical man. But the problem facing us comes within my category. We have a mystery."

"Mystery, my foot!" fumed Homer Wren. "It is obvious what has happened. I placed my plans within this safe last Friday. You, Mr. Holmes, witnessed it. Since that time I have had no access to this room." The irate inventor shot a sharp glance at Mycroft Holmes. "I've been under constant surveillance since that time, in fact. That thief, Mahler, used the idea of my timing device to construct a supposedly fool-proof safe. But he must have built something into his release mechanism which eluded me. Sometime, during the weekend my plans disappeared."

The rounded shoulders of Lord Cantlemere sagged and his already sallow face appeared paler still.

"Are you accusing Her Majesty's Government of thievery?"

Wren's face was livid with rage but his manner became calmer.

"I happen to be a loyal British subject. Therefore, I promise you that I will not reconstruct the plans of the Wren Gun and sell them elsewhere. However, I contend that the Government has the plans and I do not have the money due for them. Therefore, I shall seek legal redress." Lord Bellinger began a sentence but Wren was not to be denied. "I know that you can hold up the case, bury it under technicalities and cause endless delay, but sometime my voice will have to be heard." He turned toward Sherlock Holmes. "When it is, and when this swindle is brought to light, the reputation of the specialists you referred to, Mr. Holmes, will not be worth tuppence!"

Sherlock Holmes seemed completely unconcerned.

"As I was about to say, we are dealing with a mystery, and it is the job of a detective to solve a mystery. So I shall." As he spoke, Holmes drew a box of matches from his pocket.

"On Friday last," he said, with his commanding eyes fastened on Homer Wren, "you inspected your plans and diagrams at my insistence." The detective indicated the papers just taken from the safe. "Are you prepared to swear that these are not those plans?"

"Of course, I am," snarled the inventor. "The envelope is the same but the contents are not. My plans were workable."

"Very well," said Holmes. "Now, gentlemen, I will perform a magic trick for you. Here is the second sheet of the Wren Gun plans which were just taken from the safe." He showed the sheet to the group. "You will note that the bottom is free of words or drawings. I am now about to make my initials appear there."

Lighting a match, Holmes passed the flame close to the back of the paper moving it back and forth to prevent combustion. Faintly, at first, and then so definite as to provide no possibility of error, the initials "S.H." appeared.

"I don't understand," stammered Lord Bellinger.

"Invisible ink, gentlemen. It is as simple as that. I manufactured it myself prior to Mr. Wren's arrival in London. As you may know, the most common means of making invisible ink appear is through the application of heat. Last Friday, just after Wren inspected his plans, Doctor Watson, at my request, pretended to have a seizure.

Magic tricks by Holmes.

In the moment of distraction caused by this, I initialed the second page of the plans which then were placed into the Mahler safe. I used a hypodermic needle filled with invisible ink. You see, from the start, certain facts of this case did not ring true. My suspicions were aroused almost from the start. But that is of little importance while what actually happened is."

Every face, save one, was glued on the detective's grave visage. Homer Wren had sunk into a chair and buried his face in his hands.

"Gentlemen," continued Holmes, "there never was a Wren Gun. After his unsuccessful attempts to produce an effective time bomb, Mr. Wren busied himself with his automatic weapon theory. Many of his ideas had merit. Mr. Connaught here said his loading mechanism was effective. But Wren soon realized that a gun of the type he pictured was far beyond not only his skills but the technology of our times. However, by demonstrating certain workable parts, he was able to stimulate the interest of the Government. The plans he delivered here last Friday were not workable, as he well knew. But by contending that they had been stolen from him, he intended to threaten such a hue and cry that the Government would have been almost forced to make a settlement. I can well imagine the words of some member of Parliament if the matter had come to light. 'We spend millions on dreadnoughts but resort to thievery to secure a piece of infantry ordinance.' You see, it was all a hoax."

Ancient fires had kindled in Lord Cantlemere's eyes.

"After fifty years of official life, I cannot recall such a despicable case." He gazed at Homer Wren with loathing. "But sir, under the Security of the Realm Act, I can promise you no less than twenty years of hard labor in a military prison."

There was a unanimous growl of assent from the others which was stemmed by Holmes' upraised hand.

"Gently, gently," he said. "Because of the secrecy surrounding this affair, I presume the loyalty of Mr. Wells and Mr. Connaught are above suspicion?"

"I'd stake my life on that," replied Mycroft Holmes.

"And the same can be said of you, Lord Bellinger, twice Prime Minister of Britain and certainly of Lord Cantlemere. My brother would not hold his position without complete faith in his discretion and, certainly, Doctor Watson and I have no reason to make this matter public. That leaves only our conspirator, Homer Wren, and the threat of twenty years' imprisonment should insure his silence."

"What are you driving at, Mr. Holmes?" inquired Lord Bellinger.

"Simply, gentlemen, that the only ones who know that the Wren Gun does not exist are present in this room at this time. Now, let us picture, not what happened, but what others might think happened. A young inventor with sufficient credentials to make it believable that he could evolve a super weapon, interests the British Government in his findings. He is known to have been employed by the Government. Perhaps he has come up with a previous discovery as yet unrevealed. He arrives in London amid elaborate security precautions. An attempt to steal his plans is forestalled. Mr. Sherlock Holmes and his known associate, Doctor Watson, are on the scene, quite obviously, too. Wren delivers his plans. He is not imprisoned but instead is put to work on some other project, perhaps at a military base where supervision would not be obvious."

Since Holmes was looking at Connaught, the Scottish armament expert nodded thoughtfully. "His spring-loading device could be of some help on an idea I'm mulling round."

Holmes' eyes returned to the entire group. "There might even be a rumor that Mr. Wren is in line for a government citation."

Lord Cantlemere bristled.

"I just mentioned a rumor," continued Holmes. "At the outset, my brother, Mycroft, requested that I place myself in the imaginary role of an enemy agent. Were I such an agent with the facts I have just outlined to you, I would be convinced that England possessed a weapon of awesome power. What I propose is that a hoax be converted into a gigantic hoax. If it is done, or by what means, does not come within my province. It is just a thought."

Thus ended the most unusual adventure which Doctor Watson chose to title, "The Hoax." It is very possible that this one incident explains why the "Diary of the Challenge Match" was secreted from the world for so long. There were direct results of both an international nature and a very personal one.

In the Sudan, a self-proclaimed prophet whose true aims were more militaristic than religious, suddenly found himself without the necessary equipment to cause the sword of Islam to rise again. Extensive cavalry maneuvers in the vicinity of the

Kyber Pass, historical gateway to India, were suddenly cancelled and rebellious Afghans found themselves without ammunition for carefully-hoarded guns. Franco-German relations took a sudden turn for the better, possibly because of the vision of a British Expeditionary Force possessing fantastic fire-power of a highly mobile, easily-transportable type.

Historically, there is precedence for this assumption since the destiny of Europe, and indeed the world, was dictated for twenty years by a phantom. The spectre of The Grand Army of the Republic and the deadly fear that it would rise again. But it never did following that final disaster known as Waterloo. In a similar vein, it is possible to imagine that the fuse was removed from the powder keg, for a time, at least, by the nightmare of an automatic weapon which never really existed.

All of these events took place during a considerable span of time. But it was the Monday following Holmes' solution that the relevation of a personal nature occurred.

Holmes and Watson had departed from the "Asiatic Import Dept." office and secured a hansom back to Baker Street. Throughout the trip, Holmes had preserved a strict and thoughtful silence though, on occasion, the corners of his mouth had twitched as though he were having difficulty suppressing laughter.

Comfortably ensconced in chairs in their sitting room, Watson finally got around to the subject that plagued him.

"Holmes, throughout this whole complex chain of events, you have hinted at things which you never mentioned to Mycroft or the others. And what, by all that is holy, do you seem to find so amusing about the incident?"

Holmes answered with quotes: 'A Simple Hoax', 'A Gigantic Hoax', 'A Bit of Guile'. " He laughed for a moment, heartily. "That title of yours crystallized my thoughts. Don't you realize, Watson, that throughout it all, we have been the victims of the hoax?"

Seldom had Watson looked so befuddled so Holmes patiently continued:

"An apple vendor on Baker Street in mid-winter? A contact with a man with an eye patch? A public meeting with Mycroft in a restaurant and in a room reserved under my name? My dear brother might very easily have sent a message to us here in Baker Street or paid us one of his nocturnal visits. Instead, he leaves a trail of clues of the type that a child could follow and on a foggy night at that. Think of the inconsistencies: An inventor with a supposedly priceless set of plans coming by train to London two days before an important meeting when he might have been brought by a military escort disguised as a soldier, if need be. Nothing made sense save the obvious fact that Mycroft was drawing all the attention possible to Homer Wren and to the fact that the two of us were involved in some matter connected with him.

"Look at the supposed waylaying of Wren on the street, where he should never have been in the first place. If this had been a genuine attempt to secure the plans, the supposedly drunken man would not have been the pickpocket. He would have been the decoy, the attention-getter, just as you were with your ersatz seizure. The other man who assisted Wren to his feet, he would have been the culprit. Yet I watched him with the utmost care and he made no attempt to pilfer Wren's pocket."

Watson was shaking his head. "But where does it all lead, Sherlock? I am more confused than ever."

"Watson, from the very beginning, Mycroft knew there was no Wren Gun. I might even make a little wager with you that Homer Wren is, in reality, an agent of Mycroft. My subtle brother was following an old idea, namely: that the most realistic deceiver is he who does not realize he is cast in that role. Think what a clever web he wove. If he could deceive two illustrious statesmen plus two dedicated public servants to say nothing of his own brother, how could he fail to deceive his opponents? I'll bet my violin that Mycroft plotted this whole thing from the very beginning. But," said Holmes, very emphatically, "I'll never ask him!"

And he never did!

(NOTE: Many of the adventures of Sherlock Holmes, as faithfully related by his dedicated chronicler, John H. Watson, M.D., were replete with the unusual. Possibly, the greatest coincidence of all was in connection with this story, especially since neither of the Baker Street duo were privy to it. Long after both Holmes and Watson were gone, two men called Sheppard and Turpin, in association with the British Government, developed a machine carbine still in use. It has only 45 parts, weighing from six pounds, six ounces, to eight pounds, and fires any rimless nine millimeter ammunition at the rate of 550 rounds a minute. It is called, "The Sten Gun".)

THE TWO WAY COUNT

```
                   SKURRY
                   ♠ 10 4
                   ♡ K Q J 5
                   ◊ 9 7 3
                   ♣ 10 8 4 3
HOLMES (Dealer)                      WATSON
♠ A K 9 6 3                          ♠ Q J 5
♡ 2                                  ♡ A 7 4 3
◊ A K 6                              ◊ 8 5 2
♣ A 9 6 2                            ♣ K Q 5
                   CASTLE
                   ♠ 8 7 2
                   ♡ 10 9 8 6
                   ◊ Q J 10 4
                   ♣ J 7
```

The bidding on this hand would not conform with that of many partnerships, confirming Holmes' statement that any time an artificiality is adopted, a natural meaning is, perforce, lost. Holmes and Watson had agreed that a bid of two hearts, in response to an opening bid of one spade, would indicate a five-card heart suit. This style had worked very well for them, allowing the opener to raise partner's hearts with but three. On this hand, the device bred some problems. Holmes opened one spade.

Normally, Watson could have shown his ten points or better by responding two hearts. However, he had only four cards in the suit. This left the good doctor with two alternatives. He was much too strong to give a simple spade raise so it was either bidding two clubs which would describe his strength or bid two notrump. Watson was a point short for the latter bid but chose to respond two notrump anyway. With a game force from partner, Holmes could afford to play the waiting game and simply bid three clubs. Now, Watson bid three spades which was what the detective wanted to hear. Holmes swung into slam action by bidding four notrump, Blackwood. On learning that his partner held the heart ace, Holmes considered bidding six spades directly but feeling that there might be a grand slam, he bid five notrump. Watson's six diamond response indicated only one king so Holmes settled for six spades. Harry Skurry made the obvious lead of the heart king and the battle was on.

When Holmes was first taught bridge by Watson, the doctor had impressed on him the necessity of counting losers in suit contracts as a means of developing a game plan. However, as he rapidly rose to the expert class, Holmes soon realized that it paid to count both losers and winners especially if your loser count did not please you. If the clubs broke unfavorably, Holmes could picture a loser in that suit and another in diamonds. But he could count twelve winners. Do you see what he had in mind?

Holmes took the heart king with dummy's ace and led a low heart which he trumped in his hand. Now he played the spade ace and then led a low spade to dummy's queen. A second low heart was led from the board and trumped in the closed hand. Now the detective returned to dummy by leading a low club to the king. Dummy's fourth heart was trumped by Holmes' last spade. A low club to the queen put him on the board again. Now he extracted the last outstanding spade via dummy's jack, discarding his losing diamond six from his hand. Holmes returned to his hand with the club ace and cashed his high diamonds, conceding a club in the end.

Reginald Musgrave, who had accompanied the Challenge Match Quartette when they had made their trip to Bath, was smiling.

"I wonder if the Duke of Cumberland would have recognized your technique on that hand, Holmes?" he asked.

"That's right," said Watson. "It was the same reversal of dummy idea you came up with when we were involved in the matter of those paintings." (See "Sherlock Holmes, Bridge Detective.")

This manner of making an apparent loser disappear later became known as the Dummy-Reversal play.

THE BLAST

WATSON (Dealer)
♠ K J 7
♡ A K 5
◇ Q J 10 4
♣ A 8 4

SKURRY
♠ 9 5 4 2
♡ J 8
◇ K 7 5
♣ Q J 10 3

CASTLE
♠ A Q 10 8 3
♡ 4
◇ 8 3
♣ 9 7 6 5 2

HOLMES
♠ 6
♡ Q 10 9 7 6 3 2
◇ A 9 6 2
♣ K

CHALLENGE MATCH BIDDING: (neither side vulnerable)

Skurry	Watson	Castle	Holmes
-	1NT	pass	6H
pass	pass	pass	

When Watson opened one notrump, Holmes faced a dilemma. His partner could have no less than two hearts so the detective knew where he wanted to play. The problem was at how high a contract. A four notrump bid by Holmes would be an invitation to slam, not the message he wished to convey at all. After a lengthy pause, he decided that it was reasonable to expect Watson to hold at least two aces. In an effort to make the best of a difficult situation, Holmes bid six hearts with the full realization that he might well make seven and he could also go down at six.

Harry Skurry led the club queen. When Holmes saw the lead and the dummy hand it was with difficulty that he suppressed a sigh of relief. Taking the first trick in the closed hand, he crossed to dummy's ace and king of hearts drawing his opponents' trumps. Now the club ace allowed him to dump his losing spade. The queen of diamonds was played from the board and finessed. While this maneuver lost to Skurry's king, the small slam was made with ease.

Holmes and Watson had a discussion relative to this hand.

"Obviously, Watson, we are lacking in bidding tools when an opening notrump bid is facing a highly distributional hand. I'll admit that it does not occur too often but we should give the problem some thought. The moment you opened with a notrump bid, I was interested in only one thing: the number of first round controls you held."

"Do you have a thought relative to this, Holmes?"

"Well, we could fall back on the wasted bid concept and use four clubs as ace asking when the previous bid has been one or two notrump. The responses would be in steps similar to Blackwood." Suddenly, Holmes smiled. "However, this rather interesting thought would have dealt us an ill service in this particular hand."

"How so, Holmes?" inquired Watson.

"Had I bid four clubs over your notrump opening, a response of four diamonds would have shown no aces; four hearts would have indicated one . . ."

"Therefore, I would have bid four spades," interjected Watson, "since I held two aces."

"Betty Castle would certainly have doubled this artificial bid demanding a spade lead from her partner. And a spade lead by Harry holds me to eleven tricks no matter how I play it. There is something to be said for bidding the limit on the theory that your opponents are on a guess as to the killing lead."

In modern times, Holmes' six heart bid would be called "blasting".

It is also of interest that the great John Gerber of our times evolved the Gerber Convention which is an ace asking bid of four clubs to be used opposite opening notrump bids. Most experts use Gerber in conjunction with Blackwood in the manner suggested by Holmes.

The Challenge Match.

THE LONDON CUP

By now, the most recent Holmes discovery was common knowledge in London's bridge world. Journalists made much of it and served to popularize it outside of Britain proper. Ezra Maize's widely syndicated writings had brought knowledge of this bridge innovation to America and the convention was a hot subject of conversation at Le Club Bridgeur in Paris. But something was missing. The "Two Club Convention" was the title given to this bidding aid by Sir Guy Gorman. Holmes himself called it "Clubs Over Notrump". Various other terms were used, some, by very hidebound players, which were not too complimentary. In an indirect fashion, one of the outstanding social events of the London season had an effect upon this situation.

It was the custom every year for the Duchess of Paisley and Lady Windermere to co-sponsor a large charity entertainment, the proceeds of which went to the families of indigent Welsh and Cornish coal-miners. Much to the indignation of the most aristocratic co-sponsors, the affair had acquired the name of "The Miners' Ball".

In an effort to bury this undignified title, the Duchess and Lady Windermere came up with the idea of presenting a bridge tournament on this one particular year. The illustrious Septimus Shinegold was appointed *charge d'affaire*. Lord Arthur Saville agreed to head up the ticket sale committee and Lord Balmoral generously agreed to donate The London Cup which would go to the winners. The cup, an elaborate piece of craftsmanship in silver and gold, secured much-needed publicity for the contest. Lord Saville, with an eye to a sellout, immediately secured the promise of Holmes and Watson that they would participate in this one evening of play. Betty Castle and Harry Skurry secured entry blanks along with their opponents. Skurry, in particular, was enthusiastic about the charity evening stating that it would be a relief not to have to play constantly against "that devilishly clever Holmes".

Well-planned and promoted, the tournament drew players from everywhere. Sir George Gooden-Gooden came from his estates in Baden-Baden to play with his regular partner, Sir Alden Pursuit. Chief Constable Fenwick-Trescott, who had taken up the game at Holmes' suggestion came to London from Bath bringing his famous Scottish partner, H. Ewing Belsey. Miss Dorothy Hoyden of Croyden was an entry partnered with Lady Carrell-Hewes, later a client of Holmes on a much different matter. It was agreed that the play would follow the plan established by Henry Jones in 1857. Much to the delight of the Duchess of Paisley and Lady Windermere, the much-heralded event was referred to in the journals as "The London Cup Duplicate."

The Challenge Match continued play but, for a brief period, The London Cup captured the imagination of the bridge world.

When play finally began on the gala evening, fully half the players present were informing their opponents that they played the "Holmes' Two Clubs", or "The Two Club Convention, or whatever name they used.

Those two-man teams seated North-South remained in their places. Their East-West opponents played two hands against them and then moved to an adjacent table to be replaced by another team.

Holmes' and Watson's first opponents were Fenwick Trescott and H. Ewing Belsey. Naturally, the table of the great bridge-playing detective was completely surrounded by onlookers but then, the rest of the vast Windsor Ballroom which was the site of the affair was crowded to the very walls. Septimus Shinegold was among those surrounding the number one table. The importance of this fact will be revealed shortly.

HALT MON

WATSON
♠ 10 9 3
♡ Q 9 8 4
♦ Q 5 4 3
♣ 6 4

BELSEY
♠ K 6 2
♡ K 7 5
♦ J 9 8
♣ Q 10 5 3

TRESCOTT
♠ 8 7 4
♡ J 3
♦ 10 7 6 2
♣ A 9 8 2

HOLMES (Dealer)
♠ A Q J 5
♡ A 10 6 2
♦ A K
♣ K J 7

Holmes	Belsey	Watson	Trescott
2NT	pass	3C	pass
3S	pass	3NT	pass
4H	pass	pass	pass

Belsey's ruddy Scottish face had been looking from Holmes to Watson as the bidding progressed but when Watson passed Holmes'. four hearts, incredulity flooded his features. "Halt, Mon!" he said loudly, in a thick burr. He regarded Watson with puzzlement. "Ye be passin' a suit which ha' just been called by the mon on me right for the fust time?"

As Watson nodded, there was a sudden flash of understanding in the Scot's eyes. "Be this that club fandango that I be hearin' aboot sae much o' late?"

Watson agreed. "My partner and I are playing an artificial club response over notrump bids and stated the fact prior to play."

67

As Fenwick Trescott nodded to confirm this statement, Belsey continued. "A wee moment of your time, please. Would ye be explainin' to me the biddin'?" He was still addressing Doctor Watson.

Watson smiled pleasantly. "My partner's two notrump opening bid was standard. My response of three clubs requested him to name a four card major suit if he had one. His bid of three spades indicated four spade cards. I denied the spade suit by bidding three notrump whereupon Holmes bid four hearts."

"Hmm!" said Belsey. "Then it would be correct for me to assume that Mr. Holmes here holds four spades and four hearts? Be that so?"

Watson agreed. "Sitting West, as you are, sir, I would make that assumption."

Belsey led the three of clubs.

Holmes saw a possible loser in each black suit so his problem was to lose only one trump. He played a low club from dummy with Trescott taking the trick with his ace and returning the club two. Holmes rose with his club king. Wanting to avoid a guess in the trump suit, the detective decided to try and lay an elementary false trail feeling there was little to be lost by doing so. He played his ace and then king of diamonds. Now he led a low heart towards dummy's queen trying to create the impression that he wanted to get to dummy to cash the diamond queen. However, the Scot did not fall for this. He knew Holmes started with five minor suit cards. If he held three clubs, the diamond queen was of no use since he could ruff this loser. If he held three diamonds he could easily lead to dummy's queen when he so desired. Belsey played a low trump. His partner could hold the trump jack or ten and Holmes might try a deep finesse in the suit. Holmes hopefully played dummy's trump queen which took the trick. He returned a small heart to his ace. Holmes now abandoned the heart suit and trumped his last club in dummy. He played dummy's spade ten, dropping the five from his hand. Belsey ducked the trick. Holmes continued the spade nine to his jack and now the Scot had to take his spade king. Belsey played his heart king removing dummy's last trump but it was all over for the defense. Holmes had lost but a spade, heart, and one club, making four hearts.

Belsey was very thoughtful. "Three notrump wi' the same club lead cannot be made. We take three club tricks for sure plus the two major suit kings. I'm a-thinkin', Mr. Holmes, that they'll be hearin' some wurrrds aboot your biddin' gadget round Edinburgh way."

Septimus Shinegold had heard the entire discussion and one of the reasons his bridge column was syndicated as far as Afghanistan was that he wrote in a jovial manner and did not overlook the element of human interest.

It was not long after the London Cup Duplicate that Shinegold wrote up the hand including Belsey's "Halt Mon!" query. Public taste is an unpredictable thing. Somehow bridge players associated the club convention with "Halt Mon" and it soon became known as "The Haltmon Convention."

How singular that when a great modern player, thinking along the same lines as Holmes, revived the "Two Club Convention" his name was Samuel Stayman and the convention is now known as "Stayman"!

The second hand played on this first round prompted H. Ewing Belsey to make some further inquiries.

LESSER OF EVILS

WATSON
♠ A 9 6
♡ Q 8 7 2
◇ K J 4
♣ A Q J

BELSEY (Dealer)
♠ J 5 2
♡ K 6 3
◇ 9 8 7 6
♣ 6 5 3

TRESCOTT
♠ 8 7
♡ J 10 9 5
◇ A Q 10
♣ K 10 9 4

HOLMES
♠ K Q 10 4 3
♡ A 4
◇ 5 3 2
♣ 8 7 2

Belsey	Watson	Trescott	Holmes
pass	1NT	pass	3NT
pass	pass	pass	

Against Watson's three notrump contract, Fenwick Trescott led the heart jack. When Holmes' dummy hand was exposed, Belsy took a long look at the great sleuth and his brow was furrowed. But he remained silent. Watson played dummy's heart ace and then led a low club finessing the queen In his hand. Trescott won the trick and led another heart which Belsey took with his king. However, Watson's queen took the return of the suit. Now Watson was able to cash five spade tricks and two club tricks to go with his two winners in the heart suit.

Belsey was shaking his head. "I dinna ken," he said. "I thought yourrr convention, Meester Holmes, was to try and find major suit fits. Would ye nay bid yourrr two clubs and then show the spade suit? If ye be playin' this gadget the way ye explained it?"

"Your thought is correct," responded Holmes. "But consider my problem after Watson opened one notrump. My hand is balanced and gains but one distributional point should the contract be in spades. Opposed to this is the risk of my partner's minor suit holdings being led through rather than to. To me, this risk outweighed the slight advantage of playing in my five card suit. However, if you feel our bidding was misleading, we should certainly call the director."

Belsey was shaking his head negatively. "Mon, I canna argue wi' common sense. Were ye playin' in four spades, we should ha' taken two diamonds along with a club and a heart. Should we play against each other again, Meester Holmes, could ye possibly stay away from notrump bids? Yourr wee gadget is givin' me no luck at all."

But Belsey had given the "wee gadget" a title though he had no way of knowing it at the time.

The London Cup Duplicate provided a veritable field day for Doctor Watson. With the cream of British bridge players all anxious to use what later became known as the Haltmon Convention, numerous hands involving this bidding aid occurred. Watson makes note that he was greatly aided by Baroness Jeurdon and Lady Beatrice Lind-Mead who assisted him in collecting hands relative to Haltmon which were painstakingly listed in Watson's Diary of the Challenge Match. While the hands were not played in the Challenge Match and some did not involve Holmes and Watson, still the Convention found birth at the Grosvenor Square Bridge Club and Watson felt that fact warranted their inclusion in his Diary.

THE THOUGHT-PROVOKER

This hand was played by the aforementioned Miss Dorothy Hoyden of Croydon partnered with Lady Carrell-Hewes. Their opponents were star players from the Old Chelsea Bridge Club, Freda Fright and Lorraine Loftus.

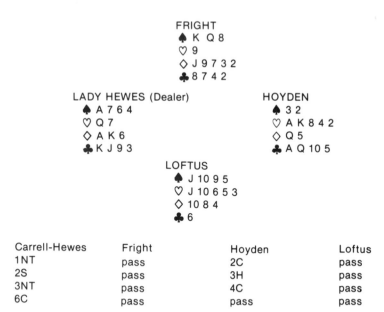

```
                        FRIGHT
                        ♠ K Q 8
                        ♡ 9
                        ◇ J 9 7 3 2
                        ♣ 8 7 4 2

   LADY HEWES (Dealer)               HOYDEN
   ♠ A 7 6 4                         ♠ 3 2
   ♡ Q 7                             ♡ A K 8 4 2
   ◇ A K 6                           ◇ Q 5
   ♣ K J 9 3                         ♣ A Q 10 5

                        LOFTUS
                        ♠ J 10 9 5
                        ♡ J 10 6 5 3
                        ◇ 10 8 4
                        ♣ 6
```

Carrell-Hewes	Fright	Hoyden	Loftus
1NT	pass	2C	pass
2S	pass	3H	pass
3NT	pass	4C	pass
6C	pass	pass	pass

Lady Carrell-Hewes found no difficulty in opening one notrump. Her queen, small doubleton did not bother her since the new club convention did provide the

70

notrump bidder with additional protection. At a later period, Holmes even advocated opening one notrump with a jack, small doubleton. Dorothy Hoyden immediately recognized her holding as a problem one. Opposite her partner's known strength, she had points galore but a distributional hand. She chose to bid two clubs as a forcing measure to see what would happen. Lady Hewes responded two spades, naturally. Now Dorothy showed her five hearts. Her partner denied the suit by bidding three notrump. Dorothy realized her partner had to have seven cards in the minor suits and now showed her clubs. Dorothy's energetic bidding plus a four-card club fit prompted Lady Hewes to go right to a small slam.

Lorraine Loftus from her holding and the bidding could count out the heart suit. She knew dummy held two and Dorothy had five. She was tempted to open a heart to dispose of her partner's singleton but quickly realized that her hand was singularly lacking in entry cards. She chose the spade jack as her opening lead.

See if you can plan the play as well as the ace player from Croydon.

Dorothy took the spade lead with dummy's ace. The cards looked good and she had thoughts of making seven. She played a low club to her ace and a trump back towards the board. With South showing out, the adverse trump situation was revealed. Now Dorothy, playing with great care, took the second club with a high card in dummy. She shifted to a low diamond taken by her queen. then a diamond back to dummy's ace and she played the diamond king which provided a resting place for her losing spade. Dummy's heart queen was cashed. Dorothy now led a low heart.

Freda Fright had a problem. She knew from both bidding and play that Dorothy had originally held doubletons in both the spade and diamond suits. If Freda did not trump, it was obvious that her opponent would simply cross ruff the major suits for the necessary twelve tricks. Freda trumped the heart lead with Dorothy playing a small heart. Miss Fright now led her last club. Dorothy took the trick in her hand and played her heart eight which she ruffed with dummy's last club. A spade lead, ruffed in the closed hand, allowed Dorothy to cash her good ace-king of hearts and score her slam.

When Holmes and Watson played the uninteresting North-South hands they did not face such a talented declarer. In fact, their opponents bid to six notrump going down on a spade lead. Therefore, Dorothy's expert bidding and play gained a large number of points for Holmes and Watson.

This hand, much later, gained fame. Dorothy Hoyden had learned much by kibitzing Holmes and Watson when they played in Bath, England. Returning to her home in Croydon, she soon became the city's top player. Following the London Cup Duplicate, it was this particular hand which prompted her to evolve an extension of Holmes' major suit asking bid. She employed a bid of two clubs opposite a no-trump opening as asking for a major but showing less than game-going strength. A bid of two diamonds was used also in quest of a major suit but was game-forcing. Her innovation became known as "Two Way Haltmon". Miss Hoyden employed her idea with great effectiveness when she represented England on the all-female team which played the "Signoras Azzura", the Italian woman's team, for the world championship. When Samuel Stayman gave birth to the modern "Stayman Convention", I am given to understand that he did not choose to use the two-way variety on the theory that it was too revealing to the opponents. This is a subject of much interest to modern bridge theoreticians.

THE DOUBLE SURPRISE

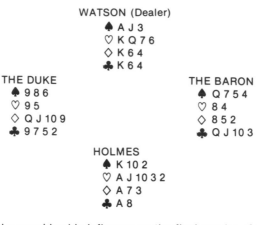

WATSON (Dealer)
♠ A J 3
♡ K Q 7 6
◇ K 6 4
♣ K 6 4

THE DUKE
♠ 9 8 6
♡ 9 5
◇ Q J 10 9
♣ 9 7 5 2

THE BARON
♠ Q 7 5 4
♡ 8 4
◇ 8 5 2
♣ Q J 10 3

HOLMES
♠ K 10 2
♡ A J 10 3 2
◇ A 7 3
♣ A 8

This hand had a considerable influence on the final results of the London Cup Match. The bidding revealed an interesting theory of Holmes and also supplied him with several surprises. A great follower of Holmes, the Duke of Cumberland, was sitting West playing with his intimate friend, Baron Roth-Stone.

The Duke	Watson	The Baron	Holmes
-	1NT	pass	2C
pass	2H	pass	4NT
pass	5D	pass	6H
pass	pass	pass	

Pretend you are Doctor Watson sitting North. How would you play this small slam in hearts? Baron Roth-Stone opened the club queen.

Relative to the bidding, when Holmes picked up his very strong hand he was much surprised to hear Watson open one notrump. Holmes was now intent on reaching a slam but he could not bid three hearts at this point since he and Watson had agreed that while this bid would have strong slam overtones, it would also indicate six heart cards. Holmes temporized by bidding two clubs. His second surprise, nay almost shock, came when Watson responded in hearts, Holmes' own suit. Four notrump, Blackwood, was almost automatic at this point. When Watson showed one ace, the great detective knew the partnership held all four. He paused for a long moment and then, for reasons of his own, concluded the bidding with six hearts.

Watson was surprised as well when the dummy hand showed up with three aces. However, he played the hand with speed and dispatch, as I am sure you would.

Watson took the club lead with dummy's ace. A low heart from dummy went to his king and a low heart back was taken by dummy's ace, exhausting the defenders of their trump cards. Now Watson played the club eight from dummy which he took with his king. A low club back was trumped in dummy. Watson played off the ace and king of diamonds and then a low diamond taken by the Duke of Cumberland. The Duke was in an uncomfortable position. A minor suit lead allowed a ruff and sluff. With a sigh of resignation he led a spade and the Baron's spade queen was trapped.

Perhaps the most interesting point of the hand was Holmes' bid of six hearts. With the same cards, the bidding of Harry Skurry and Betty Castle proceeded along the same lines till Skurry found out the North-South hands held all the aces. He then bid five notrump and finding his partner with three kings, went to seven hearts which could not be made.

Back at the Grosvenor Bridge Club the following day, Skurry asked Holmes how he had resisted the temptation of a potential grand slam.

"It wasn't easy," admitted the great detective, "but despite my five hearts, my hand was still a balanced one. Watson's opening notrump signalled the same type. I did not want to be in a seven-contract even if our side had all of the aces and kings. I have noticed that a balanced hand opposite a balanced hand does not play as well as one might suspect."

"Now he tells me," growled Skurry. He had good reason to feel disappointed. Skurry and Betty Castle enjoyed a fine round at the London Cup Match but the results of this one hand proved their undoing.

THE WRONG CHOICE

WATSON
♠ K J 4
♡ K 2
◇ 8 2
♣ A K Q J 8 4

THE DUKE
♠ 10 9 8 5 2
♡ A Q 9
◇ A K 5
♣ 7 6

THE BARON
♠ A Q 7 3
♡ 7 4
◇ Q J 10 9 7 6 4
♣ void

HOLMES(Dealer)
♠ 6
♡ J 10 8 6 5 3
◇ 3
♣ 10 9 5 3 2

Holmes	The Duke	Watson	The Baron
pass	1S	2C	2D
2H	2S	3C	4S
5C	5S	pass	pass
pass			

Opening lead: Club king.

The Duke of Cumberland and Baron Roth-Stone did not cover themselves with glory in the bidding of this hand and, alas, the play was no better. The Duke, whose admiration of Holmes had prompted him to try and think like a bridge player, studied his cards carefully. With no minor suit losers, he felt that he had two available finesses and if but one was successful, a twelve trick result was possible. Trumping Watson's club king, he promptly led a low heart from dummy. His heart queen lost and Watson made the excellent return of the club ace. The Duke trumped in dummy again and led a heart to his ace. Now a low spade was played. When dummy's queen held the trick, Cumberland played the trump ace. But the spade king did not drop and even the five spade contract was in danger. At long last, the Duke played a diamond to his ace and king. The diamond five from the closed hand was trumped by Watson's spade king and back came the club queen. Cumberland was shut out of dummy and still had a losing heart so his contract was defeated.

The Duke turned to Holmes somewhat red-faced. "I rather butchered that, didn't I?"

"The play could certainly have followed different lines," agreed Holmes, "as well as the bidding."

"How would you and doctor Watson have bid the hand?" asked Baron Roth-Stone.

"There can be no complaint about the opening spade bid. According to our methods, Watson had sufficient strength to double and then show his splendid suit later but my original pass prompted him to mention clubs immediately. The bidding progressed reasonably to three clubs. At this point, Baron, I would have been inclined to bid four clubs indicating spade support and your very powerful holding. Over my five clubs, the Duke could very well bid five diamonds. A response of five spades would show, by inference, your heart losers. Holding the heart ace, the Duke could then progress to six spades.

"On the play, I am reminded that obvious finessess could be listed under a heading of 'dangerous weapons.' Trumping the club lead is obvious but the heart finesse was completely unnecessary. Instead, a low diamond to your king and a spade back for the trump finesse. When this succeeds, play the trump ace and then switch to diamonds. Watson can trump in when he wishes but you still have entry to dummy and the diamonds provide more than enough discards for your losing hearts."

The Duke shook his head. "I thought I had it figured out so well."

Holmes had a twinkle in his eye. "Well, the way my good partner attacked dummy's entries was excellent defense you know. Mark it down to bad luck."

The Duke matched Holmes' smile. "I think not, Sir. I shall mark it down to bad play on my part and kindness towards opponents on yours."

"I wonder if he realizes how kind?" thought Watson to himself. "It would have involved a risky line of play but if Holmes had been declarer at seven spades, he would have brought in the grand slam."

You see, of course, what Watson was thinking about.

DOUBTFUL VALUES DENIED

The following hand pitted Baroness Jeurdon and Lady Lind-Mead against the unsavory team of Winhaven Hyde and Jerome Jeckle. While the bidding did not involve "Haltmon" it was made possible by the fact that both ladies played Holmes' convention.

BARONESS JEURDON
♠ A 9 3
♡ A 10 7 3
◇ A K J 2
♣ Q 8

JEROME JECKLE (Dealer)
♠ Q J
♡ K 9 4 2
◇ 9 5 3
♣ 10 6 4 2

WINHAVEN HYDE
♠ K 10 5
♡ Q J 8 5
◇ 8 7
♣ K J 7 5

LADY LIND-MEAD
♠ 8 7 6 4 2
♡ 6
◇ Q 10 6 4
♣ A 9 3

Jeckle	Baroness Jeurdon	Hyde	Lady Lind-Mead
pass	1NT	pass	2S
pass	3S	pass	4S
pass	pass	pass	

Opening lead: Spade queen.

Were you playing this hand, would you exhibit the skill of Lady Lind-Mead?

Baroness Jeurdon's opening notrump was an absolute maximum. her partner's response of two spades showed a five-card suit at least but a bad and unbalanced hand. The Baroness with three reasonable spades, gave her partner a single raise. Lady Lind-Mead, knowing her partner would not raise her "drop dead" bid without top values, went on to game.

Lady Lind-Mead ducked Jeckle's opening trump lead and he continued the suit. Dummy's spade ace took the second trick. Now the heart ace was played from dummy and a low heart trumped in the closed hand. A low diamond went to dummy's ace and another heart was trumped in declarer's hand. Again Lady Lind-Mead returned to dummy via the diamond king. Playing dummy's last heart, she trumped it with her own last spade. She now played the diamond queen. Muttering

75

under his breath, Winhaven Hyde trumped the diamond lead and returned a low club. The declarer let this ride around to dummy's club queen. A low club from dummy was taken by declarer's ace and she now led the club nine which was trumped by dummy's remaining spade.

"Nice dummy reversal end-play," complimented the Baroness.

"It brought home the bacon," replied Lady Lind-Mead.

This proved to be a prophetic remark since Lady Lind-Mead later went to America and married a rancher in New Mexico. Baroness Jeurdon also went to America and descendents of both these titled ladies are now active in modern day bridge.

Both Jeckle and Hyde were livid at the results of the hand. But they had other problems in store for them since their next opponents proved to be Holmes and Watson.

COMPETITIVE HALTMON

```
                    WATSON(Dealer)
                    ♠ K Q 8
                    ♡ A Q 8 5
                    ◇ 8 7 4
                    ♣ A J 2
        JECKLE                      HYDE
        ♠ 9 4 3                     ♠ A 7 6
        ♡ J 6 3                     ♡ 7 2
        ◇ A 9                       ◇ K Q J 10 5 3
        ♣ 10 8 6 5 3                ♣ 9 7
                    HOLMES
                    ♠ J 10 5 2
                    ♡ K 10 9 4
                    ◇ 6 2
                    ♣ K Q 4
```

Jeckle	Watson	Hyde	Holmes
-	1NT	2D	3D
pass	3H	pass	4H
pass	pass	pass	

When Holmes saw Jeckle and Hyde approach their table exchanging angry words, he resolved to get into the bidding if at all possible. The great bridge-playing detective, as previously mentioned, felt that balanced hands did not play too well opposite each other. He had another theory that angry players cannot fight each other and their opponents at the same time. At least, not effectively. When Watson opened one notrump, Hyde overcalled with two diamonds. Holmes and Watson had not discussed a situation like this but the detective chose to bid three diamonds feeling that Watson would get the idea. The doctor did some thinking. If Holmes actually held diamond strength he might well have doubled Hyde's overcall. Watson divined that his partner was looking for a major suit fit and had chosen a cue bid of the opponents' suit as the only means available. He bid three hearts and was rewarded for his inventiveness when Holmes raised him to four.

76

A fuming Winhaven Hyde led his diamond king. Jeckle made the good play of overtaking with his diamond ace and returning the suit. Hyde took the trick with his ten and led the diamond queen trying to signal his spade ace to his partner. But Watson was alert and trumped the third diamond with dummy's heart king. Now Watson led the heart ten from the board. When Jeckle played low, the trump ten won the trick. Watson calmly continued with the heart nine which Jeckle covered with his jack. Watson took the trick with his ace and extracted Jeckle's last trump with his queen. He now led the spade king. Hyde ducked and the king held the trick. Now Watson led his queen of spades and again Hyde ducked. A third spade from Watson's hand fetched Hyde's ace. The diamond jack was trumped by Watson's last heart and after cashing his club ace, Watson entered dummy via the club suit to cash the remaining black suit winners. Watson had lost two diamond tricks and a spade but his contract was secure. Both Hyde and Jeckle made references to bad cards, something they could not say on the following hand.

ALL OR NOTHING

```
                        WATSON
                        ♠ Q J 10
                        ♡ 7 4
                        ◇ J 10 9 6
                        ♣ A 8 6 3
       JECKLE                              HYDE(Dealer)
       ♠ 9                                 ♠ K 6 3
       ♡ Q J 10 8 5 3                      ♡ A K 9
       ◇ Q 5 4                             ◇ A K 7 3
       ♣ K 7 4                             ♣ 9 5 2
                        HOLMES
                        ♠ A 8 7 5 4 2
                        ♡ 6 2
                        ◇ 8 2
                        ♣ Q J 10
```

Jeckle	Watson	Hyde	Holmes
-	-	1NT	pass
4H	pass	pass	pass

Opening lead: Queen of spades.

The bidding requires no comment. Watson chose to attack in the unbid major. Jeckle wisely played low from dummy. Now Holmes indulged in a long pause. The bidding marked Jeckle with a long heart suit and hence a distributional hand. Watson's lead could well be from the queen-jack-ten. If so, Jeckle could have but one spade card. Holmes knew the field was strong and the scoring might well be close. He overtook Watson's spade queen with his ace, promoting dummy's spade king into a winner. There were gasps from the onlookers at table Number One. Now Holmes returned the club queen. Jeckle's jaw tightened. It flashed through his mind that, even as a child, he had never believed in Santa Claus. He played a low club and Watson produced the eight. Holmes continued with the club jack which Jeckle covered with his king hoping for some sort of block. Watson took his ace and returned a club captured by Holmes' ten. The contract was down.

Hyde's nostrils flared. "Of course, I could have made three notrump."

Crimson crept up Jeckle's face. "Against a club lead?"

"The suit blocks," was his partner's high-pitched response.

"North could realize that and switch to a spade and your notrump contract goes down a bundle."

"But what if Holmes leads a low spade?" was Hyde's retort. "I would have ten running tricks."

It was Watson who chose to tighten the screw. "Without my partner's superb defense, four hearts makes easily."

With Jeckle and Hyde glaring at him, Watson explained.

"Suppose Holmes chose to let my spade queen hold the first trick. I would continue the suit and declarer would ruff. Now two rounds of hearts ending in dummy and the precaution of leading the spade king and trumping it in the closed hand. You can now test the diamonds. They do not break but the fourth diamond is led from dummy and declarer dumps a low club. I am hopelessly end-played and you must come to the tenth trick with the club king."

Hyde and Jeckle left the table angrily as there was a murmur of approval of Watson's shrewd analysis from the onlookers. While the scores were being totalled, Hyde and Jeckle retired to the bar and angrily drowned their sorrow to such an extent that they were asked to leave the premises, which they did with recriminations. There was only one other incident but it did not mar the complete success of the evening. London's super salesman, Grover Gitley, purchased a kibitzer ticket to the gala affair. However, he brought with him a sample case of Gitley Nail Files and was attempting to show them to onlookers when intercepted by the Duchess of Paisley. The Duchess ordered him to leave forthwith though she did offer to refund his entrance fee. The gentleman took her action in good humor, refused the proffered refund and departed with his usual beaming face.

At a later date, Grover Gitley also matriculated to America where he changed his name for some unknown reason and began to manufacture razor blades. It is rumored that his descendants are sharp bridge players indeed but there is no absolute proof of this.

Thus ended the London Cup Duplicate. Watson makes a modest note of the fact that he and Holmes won largely because of the grand slam in hearts which Holmes avoided and the detective's great defense against Jeckle and Hyde. Skurry and Castle came in second so the event proved a distinct triumph for the players in the historic Challenge Match.

Just as the trip to Bath did much to popularize bridge in the hinterlands, so did the London Cup event promote bridge even more among the social elite. Where hitherto to play good bridge had been considered a social asset, it was now considered a necessity.

At least, that is how Watson stated it in a marginal note in his famous Diary.

Grover Gitley apprehended by Duchess of Paisley.

THE ADVENTURE OF THE
SOFT FINGERS

It was a gray and overcast Sunday morning that found Holmes and Watson early risers for no particular reason. The diligent Mrs. Hudson, long used to the irregular schedule of her famous roomers, had provided the duo with a hearty breakfast. Watson was sitting at the side of the fireplace working on his "Diary of the Challenge Match". Holmes, in his robe, was standing at his oft-used post beside the window surveying the passing scene in the street below. Snow had fallen in profusion the night before. White flakes were not allowed to lie dormant on top of drifts but were seized by frequent gusts of wind and sent drumming against the glass of Baker Street windows. Holmes had just lit a Marley cigarette✦ when something caught his attention.

✦Watson makes note of the fact that Holmes was partial to Virginia Tobacco and that large shipments of American cigarettes arrived periodically through the good offices of Francis Hay Moulton of that country.

"Hello," he said, "I believe a message just arrived for us."

Watson revealed a flash of his infrequent pawkey humor.

"Delivered, no doubt, by a former coal miner from Wales whose brother is now serving in Her Majesty's Navy."

Holmes chuckled as he crossed to the door of their suite of rooms.

"You mock me, my dear Watson. No, it was a youthful employee of the telegraph office."

As the detective opened the door, the footfalls of Billy the Page Boy could be heard on the stairs. Billy appeared at the entrance, silently handing Holmes the telegram. The long thin fingers of the master sleuth extracted the message and his quick eyes darted over it.

"Thank you, Billy," he said. "No response. There will be a gentleman calling shortly and you can show him right up."

Billy closed the door as Holmes crossed to Watson, handing the telegram to him. The doctor read it aloud:

"Sherlock, I trust this finds you at home and that you will remain on the premises. A certain Mr. Wakefield Orloff will call on you shortly. I can vouch for his character and motives and trust that you can provide assistance through the use of your unique talents. In haste. Mycroft."

Watson rose from his chair.

"This does sound exciting, Holmes. You were commenting just yesterday about the dearth of criminal cases recently."

"There is nothing to indicate that Orloff comes to me regarding a criminal matter."

'But your brother does mention your unique talents. I hardly think the gentleman wishes to discuss Australian wool production."

As Holmes crossed to the window again, he pocketed the telegram which Watson had returned.

"Wakefield Orloff. Now I just wonder who he might be?"

As Holmes again regarded the street below, Watson joined him in his vigil. There were few passers-by and Holmes' eyes centered on a figure about a block away.

I fancy that is our bird, Watson."

The man he indicated seemed short, with a bowler and a dark top coat. He was coming at a good rate, his feet automatically finding firm footing in the shifting snow.

"Note how he glanced at the house numbers," muttered Holmes.

As Watson nodded, a curious thing happened. The wind, which had relaxed into a temporary calm, suddenly revived with a violent gust. The man's bowler started to go with it and was, in fact, airborne for a moment. But an arm shot out with amazing speed, snatching the hat brim and replacing it in one continuous movement. It was so fast that one did not quite believe it had happened. The man's stride had scarcely faltered during the split second action. Watson's eyes had widened and Holmes' breath came in with a soft hiss and then was expelled in a low whistle.

"Watson," said the detective, "before the arrival of this emissary I am taking the precaution of removing my revolver from my desk and placing it in my dressing gown pocket." He did so.

"Do you feel this man could be an enemy?" asked the good Doctor.

The man with the Bowler Hat.

"Not with Mycroft's blessings. However, anyone with reflexes as fast as that has to be potentially dangerous. Let us trust that he is dangerous to others and not to us."

When Wakefield Orloff reached the first landing of the stairs at 221B Baker Street, he found the door ajar and entered. His eyes passed over the sitting room in a seemingly lazy glance that was not lazy and missed nothing. After the street incident just witnessed, Watson took pains to study him closely. The man was on the short side and seemed a little plump. It crossed Watson's medically-trained mind that what swelled his coat could be layers of muscle and not fat. His face was round and good humored with a mobile mouth. His hair was thin but plastered artistically and he had a small, well-brushed mustache. His clothes, not new, were well-cut. Watson thought he might be a retired army officer. His eyes were very clear and a peculiar shade of green. Watson decided that, whatever he was, he wasn't retired.

He spoke in a low and pleasant voice. "Mr. Holmes, I am Wakefield Orloff." "We have been awaiting your arrival. My friend, Dr. Watson."

"A pleasure, sir," said the visitor with a nod to Watson. He removed his hat which he carefully placed on a side table. A billfold appeared from an inner pocket and was flipped open. Orloff showed it to Holmes who nodded quickly.

"Some identification," thought Watson.

Orloff was out of his topcoat in a flowing motion and removed his gloves. Holmes indicated an armchair and Orloff seated himself in it. His back was straight and his weight seemed balanced on the balls of his small feet. Watson wondered if he might have been a professional dancer at one time.

As Holmes took a chair, there was a moment of silence which the great detective broke.

"Do you know the contents of the telegram I just received?"

"Only that it mentioned my coming here."

"I assume you know my brother?" Orloff nodded. "He requested that Watson and I be of what help we can."

Watson thought it sporting of Holmes to include him, something which Mycroft had not done. He then noted that Holmes had not mentioned who they were going to help and recalled that Mycroft had been vague on this point as well.

Orloff picked up the ball which Holmes had tossed his way. "I work for the government — Foreign Trade Department — but that is not important. It was felt that the information which I bring would best be delivered in person." Orloff wasted no time on oft-used phrases, like "confidential" or "top secret". Like most experts, he assumed the obvious. "The situation relates to Sir Randolph Rapp."

"I know of the gentleman," stated Holmes.

"And therefore know that a great deal of important information passes through his hands," continued Orloff. "There is a definite indication of a leak. Certain moves of the government in the field of geo-politics have been anticipated. Pre-knowledge of these attitudes of Her Majesty's Ministers could only be possible through someone in the Rapp apparatus."

"Because Rapp himself is so instrumental in forming these attitudes." Holmes seemed on familiar ground.

"Exactly," said Orloff. "Do you know Sir Randolph's work pattern?"

To Watson's surprise, Holmes nodded. "His activities are centered around his home in Mayfair. Since he is not officially connected with any government branch, he visits various offices on occasion but uses his domicile as his headquarters."

Watson, who had never heard of Randolph Rapp, almost interrupted with an obvious question, but preserved his silence.

"What is the composition of the Rapp household?" asked Holmes.

Orloff ticked them off. "Wife, Amanda Rapp. To be a part of her husband's work, she acts as a file clerk. Rapp jokes about it saying that Amanda files phonetically rather than alphabetically but that may be apocryphal. Associate, Alexander Villers. Last living member of an old family which came with the Norman Conquest. Considered a brilliant disciple of Sir Randolph. Butler, Ralph Cord. The other servants are not in residence. Government stenographers and office personnel with security clearance come to the dwelling when needed. Actually, I . . . it was felt that the fewer people living on the premises, the less chance of a leak. Unfortunately, this precaution was not enough."

Holmes was regarding his visitor keenly, "I assume that you feel the actual residents of the Rapp household are the only ones that could be involved in this security breach."

Orloff nodded. "Sir Randolph works in the fragile world of speculation. It is important for his efficiency to feel relaxed, without pressures or restraint. Villers is a working cog in the Rapp machine. He cross-checks information for Sir Randolph and studies official reports, principally from diplomatic sources. He also acts as a sounding board of Sir Randolph's occasional speculations as does Amanda Rapp. There is one other semi-resident — a Miss Hortense Frayne, Canadian, graduate of Ottawa University, Master's degree in psychology and sociology. Lives in a flat in Berkshire Mews but frequently stays over at the Rapp mansion. There is a bedroom permanently available for her there. She keeps an eye on the S.S. and C.I.D. Central Office reports. If there is a file on a particular person which catches her interest, or Villers' for that matter, it is brought to Sir Randolph's attention."

"Miss Frayne, then, can be included in the possible suspects," said Holmes thoughtfully, "unless....."

"Sir?" Orloff's expression was politely inquisitive. Watson noted that he had not moved a muscle since sitting down. With his hands folded in his lap, he had remained completely relaxed and motionless.

"Unless," continued Holmes, "Miss Frayne also reports elsewhere."

Evidently, Wakefield Orloff had been given the green light by Mycroft Holmes. "A very clever investigator might conclude that Miss Frayne has an association with an intelligence organization, possibly in Canada or even here in Britain."

"So," said Holmes, "we have a wife, an assistant of impeccable credentials, another with friendly espionage connections, and a butler. We are to presume that Sir Randolph, himself, is above suspicion?"

"Undoubtedly," stated Orloff. "He has received high honors from his country and is extremely well-paid for his work. Upon retirement, not imminent I am happy to say, he will possibly write a sequel to his remarkable 'The Motivated Minds of Mankind.' He works with an absolute minimum of direction or interference. He is frank in declaring that the *status quo* is most satisfactory to him. As a guess I would say the same applies to Lady Rapp."

Holmes' eyes flicked briefly towards Watson. The doctor knew that the great detective was recalling the amazing matter of the Right Honorable Trewlawney Hope. (See: "The Adventure of the Second Stain *)

"Two points require answers," said Holmes. "First, a matter of procedure. Hypothetically, I am Villers, or even Miss Frayne. I bring a file on a certain person to Sir Randolph's attention. He feels the matter is of sufficient importance to demand his scrutiny and that his opinion should go to — say — the Secretary for European Affairs. What happens?"

Because of the prominence of those involved, this baffling case was kept secret for many years. It was only after Holmes retired from London and was engaged in bee-farming on the Sussex Downs, that Watson released a carefully-guarded account of the incident to the public.

Orloff's response was without hesitation. "Sir Randolph, after studying the matter, might write up an opinion immediately. He frequently does. Or he might send signals of inquiry or secure what information he needs himself. Whichever avenue he chooses, he prepares his final judgment alone. His conclusions are written in long hand while locked in his upstairs study. The material is then given by Sir Randolph to an official courier for delivery to — well, in the situation you present Mr. Holmes, to the Secretary of European Affairs. The couriers have strict orders to take nothing from an intermediary. They receive Sir Randolph's findings from his hands only."

A smile of admiration touched Holmes' face. "A nice bit, that. The mark of the security expert."

If a gleam of satisfaction warmed Orloff's eyes, it was gone in a flash.

"Are there any exceptions to this procedure?" asked Holmes.

Orloff nodded. "Frequently, Sir Randolph works late at night. Transportation of his findings would be hazardous and inconvenient. On those occasions he places his report in the safe in the living-room. It is a Harley-Mills of the latest design. Only Sir Randolph knows the combination. And the combination is changed every month," he added, with emphasis. After a short silence, Orloff continued. "You mentioned two points, Mr. Holmes."

"I can instigate certain lines of investigation now," said Holmes, "and I will. But the crux of the matter is meeting the quartet of potential suspects and viewing the Rapp mansion in Mayfair. I would be doing you and/or my brother an injustice if I did not conclude that you have a plan regarding that."

"I am just a messenger, Mr. Holmes." Orloff was a little too quick with this statement. "However, we do have a stroke of luck. Sir Randolph has become quite enamored with the game of bridge, as have his wife and associates. This interest is no doubt sparked by the exploits of you and Doctor Watson in the Challenge Match which everyone is talking about. I can assure you that if you and Doctor Watson are available, there will be a dinner party at Sir Randolph's tonight with you as the guests. Sir Randolph is certain to want to play bridge, which may prove a bore."

"*Au contraire,*" said Holmes. "It could be most revealing."

"This will not seem engineered, Mr. Holmes. Sir Randolph has already dropped broad hints to Mr. Mycroft Holmes as to how anxious he is to meet the great bridge-playing detective."

Holmes had no more questions and Orloff had no further information to impart. So the matter stood. Their visitor departed with the assurance that they would shortly receive an invitation from Sir Randolph personally.

When the door closed behind Wakefield Orloff, Holmes sank back into his chair. With his elbows on its arms, his hands steepled and his nose touching their apex, the master illusionist of the mind sat gazing at the door in deep thought. Suddenly, he shook his head quickly and looked at his confrere.

"Forgive me, Watson. We have had a tasty and interesting tidbit presented to us, have we not?"

"Indeed, Holmes."

"And yet," continued the detective, "I find Orloff himself just as interesting."

"A messenger?" Watson offered this as bait to see what rabbits Holmes might pull from the recesses of his mind.

"Far more than that, Watson. The hat which we saw him retrieve so quickly on the street and which he placed so carefully on the side table preserved its shape remarkably well, didn't it?

"It did, for a fact," said Watson thoughtfully.

"Small wonder. The brim of that bowler is reinforced with steel. In the powerful hands of Orloff, I am sure that it could be sent skimming through the air and deliver a stunning and perhaps fatal blow to whatever head it might come in contact with."

"Good heavens, Holmes! What a subtle and unexpected weapon."

"No more than the toes of his shoes which were steel-tipped. A kick to a kneecap would have a crippling effect."

Watson was goggle-eyed. 'What is the man — a walking arsenal?"

"Our departed guest, Watson, is undoubtedly one of England's top security officers. Did you notice how his voice had a tinge of satisfaction when he mentioned that the safe combination was changed monthly? He slipped a little when he mentioned that the fewer people living on the Rapp premises the better. He started to say: 'I felt' and corrected himself to say: 'it was felt'."

"Now that you mention it, I do recall that." Watson's brows were knit. "But, Holmes, who is this Randolph Rapp that you both seemed so familiar with?"

Holmes' eyes assumed a dreamy look. "It is singular that a problem involving Sir Randolph should reach my ears. The gentleman owes his present position, in part, at least, to my brother. As I have mentioned previously, Mycroft is the clearing-house for the opinions of every department. Only he can focus all the information into a tidy whole. It is Mycroft who equates how each factor will affect the other. The final conclusion, which often formulates government policy, is frequently the creature of Mycroft's meticulous mind. England, having done so well with him, decided to forge another tool. Policy may be decided by a government according to the whim of its rulers, but it is transmitted by men. A man has certain drives, certain factors which color his thinking and motivate his actions. Sir Randolph Rapp is an expert on the drives of men. He studies and then delivers an opinion as to how they will react under a given set of circumstances. He can deduce with uncanny accuracy whether a certain individual is dangerous to the state. I do not mean to imply that Sir Randolph is clairvoyant, but his record is singularly successful. His judgments of men have given England a definite one-upmanship in our foreign relations."

"Holmes," exclaimed Watson, "what an amazing situation!"

"And one which can never be revealed." The detective picked up his pipe and crossed to the Persian slipper on the mantelpiece. "Oh, but the news media would have a merry time indeed revealing that the destiny of England is decided, in part, by the supposition of a former Regius Professor of History at Cambridge. But, as in bidding theory, Watson, it is what works that counts. Pragmatic England has a long history of losing many battles but seldom losing a war."

With his pipe lit to his satisfaction, Holmes instigated the lines of investigation which he had mentioned to Wakefield Orloff. Messages flowed from his pen to unknown destinations. Billy was kept busy with comings and goings and Holmes littered the sitting-room with his volumes of newspaper clippings. Watson kept silent and out of his way, well knowing that Holmes was wandering through the labyrinth of his mind following threads of supposition, inference, and deduction anchored to the facts that he could unearth.

It was in the early afternoon that a special messenger arrived with the anticipated invitation to dinner from Sir Randolph Rapp. The distinguished author and scholar expressed his delight that Holmes and Watson would be available. Directions were included and it was a dinner at eight.

Holmes had, by this time, studied portions of his extensive files of newspaper clippings and evidently drained this source of information. With an introspective air, he left Baker Street for points unknown. Watson tried to busy himself with his cherished "Diary of the Challenge Match" but his mind kept wandering back to the strange-cloak-and-dagger affair which his friend had become involved in. It was not until early evening that the detective returned. His manner had changed and he even hummed a bit of a tune as he hung his greatcoat and deerstalker hat on the back of the entrance door. This provoked a comment from Watson.

"I rather think from your manner, Holmes, that you have uncovered some valuable information."

"As to its value, I cannot say," responded Holmes, "but I have added to our general fund of knowledge. I learned from a former professor at Cambridge that young Villers was a recluse. During his period at the University he had no romantic entanglements and no friends for that matter. Actually, my learned friend was somewhat vague in recalling Villers. He did mention that he affected a beard during his college days to conceal his extreme youth. From other sources, I learned that Villers is now clean-shaven."

"But what possible value could that . . !" Watson did not finish his sentence as a thought occurred. "Oh, I see what you're getting at.

"Please tell me, Watson. I don't see it at all."

"You think this studious pose was a false front to cover some other activity."

"An interesting thought, Watson, but facts don't bear it out. Villers was one of the most brilliant graduates in Cambridge history. He studied, all right, and his marks proved it." Since Watson looked disappointed, Holmes advanced another thought. "Relative to the butler, Ralph Cord, it might interest you to know that he was a long time member of the Villers household."

Watson brightened. "Well, Holmes, that could indicate collusion."

"I don't know what it indicates but these are things we can bear in mind tonight."

Since the detective seemed prepared to drop the conversation, Watson posed a question. "Did you learn anything about the Rapps or Hortense Frayne?"

"Didn't bother," responded Holmes. "I rather imagine the capable Orloff knows everything important about them already."

This proved all the information Watson was able to secure prior to their departure for dinner.

Night had long fallen when Holmes and Watson arrived at the entrance to the Rapp estate. An impressive iron spike fence surrounded the rambling house and grounds. The gate was locked but the gate house within was occupied by a big, broad-shouldered, truculent-looking man who opened the outer portal when they identified themselves. As they walked up the broad roadway to the house, Holmes indicated the watchman behind them.

"A loan from the Criminal Investigation Division, I'll wager."

The lawns were close-cut and almost devoid of trees offering an open area between fence and mansion. Behind stout wire close to the dwelling, Watson spied luminous eyes gazing at them. Low and ominous growls emanated from that direction.

"Doberman Pinschers," stated Holmes. "They let them loose when the household beds down for the night."

Watson shuddered. "Pity the poor swagman caught between fence and house."

A massive front door was opened by the butler, who ushered them into a brightly-lit drawing room. The fort-like exterior dissolved into a picture of comfortable English home life. Watson's feet sank into costly oriental rugs and he noted original art works on the walls. As the butler retreated with their hats and coats, Sir Randolph Rapp greeted them. Watson was surprised. The former professor, now motivational specialist, resembled a jolly toy-maker. His face was ruddy and wreathed in smiles. His figure indicated a sedentary life and his hair looked designed to defy a comb.

"Casualness seems the keynote here," thought Watson but he noted that when Sir Randolph introduced his wife, he managed to have Lady Rapp in the best light possible as she greeted the guests. Amanda Rapp was quite tall with flaxen hair and a Dresden doll face. She moved with the willowy grace that some English ladies seem born with.

"Looks like she could kick up her heels if she wanted to," thought Watson. He had not forgotten Lady Hilda Trelawney Hope who had become entangled in the web of the international blackmailer, Eduardo Lucas.

Sir Randolph seemed alien to formality and bypassed customary small talk. Over some excellent sherry, he launched into a series of questions relative to the Challenge Match. This subject dominated the conversation with the enthusiastic cooperation of Amanda Rapp.

It was shortly before dinner that Alexander Villers and Hortense Frayne made their appearance. When the butler, Ralph Cord, materialized from the dining-room with a significant glance at his mistress, and Lady Rapp rose to gather eyes and lead the parade to the festive board, Watson resolved to study his fellow diners with care in the hope of presenting a shrewd observation to Holmes

Over a sumptuous repast, Holmes fielded most of the queries that his fellow diners batted his way. Sir Randolph had numerous questions regarding Holmes' two club convention opposite an opening notrump bid.

"Supose the bidder wants to play in a club partial? Does the convention operate opposite an opening three notrump bid?"

This recent Holmes innovation seemed to fascinate him.

Watson had time to consider the others at the long, oaken table. Alexander Villers was meticulously dressed and had a wiry, well-put-together body. From the neck down, he looked like a fencer. But his head was that of a scholar and his face was dominated by large, almost myopic, brown eyes. Smiling did not come easily to him but his manner was affable enough. Hortense Frayne, from Ottawa, was small and quite dark.

"Some Basque blood there," thought Watson.

Her movements were quick and nervous and her figure was underslung with a long waist and rather short legs.

"She doesn't look like an espionage agent," thought Watson, "but then what espionage agent does?"

The good doctor wondered what a spy was supposed to look like and didn't come up with an answer. He tuned back in on the conversation.

"We are an unfortunate number for bridge," Sir Randolph was saying.

"Let's play cut-in, Randolph." It was Lady Rapp speaking.

"And that way, we can all play with Mr. Holmes," Hortense Frayne colored slightly, and added, with haste: ". . .and Doctor Watson, of course."

"Holmes is the attraction," thought Watson, "so now he will have to play for his supper." Then another thought crossed his mind. "The wily fox is going to study their reactions at the table. Sir Randolph may just be motivating himself onto a slide of Sherlock Holmes' mental microscope."

After coffee and some excellent brandy, the group gathered in the drawing room where the butler, Cord, had arranged a card table and chairs. Holmes spread a deck but, with a movement singularly clumsy for him, managed to allow a number of cards to spill over the side of the table and onto the floor. The alert butler retrieved the pasteboards and Holmes secured them from his hand. An expression akin to alarm flashed through the servant's eyes but Holmes seemed embarrassed and the look faded to be replaced with the impassive visage, seemingly a trademark of that particular and unique species known as "the perfect English butler."

The luck of the draw found Holmes paired with Villers against Amanda Rapp and Hortense Frayne. It was Villers' deal and Watson noted for the first time that the third and fifth fingers of Villers right hand were deformed. However, he dealt the cards easily enough and play began with Watson and Sir Randolph as spectators.

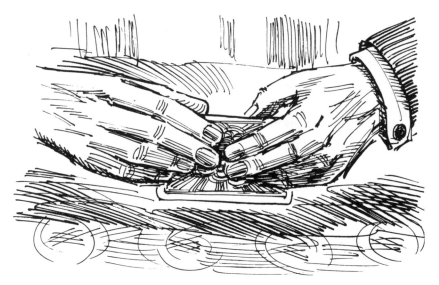

The Soft Fingers.

88

THE LOOPHOLE

North dealer: Neither side vulnerable

VILLERS (Dealer)
♠ J 5 2
♡ 10 7 6
◇ J 2
♣ A K J 10 2

AMANDA
♠ Q 10 4
♡ J 9 5 3
◇ K 9 8 7
♣ Q 5

HORTENSE
♠ A K 9 7 3
♡ 2
◇ Q 10 5 4
♣ 8 6 3

HOLMES
♠ 8 6
♡ A K Q 8 4
◇ A 6 3
♣ 9 7 4

Villers	Hortense	Holmes	Amanda
pass	pass	1H	pass
2C	2S	pass	pass
3H	pass	4H	pass
pass	pass		

Hortense backed into the bidding after her original pass. Holmes indicated his minimum values by passing on the second round. Villers felt his cards warranted one more try so he gave Holmes a belated raise and the detective went to game. Holmes had wanted to rebid his sturdy suit on the second round. Being unsure of his partner, he had chosen the cautious view.

Amanda Rapp led the spade four. Hortense cashed her two top spades. A diamond shift at this point would have defeated the contract but Hortense stubbornly continued with a third round of spades which Holmes trumped. To give a player of Holmes' calibre a loophole often proves fatal and so it was with this hand.

Holmes cashed two rounds of hearts revealing the adverse split. He now led a low club, finessing dummy's jack successfully. The ace of clubs from dummy dropped Amanda's queen and Holmes saw a clear road ahead. Returning to his hand with the heart queen, Holmes now led his last trump. Amanda took the trick but had nowhere to go. She led the diamond seven and Holmes captured Hortense's queen with his diamond ace. The detective led his last club to dummy and cashed out the suit discarding two diamonds from his hand. The game was in the bag.

"You are daring," said Amanda Rapp. "Playing your last trump might have allowed us to run the spades."

"Impossible through both bidding and play," said Holmes. "Miss Frayne overcalled in spades indicating at least five. This was confirmed by your low lead of the suit, Lady Rapp. The point of the hand was not to lose access to dummy's clubs. Had I continued clubs after learning of the adverse trump split, you would have ruffed. A heart return would have shut me out of the dummy and the contract would have been defeated by two tricks."

"Of course, a diamond shift by Hortense at the third trick would have set up a trick in that suit in time," Villers had been watching the cards carefully.

"How was I to realize that?" argued Miss Frayne.

"The powerful side suit in dummy was the clue." Holmes voice was gentle. "The minute the North cards were revealed, it was obvious that a club finesse, if necessary, was pre-destined to succeed. An attacking defense was mandatory."

"Cheer up, Hortense," said Sir Randolph. "We are but novices, you know, in hopes of better things."

The next hand was passed out. The third deal resulted in a fifty point set for the ladies. On the last deal of the four-hand rubber, the following cards appeared:

PLACE THE CARDS

West Dealer — Holmes-Villers vulnerable

```
                    VILLERS
                    ♠ Q 9
                    ♡ A 3
                    ◇ A K J 8 3 2
                    ♣ Q 8 3
AMANDA(Dealer)                      HORTENSE
♠ A K 10 8 4                        ♠ 7 6 5 2
♡ J 10 6                            ♡ K 8 7 4 2
◇ Q 7 6                             ◇ 4
♣ J 2                              ♣ 10 6 5
                    HOLMES
                    ♠ J 3
                    ♡ Q 9 5
                    ◇ 10 9 5
                    ♣ A K 9 7 4
```

Amanda	Villers	Hortense	Holmes
1S	2D.	2S.	3D.
pass	4D	pass	5D.
All pass			

90

Lady Rapp's opening bid was minimum indeed but she did have the boss suit. Villers immediately discounted his spade queen but knew that Holmes would read his vulnerable two level overcall as strong. Following raises by East and South, West was very content to pass. Villers felt his hand was worth another try and Holmes was delighted to go to game with his ample values. The spade two was opened and Lady Rapp cashed her two winners in the suit and shifted to the heart jack.

Villers placed the heart king with Hortense Frayne and realized that was the only card of importance she held. Surely, the diamond queen was with Amanda to justify her opening bid. But Hortense had contributed a spade raise to the auction. The bid must have been based on distributional values. Figuring Miss Frayne for a trump shortage, Sir Randolph's assistant embarked on a well-conceived game plan. He rose with the heart ace, crossed to dummy with a club and played the diamond ten. When it was not covered, he let the card ride. With the successful trump finesse and a club suit that behaved well, the game was assured.

After a number of fairly flat hands, the following combination was dealt. Sir Randolph and his wife were pitted against Hortense Frayne and Holmes.

WASTED MOTION

North Dealer — Holmes-Hortense Frayne vulnerable

AMANDA(Dealer)
♠ A K 3
♡ 8 7 6 3
◇ 8 5 3
♣ A J 7

HOLMES
♠ 9 7
♡ K 9
♤ A Q 7
♣ K 10 9 8 4 3

HORTENSE
♠ 10 8 6 5 4
♡ 5 4 2
♤ 10 9 6 2
♣ 2

SIR RANDOLPH
♠ Q J 2
♡ A Q J 10
◇ K J 4
♣ Q 6 5

Amanda	Hortense	Sir Randolph	Holmes
pass	pass	1H	2C
4H	pass	pass	pass

As the best of a bad lot, Holmes opened the spade nine. Sir Randolph took the trick in dummy and led a heart for an unsuccessful finesse. Holmes returned his last spade. Two rounds of hearts drew trumps. Sir Randolph now finessed dummy's club jack. When it won, as he knew it would, he played the club ace and then another club putting Holmes on lead. But the great detective had been counting and simply returned a low diamond. Sir Randolph won the trick but lost the contract. He was forced to accept two diamond losers for a one trick set. There was some discussion about this hand.

"You held every important card," Sir Randolph was looking at Holmes.

"As you might have known I would," responded Holmes. "I did make a vulnerable overcall with a suit lacking three honor cards. The bidding marks the trump finesse as wasted motion."

"The contract," said Watson with a small shudder, "can be made."

"Do tell us how, Doctor," said Lady Rapp.

"If Holmes is forced to lead a minor suit card, the defense suffers. Sir Randolph might have taken the spade lead and played to his heart ace. Now another spade and then a second heart. Holmes is now on lead with a trump throw-in. Say he returns a diamond, Sir Randolph takes the trick and successfully finesses the club jack as he did. The ace of clubs and a club continuation puts Holmes on lead again. A club from him allows Sir Randolph to limit his diamond losers to one and a diamond lead by Holmes performs the same function."

Villers had a comment. "Actually, an opening club lead sets the contract."

Holmes agreed. "Septimus Sheingold might find that lead but I doubt if I could." Diplomatically, he added another thought. "The bidding did leave something to be desired. I would have opened with Lady Rapp's hand but that is neither here nor there. Surely, Sir Randolph, your hand called for an opening bid of one notrump. The three notrump game is ironclad."

Sir Randolph sighed. "I was infatuated with my hundred honors. Your coming tonight has certainly shown us how much we have to learn."

Sir Randolph learned something else in a hand that came up later in the evening. At this point, the big team was re-united and Sir Randolph and Miss Frayne were nervously facing Holmes and Watson.

THE KILLING LEAD

North Dealer — Sir Randolph and Miss Frayne vulnerable

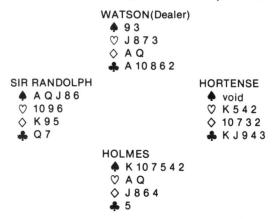

WATSON(Dealer)
♠ 9 3
♡ J 8 7 3
◇ A Q
♣ A 10 8 6 2

SIR RANDOLPH
♠ A Q J 8 6
♡ 10 9 6
◇ K 9 5
♣ Q 7

HORTENSE
♠ void
♡ K 5 4 2
◇ 10 7 3 2
♣ K J 9 4 3

HOLMES
♠ K 10 7 5 4 2
♡ A Q
◇ J 8 6 4
♣ 5

Sir Randolph	Watson	Hortense	Holmes
-	pass	pass	1S
pass	2NT	pass	4S
Dbl	pass	pass	pass

After opening with very limited values, Holmes' hand improved greatly when Watson bid 2 notrump. Holmes knew his partner had at least two spades and was close to opening bid strength. Holmes bid game.

As the bidding progressed, Sir Randolph felt he finally had his expert opponents drawn and quartered. It was with difficulty that he doubled in an even tone of voice. Content to sit back and wait for his tricks, he opened the heart ten.

Holmes knew he was facing a trump stack. He took the heart lead with his queen and led a diamond, successfully finessing dummy's queen. The ace of diamonds took the third trick. Holmes now led a low heart to his ace and trumped a diamond on the board. A heart ruff followed and a club was led to the ace and then a club ruffed in the closed hand. Now Holmes led the diamond jack. With the trump nine still in dummy, Sir Randolph ruffed with the spade jack. He now played the trump ace and exited with a low trump. Holmes could not be prevented from taking ten tricks.

"I don't believe it," cried Sir Randolph. "I thought I had you for sure."

"You did," replied Holmes. His eyes twinkled. "The opening lead of the spade ace followed by the queen prevents me from ruffing in dummy. You still score your three trump tricks and your king of diamonds defeats the contract."

Sir Randolph proved a graceful loser and he laughed boisterously. "Mr. Holmes," he said, gasping for breath, "this can be a very frustrating game."

On the last hand of the evening, Holmes and Hortense Fayne were kibitzing. Sir Randolph, again partnered with his wife, played against Watson and Villers. Holmes made reference to the hand at a later date as Watson indicated with an underlined footnote in his "Diary of the Challenge Match."

The home of Sir Randolph Rapp.

THE EXOTIC AUCTION

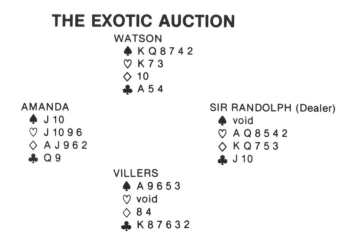

WATSON
♠ K Q 8 7 4 2
♡ K 7 3
◇ 10
♣ A 5 4

AMANDA
♠ J 10
♡ J 10 9 6
◇ A J 9 6 2
♣ Q 9

SIR RANDOLPH (Dealer)
♠ void
♡ A Q 8 5 4 2
◇ K Q 7 5 3
♣ J 10

VILLERS
♠ A 9 6 5 3
♡ void
◇ 8 4
♣ K 8 7 6 3 2

Sir Randolph opened with one heart. Villers surveyed his hand thoughtfully, then passed. Amanda gave her husband a single raise and Watson came into the bidding with two spades. Sir Randolph bid four hearts but this time Villers was not to be denied. He bid five hearts leaning heavily on his experienced partner to divine what was going on. Amanda's expressive features indicated that the auction was too exotic for her and she passed. Watson with his club control and singleton diamond bid six spades. Sir Randolph did not heed the bidding and led his heart ace which Watson promptly trumped in dummy. With clubs behaving, thirteen tricks rolled in.

"A diamond lead would hold us to six," commented Villers. "But the slam was there." He looked at Holmes questioningly. "I wanted to take some action at my first turn but lacked the bidding tools."

"The two-suited hand presents difficulties," said Holmes. "I have had some thoughts regarding such holdings."

"Oh, do tell us, Mr. Holmes," Amanda looked very interested and even Hortense Frayne perked up. She had grown more silent as the evening progressed and considering her cards who can blame her.

"I have not consolidated my thinking as yet," admitted the detective. "But there is certainly a crying need for a more definitive bidding structure. In the defensive positions, I mean."

This terminated the discussion and, indeed, the evening of bridge.

With play concluded for the evening, Sir Randolph expressed his gratitude. "I know this must have seemed like child's play to you gentlemen, but I hope you realize how much we have learned by being able to observe experts in action." His manner was most sincere and it was obvious that his interest in bridge was not a fancy of the moment. Both Holmes and Watson murmured encouraging words regarding the skills of their fellow-players of the evening, followed by their farewells.

Walking towards the gate, Watson was thankful that the Doberman Pinschers had not been released for their nightly patrol. As the burly watchman closed the gate behind them, the Baker Street duo found a hansom that just happened to be there.

"Mycroft thinks of everything," stated Holmes.

As soon as they were seated within the cab, it assumed motion. Without a directive from the passengers, it headed for Baker Street.

"Did you learn anything, Holmes?" asked Watson, eagerly.

"As much as I could hope to," responded Holmes. "What about you, old friend. Any conclusions?"

Watson's response surprised the detective. "The going was a bit thick so I fell back on a known fact. I may be in error, Holmes, but I have formed an opinion."

"Excellent, Watson! And where does your finger of guilt point?"

"When we return to our rooms, I will write down my prime suspect and put the name in an envelope. Then, after you have worked your cerebral magic, we shall see if our theories agree."

"Capital, Watson! It shall be so. But, and this in no way interferes with your idea, did you make note of anything during our evening of bridge?"

"Let me see," said Watson, carefully. "Hortense Frayne seemed very cautious in her bidding and play. Making the right move did not seem as important to her as not making a wrong one."

"An excellent analysis, Watson, with which I concur."

"How does she fit into this picture, Holmes? Wakefield Orloff as much as told us that she was a member of British Intelligence?"

"As is common in matters of this kind, there is a watchdog within the house as well as the Doberman Pinschers outside."

"Oh?" said Watson. "Miss Frayne."

"I'm sure she is well-qualified for her duties. She would have to be, working with Sir Randolph. But her prime function is to provide a pair of watchful eyes within to augment those without."

"You don't seem too interested in her, from the suspect angle."

"Not especially." Holmes showed unusual frankness. He tended to reveal little until his analysis was complete. "What is your opinion of Lady Rapp?" he asked.

"Her aproach was refreshing, as was Sir Randolph's. They both made mistakes which was inevitable since they are new to the game. However, this did not interfere with their enjoyment nor, better still, prompt them to adopt a futile defense of their errors."

"They treated the game as a game and were pleasant partners despite their shortcomings. Your observations are really excellent, Watson. If my schedule becomes crowded, I must place you in charge of a case."

"I didn't cover myself with glory in that Lady Carfax affair. (See: "The Disappearance of Lady Frances Carfax".) As I recall you said that I made a very pretty hash of it."

We all make mistakes, Watson. Did you have any thoughts regarding Alexander Villers?"

"He has potential," stated Watson. "He places cards and showed inventiveness in his defense. Too bad about the chap's fingers."

"Deformity in the hands is an hereditary defect of the Villers family. They date back a long way, you know. Unless Alexander has an heir, the family dies with him."

One of the most remarkable characteristics of Holmes was his ability to turn his brain off like a water faucet when he felt he could no longer work to advantage. The remainder of their return trip to Baker Street was spent in conversation unrelated to the case at hand.

As they descended from the hanson, Holmes reached up with a coin towards the driver. This top-hatted individual shook his head.

"Thanks, Guv. But loike they sye — hit's on the 'ouse!"

Touching his hat brim with the butt of his whip, the worthy shook his reins and the horse clattered off down the dark street.

Watson took this moment to return to the Rapp matter. "I rather expected Orloff to be present tonight."

A tight smile creased Holmes' face as the flickering street lamp threw strange shadows on his hawk-like visage.

"True to his instincts, the singular Mr. Wakefield Orloff faded into the background. But I would hazard a guess that we have not seen the last of him." (It will surprise absolutely no one to learn that Holmes' thought was correct. Orloff did appear again, according to Watson's Diary of the Challenge Match, but on a completely different matter.)

As Watson fitted his key in the lock, the door opened suddenly revealing the face of Billy. The Page Boy said:

"Doctor Watson . . . .Mr. 'Olmes — glad yer back." He opened the door wide allowing their entrance. "Batch of messages fer you, Mr. 'Olmes."

"I'm glad of that," said the master manhunter.

In their comfortable sitting-room, Holmes went over the harvest that his communiqués of the day had reaped. One large package produced an impressive pile of clippings which he selected for study. As he progressed, Watson noted that he tossed most of the neatly clipped newspaper columns aside, though he did retain several which he placed under a seashell by his right hand. (The seashell was from the island of Uffa where Holmes and Watson almost perished.)

As Holmes lit a cigarette, he indicated the printed matter.

"Carruthers of the Standard has been most helpful. But I do wish he would train his reporters differently." Watson's blank stare spurred him to continue. "Young newspapermen are told to consider a story from five angles: Who, What, Where, When, Why. For our purposes I wish they would add the word, 'How'!"

"I am not following you, Holmes."

"How did people look? How did they react?" Holmes picked up another clipping. "It must have occurred to you, Watson, that in most of the matters that come to our attention, we are cast in the role of the 'Johnny-come-lately'. Other hands have fingered the evidence. Other minds have already considered the facts. We must often look where they have not. The little things."

Holmes' eyes became riveted on the clipping in his hand. "He's indicating a considerable amount of interest in that one column," thought Watson.

As though he had read the doctor's thought, Holmes spoke again: "Now here is something. The account of a famous wedding. 'The bride wore blue to match her dancing eyes.'" Holmes read for a moment and then quoted again. "The groom was in the traditional family kilts but looked very Irish with his raven black hair and piercing blue eyes." The detective mused over the clipping for a long moment, then tossed it on the desk top. He swept the others back into the envelope in which they had come.

"Watson, would you be good enough to hand me that box over there?" He indicated a cardboard container which he used from time to time as a repository for certain news items. As Watson complied, a thought came to Holmes. "I say, ol' boy, have you jotted down your suspect?"

"I have not, but I shall right now." Watson did so.

Holmes was considering the contents of the cardboard box. "There are some rare birds here, Watson. Criminals of note who have been out of circulation for some time."

"Incarcerated?" asked Watson.

"No. Just missing."

There was a discreet knock on the door which then opened to allow Mycroft Holmes to enter. The second most powerful man in England had *carte blanche* regarding access to Holmes' abode.

"I thought you might drop by," said Sherlock.

With a word of greeting to Watson, Mycroft lowered his unwieldy frame into a chair and fastened his alert, steel-gray eyes on the younger Holmes.

"An annoying business, Sherlock," he said. "Have you arrived at any conclusions?"

I have. So has Watson."

"Are you in agreement?"

"We shall soon know. Let me present a compendium of the matter." Sherlock began pacing the room slowly, pausing from time to time to make a point.

Mycroft relaxed his tall and portly form. The subtle play of expression on his massive face suggested patient attention. "I wonder how much he already knows?" thought Watson.

"Regarding this security leak which could seriously affect affairs of state, we got off to a good start. The idea of using a bridge game as a means of meeting the principals was excellent. It also gave me an insight into their personalities. I was puzzled by the outline of the situation presented by your security agent, Wakefield Orloff."

"I didn't call him a security agent," said Mycroft.

"You didn't have to." Sherlock's tone was dry. "Orloff gave us five suspects, if we include Sir Randolph. Then he promptly narrowed the field to two, pointing out that Sir Randolph and Lady Amanda lacked motive and Hortense Frayne was actually an agent of the government. I began to wonder why my astute brother had bothered to involve me in the case at all. The process of elimination gave us a good prima facie case against Alexander Villers. Prior to the bridge game tonight, I was diverted from Villers momentarily but had to come back to him. The bridge game provided an immediate inconsistency. Alexander Villers was a scholar from early youth, and, like many others of the type, was withdrawn from the world. His Cambridge professors described him as a 'loner'. How was it that this introvert was such a good bridge player? Villers is no newcomer to the game. His play proved it. But bridge is a game which requires people, something that Alexander Villers had shunned.

"That is an angle that we never considered," Mycroft's placid manner was, for the moment, abandoned.

Sherlock became very brisk and businesslike. "When I first learned of this puzzling affair, a gnat began buzzing around my head in an irritating fashion. Obviously, Mycroft, you had done a great deal of thinking on this matter. Obviously, Alexander Villers was your prime suspect. Why had you not done something about it?"

Mycroft's face became stern. "Sherlock, one just doesn't go around accusing the last member of one of England's oldest families without conclusive proof. There was also the problem of how Villers secured his information. He has ready access to portions of Sir Randolph's work but not the summations."

"All right," said Sherlock, "how about Cord?"

Mycroft shook his head in irritation. "The butler leads to another frustrating dead end. Ralph Cord, prior to his position with Sir Randolph, spent his entire life in the service of the Villers'. He was the only one of the servants in the Villers Castle in Northumberland who really knew Alexander. He went to work for Sir Randolph on Alexander's recommendation. What would transform this perfect butler into an agent for a foreign power? Possibly, more important, what talents would he have that would make him of any value to an espionage ring? It is an endless circle, Sherlock."

"Until you step away from it and regard it from a different angle." Sherlock Holmes had that cat-like look that Watson had seen before. "I wondered if you knew about the butler."

"We knew a lot of things," said Mycroft, with a bitter tone. "But nothing seemed to help us."

"Perhaps this will." Holmes ceased his pacing, regarding Mycroft and Watson keenly. "Tonight I chanced upon something which definitely implicated Ralph Cord. I was forced to conclude that Cord is not the man we think he is. It was but a short step to the conclusion that the same situation could exist with Villers. Having gotten this far, I needed a theory as to what had actually happened and the proof. The theory was easy and I just found the proof before you arrived, Mycroft."

Holmes resumed his nervous pacing. "Consider, if you will, this unique situation. We have a young nobleman who spent much of his childhood and young manhood away at schools. He was a brilliant scholar and graduated from Cambridge with some of the highest marks ever recorded. At this time, his parents had an unfortunate accident. Their carriage horses bolted and both perished when the vehicle crashed. To try to recover from shock, Villers took an extended trip to Europe. Now, these are all facts but when you put them together, an unusual picture emerges. In certain circles, everyone knows of Alexander Villers but, with the death of his parents, nobody really knew him. Somewhere in a far off office or embassy there was someone sufficiently perceptive to realize that young Villers presented a golden opportunity. My theory was that Villers went to the continent but never came back."

A realization was born in Mycroft's eyes. "I could not accept him as a traitor. An imposter is another thing."

"The masquerader," continued Sherlock, "was undoubtedly selected because of a strong resemblance. Everything possible was done to augment this. In school, Villers affected a beard. Now he is clean-shaven. And it must have taken a fine surgeon indeed to duplicate the deformed fingers of the right hand which were an hereditary mark of the family."

Watson could restrain himself no longer. "Holmes, what makes you so certain of all this?"

"My dear Watson," replied Holmes, "I just read you an old clipping relative to a famous wedding. It was the wedding of Alexander Villers' father and mother. The reporter made note of the fact that both the bride and groom were blue-eyed. But the imposter has brown eyes." Holmes glanced at his brother. "The name of Gregor Mendel may mean little to you, Mycroft, but it will undoubtedly ring a bell with Watson here."

"The founder of genetics," exploded the good doctor. (The fact that Watson was immediately familiar with Mendel indicates that this adventure must have taken place around 1900. Mendel's law was made public in 1865 and generally ignored by biologists. At the turn of the century, however, three of the leading biologists of the day concurred with Mendel's findings and they became the basis of the modern scientific theory of heredity.)

"Exactly," said Sherlock. "The Mendelian Law proves that two blue-eyed persons cannot have a brown-eyed offspring. Therefore, the man we know as Villers must be an imposter."

"But the information?" Mycroft was persistent on this point.

"For shame, Mycroft," said his brother. "You know the security measures at the Rapp household are extensive. The information can only come from the safe where Sir Randolph's opinions are frequently placed prior to their being handed to a government courier." Mycroft started to speak, but Holmes cut in quickly. "I know what is bothering you — the deformed fingers. The imposter is right-handed and with only three working digits he could not 'crack a crib', to use the vernacular of the light-fingered gentry. But you are forgetting the butler. I rather imagine that if Mr. Orloff takes a trip to Northumberland, he will find the true Ralph Cord still living there. No one bothered to check this possiblity. Everyone took Villers' word for the man's identity. But I find that the present butler in the Rapp home fits the description of one Cosmo Tracy. You may not know of Tracy but the Nottingham Bank people do, along with many others. Cosmo Tracy is a master cracksman and I believe it is he who opens the safe when the pseudo Villers give the word."

Watson was regarding Sherlock with a singular expression.

"Whatever alerted you to him?" asked Mycroft.

"During dinner tonight I noticed something. Later I was able to confirm my suspicions. I managed to let some cards drop from the bridge table. The butler retrieved them for me. In taking them from him, I was able to feel the tips of the fingers of his right hand. They had been sandpapered." Holmes seemed surprised by the look of amazement this prompted in both Watson and his brother. "It is an old trick. Increases the sensitivity of the fingers to the fall of the tumblers. An American safe-cracker, the greatest of them all, originated the technique. His name was Jimmie Valentine."

Mycroft slapped his knee explosively. "By George, we've got them."

"But let us not take them" said Sherlock. "You and your somewhat sinister associate, Wakefield Orloff, have the makings of a coup here, Mycroft. It will take some doing but if the reports that go into that safe are carefully doctored, I rather imagine the employers of the false Villers and his cracksman accomplice will get hopelessly confused." (In his "Diary of the Challenge Match" Watson noted that he never learned if Holmes's ingenious counterplot was put into effect. He mentions that he took pains not to inquire.)

There was a satisfied expression on Mycroft's massive face as he rose to his feet indicating that in his mind, the case was a *fait accompli*. However, Sherlock detained him.

"We still have Watson's suspect to consider."

The good doctor silently handed Holmes his envelope which the great detective tore open eagerly. Extracting the sheet of paper, he read aloud: "Ralph Cord." His eyes widened in surprise which dissolved into admiration. "Watson, you solved it. The supposed Villers pushed the button but the butler did the deed. Here I have been combing newspaper files and delving into family history and you produce the culprit like a slight of hand expert. What thread led you to unravel this tangled web?"

Watson chose his words with care. "Was it not a great Frenchman who said' 'If you can't beat 'em, join 'em?' "

"I fail to follow your ratiocination," said Mycroft.

"No matter," continued Watson. "Ever since I became Sherlock's chronicler and made certain of his exploits available to the public, there has been a rash of stories dealing with mystery, mayhem and murder. Completely fictitious, of course, but they all have one fact in common. In every story, it is always the butler who did it."

Holmes smiled. "A distinct touch, my dear Watson. A distinct touch indeed."

"THE FOUR DETECTIVES"

There never was, and probably never will be again, a bridge match as singular and as interesting as the legendary Challenge Match. Even the celebrated Culbertson-Lenz match of much later vintage was played on a consistant basis. But the Challenge Match was frequently interrupted by demands upon the time of one or all of the participants. One might say that this negated its appeal, but this would be indulging in that "first thought" analysis which Holmes shunned; both in the game of bridge and the game of life. Pauses in the match allowed kibitzers, followers, and the press, to speculate on the hands, evaluate the lines of attack and defense and anticipate the future. They provided periods of gestation and discussion which made the Match more popular than it might have been.

It was shortly after Holmes returned from Odessa. The Match was resumed with regular periods of play. At this time a singular situation presented itself. Three unrelated ingredients combined to produce a unique compound in the annals of crime detection.

The "Cordon Bleu Societe Internacionale Des Chefs Culinaires" chose, on this particular year, to have its annual convention (they used the word "congress") in London. As a ranking officer of the group, as well as an amateur chef of world-wide repute, Arséne Pupin of Paris was in attendance. This required a temporary leave of absence from his duties to the Republic of France and many a larcenous soul breathed a sigh of relief at his absence. M'sieur Pupin was considered the finest product of the Sûreté Francaise. His efforts had filled half the prisons of France and contributed to the population of the penal colonies abroad. Pupin was a name to be conjured with in the esoteric group of crimefighters of world renown.

As gourmets from all over the world gathered in London, Her Majesty's Government was involved in a difficult, tedious, and tender matter. It dealt with spheres of influence on the dark continent of Africa. The views of Britain were not shared by the Kaiser of Germany. However, the recent Egyptian campaign had proved costly so it was decided that the British Fleet would not become involved in strategic maneuvers providing a show of strength in the North Sea. In a similar vein, the Field Marshals of Germany did not muster reserves or place elite troops on parade. Bismarck's eyes were not gazing south towards Africa. He had other and more convenient targets in mind. Since both viewpoints were in agreement that the cumbersome display of the sinews of war was not expedient, a German delegation was sent to England to discuss the situation in depth with Her Majesty's Government. Now said delegation needed as much protection as a pack of wolverines. However, as a gesture to indicate that the Kaiser's government considered the negotiations to be of paramount importance, Germany summoned from Berlin's Alexanderplatz, Herr Wolfgang Von Shalloway, as, Security Officer. The deadly, machine-like German logic of Herr Von Shalloway was offended. To be removed, if only for a short time, from the direction of the Criminal Investigation Department of the Berlin Police Force, to act as a piece of window-dressing, was inconceivable. However, when Bismarck said "Jump!", the German officials said: "How high?" So Von Shalloway left his Meldwesen, that precisely catalogued collection of twenty million cards dealing with criminal cases. He said good-bye to his "Kriminal Archiv", the clipping collection on similar matters from all over the world. This man, considered by many as the greatest of detectives, docilely departed for London. No clue as to his thoughts regarding his mission was evident in his stoic Teutonic face. However, his subordinates, a group of singularly-endowed men now in charge of the Berlin investigation machine, walked very softly immediately prior to the departure of "The Chief".

Public taste is always a factor to be considered. The English were indicating a certain restlessness as though sated with the discoveries from the Valley of the Nile. Mummies were, for the moment, old hat. With an eye constantly cocked towards legacies, endowments, and similar types of usufruct, the British Museum pulled off a coup. After lengthy negotiations with the Government of China, it was arranged that a considerable collection of vases of the Tang Dynasty vould be transported from the Orient and placed on display. Much was made of this by the news media, and reasonably so. The worth of the vases was beyond calculation. Suddenly, the prices of Chinese furniture escalated. Oriental prints and bric-a-brac became the vogue. Modish ladies of fashion re-decorated madly. The shops of Limehouse never had it so good.

The vases did represent, in actual value, part of the national treasure of a nation. While the Chinese held the talents of Scotland Yard in high esteem, because of the fine record of the British police forces in Hong Kong and Singapore, a little something extra was needed as a balm to uncertainties while such objects of value were on foreign soil. The hands holding the reins of China beckoned to Chan Chow Lee. In the western world, little was known of this Oriental master manhunter. But that specialized group at the head of the forces of law and order knew of him. His solution of "The Case of the Manadarin of Panderin", without the slenderest gossamer of a clue, had elicited the admiration and respect of those "in the know." Inspectors Gregson and Lestrade of Scotland Yard were quivering with anticipation when officially notified that the wily sleuth from Peking would accom-oany the shipment of Tang vases to the British Museum.

Chan Chow Lee did not consider his mission vital. He realized that the British police would take the same security measures which he would set into motion were some English treasure to be displayed in China. Furthermore, they had the advantage of more trained personnel. However, he was in accord with the idea that some precautions before the fact were superior to desperate measures after it. At least, that is the idea he advanced publicly. Privately, another thought was flitting through his inscrutable mind. London, to him, was not a city but a person. Possibly, he might meet this man he admired so much. He was thinking of none other than Mr. Sherlock Holmes of Baker Street.

The ingredients for the compound were there. All that was required was the catalyst. Singularly enough, it was the good Doctor Watson who provided it in the form of a thought.

"I say, Holmes," the Doctor said, looking up from his paper, "doesn't this strike you as a trifle odd?"

Holmes put down the scissors with which he was cutting a clipping for his voluminous files and removed his pipe from his mouth. But he said not a word. His inquisitive glance was sufficient, and Watson continued, indicating the newspaper in front of him.

"This gourmet society that is to hold a congress at The Archery Tavern shortly — their vice-president is none other than Arséne Pupin."

Holmes nodded. "Pupin has been all wrapped up in cookery for years. Doesn't interfere with his effectiveness, however. It will be a sad day for France when he leaves the Sûreté. He solved a case in Le Havre some years ago" . . . .

Holmes' voice dwindled to a halt. Looking at his old friend and companion with that sharp, intuitive glance which was 'one of his trademarks, he shifted direction. "That was not your complete thought."

"Indeed, no," agreed Watson. "Didn't your brother Mycroft, tell us the other day about the Anglo-German discussions to take place on Downing Street?"

Holmes nodded. "He made some mention of it."

"And also that Wolfgang Von Shalloway was a member of that delegation?" persisted the doctor. "At the Bagatelle Club last night*, the Duchess of Paisley buttonholed me and I couldn't get away from her. She could talk of nothing but a display of Chinese vases at the British Museum and how she had bought a completely new wardrobe based on Chinese silk."

Holmes' chuckle was sympathetic. "I noticed your vain attempts to get a word in even though I was, at the moment, engaged in a very difficult defense with Septimus Sheingold. The contract was five diamonds and . . . ."

"A moment, Holmes." His teeth firmly implanted in a flavorsome idea, the doctor was not to be side-tracked, even by the discussion of a bridge hand.

"Two days ago, you were cutting clippings as you are now. You made comment of the fact that the Chinese display was arriving, accompanied by a chap named Chan something or other."

"Chan Chow Lee," said Holmes by way of assistance. He leaned back in his comfortable chair and regarded Watson with as close to a "small boy" smile as he could.

"I have been dense, haven't I? How clever of you, Watson. You are alluding, of course, to the fact that three of the leading criminologists of the world will be in London at the same time."

"Four," corrected Watson. As Holmes shook his head and started to say something, the doctor over-rode him: No false modesty, my dear chap. With you but recently back from Odessa, the four leading detectives of the world will . . ."

"A moment, please, old friend."

If asked point-blank, Holmes would never have claimed modesty as one of his faults.

"The three men you refer to," he continued, "all have official positions whereas I am merely a 'consulting detective.' "

"Pish, tosh!" said Watson, waving away Holmes' words. "By any name, the game's the same. I'm amazed that no one has made note of this singular coincidence. Probably never happen again. Jolly ol' London has the four greatest sleuths at its disposal. I really think something should be done about this fortuitous happenstance, don't you, Holmes?"

"If you say so, my dear boy."

Holmes' eyes returned to his scissors but his mercurial mind had flitted elsewhere. There was that idea prompted by the Odessa case; a paper relative

*THE CHALLENGE MATCH was played in the afternoons. This particular night Holmes and Sheingold partnered in an exhibition match for charity.

to "the psychological approach to the matter of motivation." Then there was that thought that he wished to discuss with Watson, after a little more consideration, realtive to a more organized system of defense bidding. His eyes grew opaque. Watson allowed the matter to drop — at least, conversationally. Besides, he had a few things to think about himself. Silence settled over the rooms at 221B Baker Street interrupted occasionally by the pop and hiss of the oak log burning vigorously in the cheery hearth fire. Outside, fog rolled off the Thames towards Baker Street. First, just faint tendrils infiltrated the area. Then, as though in receipt of a favorable report from advance guards, it came like a massed artillery barrage. As street lights dimmed and passers-by hastened their homeward steps, all was dank and wet and cold. But English builders do their work with pride and Holmes and Watson were warm and cozy within the cocoon which they had made famous by their presence. Another day in the life of the greatest deductive mind the world has ever known drew to a comfortable end.

Early morning winds dispelled the fog embracing Baker Street. Holmes had appointments with several clients who came to the rooms shared by the detective and Watson. This gave the doctor a good excuse for leaving the premises mumbling something about an old patient. While he was always intensely interested in Holmes' cases, there was nothing on the calendar of an extraordinary nature. As was his custom, the great consulting detective had a number of matters which he worked on simultaneously. If one showed a spark of interest or some crevice in which the detective could insert his probe of specialized knowledge, he brought it to Watson's attention.

Immediately prior to his departure, Watson suddenly realized that his completely fictitious patient might be miffed if he appeared without his medical bag. He retrieved this tool of his trade from its resting place beside the cane rack near the door. Opening the doors inwards*, Watson found himself face to face with Mrs. Hudson and Lady Carrell-Hews, the latter one of Holmes' clients of the moment.

The patient smile on the sometime sardonic face of Holmes was not due to the arrival of a client but to the departure of his delightfully obvious friend, for, as the door closed behind the doctor, his stethoscope hung on one of its room-side pegs.

Adjusting his bowler against the wind, Watson secured a hansom which he directed to the Diogenes Club. This somewhat peculiar men's club had a most exclusive membership roster and served as the unofficial headquarters of Mr. Mycroft Holmes, the second most powerful man in England. Watson fortunately found Holmes' brother on the premises and secured an immediate audience with him. Mycroft Holmes and the Doctor remained closeted for the better part of an hour before the Doctor left the Diogenes Club with a satisfied expression.

It was that afternoon, during the Challenge Match, when a hand Watson called "automatic" came up that prompted another Holmes innovation.

*The point is made that Watson opened the door inwards since he specifically states so in "The Diary of the Challenge Match." It has long been a source of confusion among followers of the great detective as to whether the door to his suite opened outward or inward and, indeed, as to whether it was hinged right or left. Part of this mystery is now solved via the recently revealed Diary.

THE SUREST WAY

```
              HOLMES
              ♠ K Q 4 3
              ♡ A Q
              ◇ A K 7
              ♣ Q 10 7 3
CASTLE                           SKURRY
♠ 8                              ♠ J 10 6 5 2
♡ 10 7 5 4 3 2                   ♡ K 9 6
◇ 9 5 3 2                        ◇ Q 8 6
♣ 9 4                           ♣ 8 5
              WATSON (Dealer)
              ♠ A 9 7
              ♡ J 8
              ◇ J 10 4
              ♣ A K J 6 2
```

CHALLENGE MATCH BIDDING: (neither side vulnerable)

Watson	Castle	Holmes	Skurry
1C	pass	2S	pass
3S	pass	4C	pass
5C	pass	6C	pass
pass	pass		

After his partner's opening bid, Holmes chose to show his huge hand with an immediate jump shift. His spade suit was nothing to write home about but his overall strength certainly was. Watson gave Holmes a single spade raise, waiting to see where his partner's announced power was. After Holmes raised the club suit, Watson bid the minor suit game indicating a respectable suit but a minimum hand. Holmes, who was thinking strongly of a grand slam, settled for 6 clubs with some misgivings.

Betty Castle led her singleton spade and Watson took Skurry's spade ten with his ace. Obviously, the red suits presented the only problem. Watson had two finesse positions but chose to ignore both of them. After drawing trumps in two rounds, he played dummy's king and queen of spades and ruffed a spade in his hand. Now the good doctor led a heart from his hand, going up with dummy's ace and then playing the queen of hearts which Skurry took. Harry found himself in an unenviable position. A diamond lead gave Watson a free finesse. A heart or spade lead would allow Watson to trump in dummy while discarding the diamond loser from his hand. Skurry led a diamond and the slam was home.

"Well played!" Skurry stated. "The heart king killed me. If you had just tried the diamond finesse, I could have gotten off lead by returning the suit and waited for my heart trick."

Holmes offered a gentle comment. "Watson's end play worked very well indeed, but my heart was in my mouth for a moment." Since the other three players looked at him questioningly, he continued: "Suppose Betty had held the heart·king. After taking dummy's queen a diamond return would sink our slam."

Watson's brow was furrowed. "I missed something, didn't I?"

"After you drew trumps and began playing spades, the sure way presented itself. With Harry holding all the remaining spades, simply play the three·top honors and then lead the last spade from dummy and discard a red card from your hand. Harry has to win the trick and the end play is operable and not dependent on the position of the heart king."

"Dear me!" said Watson. "It is so obvious once explained. My apologies, partner."

"Allow me to extend mine," said Holmes. "Had I taken the bull by the horns and gone to a grand slam in no-trump, Harry might very reasonably have led a club, adopting a passive defense. On the third club lead he could safely part with a heart and could drop a spade on the fourth club but what does he do when I lead the final club? He is caught in a progressive squeeze and seven no-trump comes home."

Work this out for yourself and see if Holmes was right.

Some time later, this was the hand dealt which produced a far-reaching effect on the bridge bidding of the day since it prompted another Holmes discovery.

AUTOMATIC

```
                    HOLMES
                    ♠ 7
                    ♡ J 9 8 7 5 4
                    ◇ J 2
                    ♣ Q 8 6 5
    CASTLE                              SKURRY (Dealer)
    ♠ Q 9 8                             ♠ J 10 5 4 3
    ♡ 6                                 ♡ A K Q 3 2
    ◇ A K Q 9 6 3                       ◇ 10 5
    ♣ A 10 7                            ♣ K
                    WATSON
                    ♠ A K 6 2
                    ♡ 10
                    ◇ 8 7 4
                    ♣ J 9 4 3 2
```

CHALLENGE MATCH BIDDING: (BOTH SIDES VULNERABLE)

Castle	Holmes	Skurry	Watson
-	-	1S	pass
3D	pass	3H	pass
3S	pass	4H	pass
4S	pass	6S	double
pass	pass	pass	

Harry Skurry's hand was light but had excellent distributional values and he quite correctly opened the highest ranking of his touching suits. Betty Castle had a very uncomfortable hand to bid. She felt that if she responded two diamonds, she would never be able to convince her partner how very strong she was in playing tricks. By the book, her hand was light for a jump-shift, but she chose that bid anyway as the best solution to her problem. One could fault her judgment perhaps but it is interesting to note that many modern day experts have lowered their requirements for a jump-shift response considerably. Their reasoning, certainly not without merit, being that with a 19 point hand, one is going to get to a slam opposite a partner with an opening bid anyway. It is hands like Betty's in the very good 16-17 point range that present problems.

Following Betty's game-forcing response, Harry showed his second suit and then rebid it to indicate 5 hearts and, by inference, five or more spades. Betty kept returning to her partner's spade suit for obvious reasons. Harry, picturing his partner's hand differently, ignored the fact that Betty made no slam moves and bid the small slam in spades directly. Watson, with the contract beaten in his hand, doubled. He presumed that if Betty ran to no-trump, Holmes would lead a spade. Betty and Harry allowed the six-spade contract to stand and Watson led the diamond 8.

The minute dummy came down, Harry realized that he was doomed but he made the best of an impossible situation. Taking the opening lead in dummy, he led the singleton heart to his ace. He now unblocked his club king and ruffed a heart in dummy. The club ace provided a resting place for his other small heart. He now played the diamond king and, when it held, his hand consisted of nothing but trumps and two hearts. Skurry now led a spade from dummy. Watson took the trick and returned a diamond. Harry took the trick in dummy, leading the last spade. Watson chose to duck this trick. Now Skurry led a club which he ruffed low in his hand. The spade jack drove out Watson's last high trump honor and Harry was down one as he had to be. Holmes' immediate comment was that Watson had given declarer every chance to go wrong but Skurry had played with care. His opinion went unnoticed however as Betty and Harry immediately launched into a somewhat heated discussion regarding a bidding sequence so brilliant that they ended up in a slam off the two top trump honors. Obviously, further play, for the moment, was impossible and Holmes took this opportunity to exchange some words with his partner.

"My dear Watson, this hand has sparked a chain of thought in my mind relative to slam doubles."

"Always hold the ace, king, of the opponents' suit?" queried Watson with a broad grin.

"An excellent idea," agreed Holmes, "but a rare situation indeed. Does it not occur to you that a double of an aggressively-bid slam is a losing proposition?" Before Watson could remonstrate, the great bridge-playing detective continued: "I do not refer to your double on this hand, naturally. It was automatic since you had the contract beaten before the first play. Any action from my side of the table could not affect the final result. But you will agree, I am sure, that when good players bid up to a slam, they expect to make it. Since they are good players, the defense will normally be most lucky to defeat the contract by more than one trick, if at

all. Therefore, the reward for a penalty double does not outweigh its dangers."
"Watson was chiming in with Holmes' thoughts. "The dangers being that the opponents might run to another contract or that the double will alert declarer as to how to play the hand successfully."

"Exactly," said Holmes. "Therefore, I am considering the idea of using a double of a slam for another purpose. Let me give you an example. My right hand opponent opens a diamond and I overcall a heart. The third hand bids a spade and you pass. Now the opening bidder jumps to three spades and after my pass, the next player bids six spades. You are on lead against this slam. What would your normal lead be?"

"A heart, of course," responded Watson promptly. "After all, you bid the suit."
"Exactly," said Holmes. "And if I thought our best defense involved a heart lead from you, I would pass hoping that we might be able to defeat the slam. But suppose, after the bid of six spades, I were to double? Not to attempt to exact a paltry additional penalty but to provide you with a clue as to your lead. My double would instruct you not to lead my suit."

Watson's nod of agreement was somewhat half-hearted, so Holmes expounded further:

"Most small slams resolve themselves into declarer being capable of taking eleven tricks and he attempts, by one means or another, to establish a twelfth trick. If the defense can get off to the killing lead and score two fast tricks, the slam goes down before the declarer has the chance to get his play plan in action. Therefore, I propose that a double of a slam, willingly bid by the opponents, calls for an unusual lead. It instructs the doubler's partner not to lead a trump and not to lead a suit bid by the doubler. Let me give you an instance using the same bidding sequence I just mentioned. Say Betty bids a diamond, I bid a heart, Harry bids a spade and you pass. Betty now bids three spades and Harry goes to six. I double the contract. Now, is it not conceivable that I could have overcalled with five hearts to the queen, jack, 10 and the ace, queen of diamonds? If Betty holds the diamond king, a reasonable assumption, a diamond lead by you and we might very well take the first two tricks. Another instance which could easily occur is my having a side suit void, very possible if I have made any sort of pre-emptive bid. I am asking you to find my void, usually possible since you figure to have a large number of cards in that suit."

Watson's assurance had been growing as Holmes detailed his novel thought. "This idea makes so much sense, my dear Holmes. Particularly since we take a bid of little practical use and give it a very effective and specific meaning. Your lead directing double could very well hit our opponents like lightning. I say," he added quickly, "that is a rather good name for it . . . 'The Lightning Double.' "
NOTE: How singular that in modern times, the great bridge expert, Theodore Lightner came up with the same idea evolved by Holmes. Expert bridge players of our times all use "The Lightner Double."

Slam hands are not as frequent as we would like to have them so Holmes' "Lightning Double" found use on rare occasions. To indicate its efficiency, I have selected some hands from Doctor Watson's detailed "Diary of the Challenge Match" that show the lead directional device in action.

THE LIGHTNING DOUBLE

HOLMES
♠ 5 3
♡ void
♢ K Q 9 8 7 3 2
♣ 10 8 5 2

CASTLE
♠ A Q 10 6 4 2
♡ K 9 4
♢ 6
♣ A J 3

SKURRY (Dealer)
♠ K J 8 7
♡ A Q 7 3
♢ 10 4
♣ K Q 4

WATSON
♠ 9
♡ J 10 8 6 5 2
♢ A J 5
♣ 9 7 6

CHALLENGE MATCH BIDDING: (Castle-Skurry vulnerable)

Castle	Holmes	Skurry	Watson
-	-	1S	pass
3S	pass	4S	pass
5C	pass	5H	pass
6S	double	pass	pass
pass			

The bidding deserves some comment. After Skurry opened with one spade, Betty was actually too strong with 17 support points to bid three spades. Leading experts in our time make a jump-shift with 17 points and massive support for partner or a self-sustaining suit of their own. However, Betty chose to underbid her values and then take further action. With minimum values, Harry settled for four spades but Betty kept the bidding open by cue bidding her club control. (Note: It will be recalled that Holmes originally conceived this stratagem in the famous Red Aces Hand. See: "Sherlock Holmes, Bridge Detective.") Harry now cued his heart ace thereby denying first round control of diamonds. Betty, with her monstrous spade support, a fitting king in hearts and second round control of diamonds via her singleton bid the spade slam with assurance. At this point, Holmes realized that his opponents were off one ace. Blackwood had not been employed and Betty had settled for the small slam. Obviously, if he could alert Watson to get off to a heart lead, the contract could be defeated. Therefore, he doubled in keeping with their partnership idea that slam doubles are lead directional.

Now Watson did some thinking. He and Holmes had agreed that, if in doubt when the newly-discovered "Lightning Double" was employed, the opening leader should come out with dummy's first bid side suit. However, had Holmes wanted a club lead he could well have doubled Betty's club cue bid. Watson found little difficulty in placing his heart jack on the table. Holmes ruffed and returned the diamond king which Watson overtook. A second heart ruff netted the defense three tricks. Without the double, Watson might well have led his top club and the Skurry-Castle slam would have been made.

THE DEADLY DEFENSE

```
                    CASTLE
                    ♠ 5 3
                    ♡ K J 10 4 3
                    ◇ A K 8
                    ♣ 9 8 3
WATSON                              HOLMES
♠ A Q J 7 6 4                       ♠ 10 9 2
♡ 7 5 2                             ♡ A Q 6
◇ 9 6 4                             ◇ 7 5 3 2
♣ 7                                ♣ 6 4 2
                    SKURRY (Dealer)
                    ♠ K 8
                    ♡ 9 8
                    ◇ Q J 10
                    ♣ A K Q J 10 5
```

CHALLENGE MATCH BIDDING: (Holmes-Watson vulnerable)

Skurry	Watson	Castle	Holmes
1C	2S	3H	pass
3NT	pass	pass	double
pass	pass	pass	

Harry certainly had the values for his opening bid though a gambling three no-trump bid based on a solid minor suit with scattered stoppers elsewhere would have worked out well for him on this hand. This bid is much favored by leading British players and a number of American experts as well. However, the gambling three no-trump was unknown at the time of Sherlock Holmes. Watson used the pre-emptive jump overcall which he and Holmes were playing at this time. Considering the vulnerability, his hand was somewhat skimpy for this risky bid but the good doctor took a position. Betty Castle with eleven high card points was not to be shut out of the bidding and came right in with three hearts. At this point, Skurry reasoned that if Watson led his spade suit, it would give Harry seven running tricks and surely his partner could provide two more. Therefore, Harry bid three no-trump as the easiest road to game. After Watson and Betty passed, Holmes doubled. The partnership had agreed that a no-trump double strongly called for the lead of the dummy's first bid suit. Holmes reasoned that if Watson would lead a heart, Holmes could lead through the spade stopper which he knew Skurry had. He anticipated that Watson held a spade suit of some substance inasmuch as he had made his jump-overcall when vulnerable. At this point, Skurry had mesmerized himself into thinking that he would receive a spade lead. Hence, he did not run to four clubs though this contract would also have been defeated.

The defense struck and the carnage was frightful. Watson obediently led a heart. Harry rose with dummy's king which Holmes took with the ace. Back came the spade ten. Harry played his eight spot and Watson the spade seven. The spade nine followed forcing Harry's king which Watson took with the ace. The defense scored eight tricks without stopping and Harry was down 700 points before he could gain the lead.

It is obvious that a spade lead originally would have allowed Skurry to score ten tricks and yawn in the process.

Betty Castle made no mention of a possible 4-club contract, down one, and Watson and Holmes preserved a courteous silence. The kibitzers were so stunned by the Holmes-Watson defense that Harry was, thankfully, allowed to suffer in silence.

Much later in the Challenge Match when Harry and Betty were fighting for survival, the following hand allowed Holmes' innovation to strike again with deadly efficiency.

CHAOS

CASTLE
♠ A K 10 9 5
♡ A Q 7 5
◇ K Q 7 4
♣ void

HOLMES (Dealer)
♠ 6 2
♡ void
◇ 10 9 6 2
♣ A K Q 10 8 7 5

WATSON
♠ 8 4
♡ 10 9 8 6 4 3 2
◇ void
♣ 9 6 4 2

SKURRY
♠ Q J 7 3
♡ K J
◇ A J 8 5 3
♣ J 3

CHALLENGE MATCH BIDDING: (both sides vulnerable)

Holmes	Castle	Watson	Skurry
3C	4C	pass	4D
pass	4S	pass	4NT
pass	6H	pass	7S
double	pass	pass	pass

Holmes' opening pre-emptive is obvious. Betty's cue bid constituted a massive double, forcing to game, and well-warranted by her huge holding. Skurry bid his longest suit knowing that Betty would produce another bid since game had not been reached. With his own opening bid values, Harry could smell the sweet scent of slam. Betty now showed her fine spades which was all Harry needed to hear. He unleashed Blackwood. Betty's 6 heart bid showed two aces plus a void since she had jumped a level. On the bidding, Harry had no problem figuring out her void suit and contracted for a grand slam in spades. Holmes' double was again lead directional. Since he had shown a 7-card club suit already, it was obvious to Watson that Holmes' extremely distributional hand must include a void suit. With his long string of hearts, the Doctor might very well have led the suit anyway but his partner left nothing to chance. Out came the heart-10 as the opening lead and Holmes' ruffed it. Knowing well that Betty's void was in clubs, Holmes led back the diamond-10 which Watson gleefully ruffed. Reading Holmes' return of the diamond-10 as an indication that he could ruff another heart, Watson came back with the red major which Holmes ruffed for the second time. A club lead originally and Betty Castle could not fail to take 13 tricks. But, alas, the reasonable grand slam was defeated 3 tricks and doubled to boot for a penalty of 800 points.

Harry Skurry just buried his head in his hands and groaned. The kibitzers were buzzing, of course. By now "The Lightning Double" was the talk of London and another great triumph for the bridge-playing detective. However, in all honesty, it does not rank with the bread and butter plays of bridge which are the real winners. Since it took unusual hands to operate, this colorful device gradually faded from the minds of bridge players, especially since Holmes did not choose to write a pamphlet on it. However, as previously mentioned, it was rediscovered in modern times by Theodore Lightner and is a tool in the modern experts' bag of tricks.

Having digressed momentarily to present hands involving a specific defensive innovation of Holmes, let us return to the day in question in the career of the great bridge-playing detective. It was the last hand of the afternoon's play in the Challenge Match which may explain why Holmes and Watson bid with considerable daring.

Holmes busy brewing "guile" in "The Hoax."

SCANTY VALUES

HOLMES (Dealer)
♠ 7 4
♡ A Q 8 3
♢ A Q 7 2
♣ K 10 4

CASTLE
♠ Q J 3 2
♡ 7 5
♢ K
♣ J 9 7 5 3 2

SKURRY
♠ A 8 6
♡ K J 10 9 6 2
♢ J 10 6
♣ 8

WATSON
♠ K 10 9 5
♡ 4
♢ 9 8 5 4 3
♣ A Q 6

CHALLENGE MATCH BIDDING: (neither side vulnerable)

Castle	Holmes	Skurry	Watson
-	1H	pass	1S
pass	1 NT	pass	2D
pass	3D	pass	3NT
pass	pass	pass	

Holmes with 15 points in high cards opened a heart and Skurry promptly passed since his opponent had opened his own best suit. Watson chose to bid a spade to keep the bidding low. Holmes now showed his minimum values and balanced hand by bidding one no-trump. Watson's bid of two diamonds, while a change of suit, was in no way forcing since Holmes had limited his hand with his second bid. Angling for a no-trump game, Holmes showed his four card diamond support and Watson took the auction to three no-trump.

Skurry considered his opening lead carefully. He hoped to bring in the heart suit by having Betty lead through declarer. But his spade ace was vital as a re-entry card. He made the excellent lead of a low spade in an attempt to get to his partner's hand. Holmes played dummy's spade-10 taken by Betty's jack. Dummy's singleton heart plus her own shortage in the suit alerted Betty to the fact that Harry must be loaded in Holmes' first bid suit. She returned her heart-7. At this point, the detective realized that he must keep Betty off lead at all costs. He rose with his heart ace and crossed to dummy by leading a low club to the ace. A diamond from the board fetched Betty's king which Holmes took with the ace. He was not at all surprised when Betty showed out on his diamond queen lead. Now he led a small diamond which Skurry took with his jack. Harry now put Holmes to the

114

guess by playing another small spade. Holmes easily divined that if Betty held the spade ace, her heart return would defeat his contract so he rose with dummy's spade king which held the trick. He now cashed dummy's two established diamonds and fulfilled his touch-and-go contract with two more club tricks.

During the play of the last few hands of the day, Mycroft Holmes joined the group of observers. The glance he exchanged with Doctor Watson was accompanied by a brief nod.

When the players rose after the conclusion of the final hand, Mycroft Holmes spoke to his brother briefly while Dr. Watson compared total scores with Harry Skurry. After a few pleasant words with kibitzers, the great detective joined Mycroft and the good Doctor and leaving the club they entered a waiting hansom.

"As a pair of conspirators," said Holmes, while they rattled and bumped down the street, "you won't do." He shot quick glances at his brother and Watson.

Mycroft Holmes' face remained pleasantly uncommunicative but Watson came forth with a groan.

"Really, Holmes" he said, "it is exasperating. One tries to give you a pleasant surprise . . . ."

". . . And leaves a broad path of clues. Cheer up, old friend," interrupted the detective. "Your thought is appreciated and surprise is an unnecessary adjunct."

"How did I alert your suspicions?" queried Watson.

"Dear me," said Mycroft. "We shall now have ten minutes of inference and deductions."

Holmes' eyes were somewhat icy as they rested on Mycroft momentarily. Then he turned to Watson.

"This morning you left to visit a patient, as an afterthought taking your medical bag. But you left your stethoscope behind. Sticky wicket there, ol' boy. A doctor without his stethoscope is like a bird without wings. Then you arrived for the Match at the club with a residue of dust on your coat. I know for a fact that the outside of the Diogenes Club is being cleaned and the dust is identical to that produced by a sand-blaster. See, there is some on Mycroft's coat now." Holmes demonstrated, working the gritty substance between his fingers. "So my brother's arriving at the club came as no surprise nor did his dinner invitation. Twice, while kibitzing, he lit up a French cigarette."

"I smoke them on occasion," interrupted Mycroft irresistably drawn into Holmes' analysis.

"But do not order them. Someone gave you a pack, probably a Frenchman."

"You are right, but I don't see where it is obvious that they were given to me or by a Frenchman necessarily. I might have secured them from a tobacco shop."

Holmes was patient. "There is no export stamp on the pack in your pocket."

The sleuth continued as Watson and Mycroft exchanged a glance of resignation: "Your mention of the presence of the three foreign detectives, Watson, plus a contrived excuse to leave Baker Street. Mycroft with his French cigarettes. It all adds up to the fact that we will be joined at the Archery Tavern by Chan Chow Lee, Arséne Pupin and Wolfgang Von Shalloway."

As his brother nodded, Holmes produced an afterthought.

"Besides I had an errand of my own today, relative to a case. It took me to the vicinity of Downing Street and I saw you, Mycroft, talking with Wolfgang Von

Shalloway outside the German Embassy."

Mycroft's habitual calmness was shaken.

"That alone would have gotten the wind up for you. You mean all this other . . . ."

". . . Tut, tut," admonished Holmes. "The mind, like any other muscle, requires exercise. Inference, deduction, logic; they are all womb mates of solution."

Mycroft was shaking his head as the carriage drew up at the Archery Tavern.

Holmes gave no sign that he was not surprised when introduced to the trio of eminent criminologists in the private dining-room in the Tavern secured by Mycroft. Also, he indicated much delight in meeting his contemporaries from other lands. While he knew Von Shalloway because of his association with the Hamburg Hamster Case*, the other two were strangers to him by face if not by reputation.

At first, the atmosphere was a trifle formal, even strained, as the quartet sized up each other. But this soon disappeared after large whiskeys and sodas followed by a sumptuous meal. The arm of Mycroft Holmes, backed by the prestige of the foreign office, was long. The service and fare in the private dining-room was superior. Arséne Pupin was especially interested in the Quiche Lorraine (known in the colonies as "Egg Flan"). The Frenchman absented himself from the festive board to have a few words with the chef regarding his pie shell.

"C'est magnifique" was Pupin's description. The chef, quite overwhelmed by the visitation of such an illustrious guest, proceeded to outdo himself. The table groaned as did those seated at it.

Watson commented to Mycroft, *sotto voce*, that nobody looked like they should. Arséne Pupin was singularly tall for a Frenchman. The German was small and dapper with a head that seemed slightly oversized for his body. Chan Chow Lee was garbed in the tailoring of Savile Row and looked very occidental indeed. With a degree from Oxford, the oriental was not on unfamiliar ground. Inasmuch as Chinese names consist of the family one first, he requested that his fellow criminologists address him in the style of the west by his given name of Chow Lee.

Prompted by Chow Lee Chan's gesture towards casualness. Wolfgang Von Shalloway revealed that his friends called him "Wolfie". This completely broke the ice and the four sleuths were soon busy discussing crime like old friends. Arséne Pupin cleared up several points relative to his famous Le Havre fishmonger murders to the satisfaction of Holmes. Chow Lee told some interesting stories regarding crime in the east. Wolfie, between steins of dark beer which he drank like water, told his new friends about the Morenstrausse Robberies, a recent case which he had brought to a successful conclusion.

Holmes' contribution conversationally had a familiar ring to Watson.

"I find, gentlement, the criminal mind singularly lacking in inventiveness. As I wearily go through those cases which come to my attention, I find few indications of a creative spark. If one such ingenious approach does manifest itself, the creator sticks to his *modus operandi* as if in deadly fear of deviation. I must confess that frequently, when dealing with a dull event, I find myself looking with envious eyes at the cases in which you are involved."

*How singular that Holmes was involved in the "Hamster Case" during the same period that he solved the shocking affair of Wilson, the notorious canary-trainer. It would seem this was a wildlife period in our detective's career.

"*Mon dieu,*" exclaimed Pupin, "you 'ave,-'ow is zee expression? — been reading my mail. I deal wiz fishmongers while you, 'Olmes, come to grips wiz Moriarty."

A chorus of agreement from the others buttressed his statement.

"It is true," replied Holmes, "that Moriarty was brilliant. For that reason he rapidly became the Napoleon of the underworld. But with the passing of the professor, I find a singular dearth of imaginative crime."

Holmes had touched a universal complaint and his audience erupted in agreement. None of the foreign detectives could recall a recent case which they felt was a true test of their skill.

"What a shame!" advanced Chow Lee through a cloud of smoke from a Melachrino cigarette, "that there is not a case at this moment which we could discuss."

"And perhaps solve," added Wolfie. "In reading the foreign journals I have often thought: 'Ah, if I were in charge of that one!' "

"Exactly," said Arséne Pupin. "We all look towards ze - 'ow you say - fields greener. Give us ze crime to test our skills, *mes enfants,* and you give us ze game to play."

There seemed to be an added sparkle in Holmes' eyes.

"We should," he said slowly, "consider a case none of us has been in contact with."

"Agreed," stated Wolfie. "Something intriguing but beyond the jurisdiction of all of us."

"For the sake of ze fairness," commented Pupin as Chow Lee nodded.

Mycroft Holmes, who had remained mute during the animated discussion, along with Watson, now had a thought which he made vocal.

"Gentlemen, this may interest you. A Reuter's report I received stated that Hugo Bessinger died in New York yesterday."

Sound swelled as each of the others exchanged comments.

"And ze cause of death?" queried Pupin.

"Natural," replied Mycroft. "The New York police were extremely diligent since Bessinger had many enemies. However, there is no doubt. The self-styled 'World's Greatest Detective' died in his sleep."

Holmes had an aside for Watson.

"Bessinger was an American private investigator with an extraordinary record of success. This was a fact which he was very quick to mention to anyone available."

Watson nodded in understanding of both Holmes' statement and the dry tone in which it was delivered.

"But if Bessinger was not murdered," Wolfie's voice died out and he regarded Holmes' brother with new respect. "Ah - you are thinking of the two cases . . ."

". . . Which were tied together as if by an umbilical cord." Chow Lee finished the sentence.

"Ze disappearance of Junius Crane from ze 'Satanic' " interjected Arséne Pupin, "and ze disappearance of James Crawford."

"A distinct touch Mycroft," stated Holmes. "Gentlemen, I believe my brother nas given us an excellent thought. The death of Junius Crane was never resolved, at least to my satisfaction."

"And the disappearance of Crawford was never solved." One could almost visualize Wolfie's mind busy ticking off items of interest.

117

It was as if a tocsin had been sounded. The casual atmosphere disappeared like worn-out clothes as the four manhunters responded to the call. With a rapidity ᴜnly possible via long association with arriving at decisions, the quartet established the ground rules. Each was free to use those contacts which they had. Each would attempt to shed some light on the unsolved disappearance of James Crawford, attorney-at-law of New York City. They would meet again in four days and go over their findings in concert. The meeting of the four great criminologists was adjourned with amazing rapidity, each one departing with a livelier step than that with which he had arrived. The hounds had been "loosed" on the fox.

It was back at their rooms on Baker Street that Holmes came to the assistance of a perplexed Doctor Watson.

"I feel like a dolt, Holmes."

"No more than I would at a medical convention, Watson. Let me refresh your mind regarding the bizarre affair which captured our attention at the tavern.

"We must go back in time a little for the complete picture. Junius Crane and Charles Storm were senior partners in a brokerage house in New York aptly named 'Crane and Storm.' They, along with Inez Crane, Junius's wife, were passengers on a holiday cruise to the Mediterranean aboard the 'S/S Satanic'. The cruise for the Cranes and, to a certain extent, Storm as well, was a signal for one long party. The wine flowed red and Junius Crane drank deeply. It got so bad that before the ship cleared Gibraltar on its return to New York, Crane fell down a companionway stairs injuring his leg. The ship's doctor diagnosed a hair-line fracture and placed Crane's leg in a cast and the owner in a wheel-chair. This did not seem to interrupt the almost frantic festivities in the least. There were the usual shipboard rumors, in this case involving Inez Crane and Charles Storm.

"The night before the ship was to dock in New York, was a dark and cold one. Around one in the morning, a cabin steward decided to brave the elements for some air before retiring. From an upper deck he said that he saw two figures appear below. One in a wheel chair and the other pushing it. The steward, a volatile Italian, was sure the second figure was a women. He did admit that the figures were indistinct in the darkness. He then saw, according to his testimony later, the wheel-chair being pushed to the side of the ship. The female figure pulled the body from the wheel-chair and succeeded in pushing it over the iron railing and into the sea below. Taking the wheel-chair, the figure then swiftly returned to the passenger cabin area. The steward was completely shocked by what he had seen."

"I should think so," murmured Watson.

Holmes continued: "He retired to his cabin to think things over. Evidently, he was a slow thinker since he did not reveal this incident until late the following day. By this time, the police were aboard the docked ship and his story got plenty of attention.

"When the 'Satanic' docked the following morning, Charles Storm became very concerned at the absence of his partner. Inez, somewhat the worse for wear from her voyage, was in no mood to consider it important. She expressed the thought that her husband was sleeping it off somewhere. However, the presence of the wheel-chair in their cabin did force her to realize that something was amiss. The captain was informed, the ship was searched, and the authorities summoned.

"When the story of the room steward came to light, the police took a very dim view of Inez Crane. After lengthy questioning and investigation, the State of New York charged Inez Crane with homicide and the district attorney prepared his case.

"When the trial began, all the shipboard gossip, the drinking, the carousing, was brought forth, somewhat gloatingly, by the prosecution. There was an attempt by the district attorney to tie Inez Crane and Charles Storm in with Junius's fall and injury but this did not come off. However, the prosecution did not press this since it seemed to have a trump ace in the room steward's testimony. Because of the social prominence of those involved, the press had a field day and the Crane case proved a circulation bonanza. After the testimony of the steward, the odds on Inez Crane's acquittal were rather long."

"I would think so," stated Watson. "Thus far it is so open and shut I should think the case would have been boring to you, Holmes."

"Not so," replied the detective. "I followed it carefully. I kept wondering why the defense had not tried to enter a plea of temporary insanity or some other such gambit. Charles Storm, whose intimate association with Inez Crane was never proved or disproved, stood by his partner's wife loyally. They hired a young lawyer, James Crawford, for the defense. Crawford instigated a shrewd move. He secured the services of Hugo Bessinger, self-styled 'Crime Analyist.' "

"So that's where he fits in," said Watson, on tenterhooks.

"Exactly," continued Holmes. "Hugo Bessinger was something of a phenomenon. He reeked of the showman and had an almost psychotic pride in his record and reputation. He was undoubtedly an unmitigated bore but he held the cards. He could prove his credentials. Bessinger never lost a case in court or a settlement outside one."

"Is this possible?"

"One would not think so," responded Holmes. "I felt, without proof, that Bessinger must have been very cautious of the cases he accepted. If not, he had to be inordinately lucky, a possibility, or the possessor of some second sight, a distinct impossibility.

"In any case, Bessinger appeared as a friendly witness for the defense. The district attorney felt it wise to accept his status as a specialist in crime without question since Bessinger was very much in the public eye at the moment. Bessinger put on a show for the court and the public. He appeared with various intricate machines designed to record weight and stress. He had as much equipment as a magician and he dazzled the jurors with technical phrases delivered with great conviction. He ended up convincing the court and jury that a frail woman of Inez Crane's size and weight was completely incapable of lifting or shoving an object the size and weight of her husband over the railing of the 'Satanic'. All of the prosecution's points about dissipation and excesses now came to the aid of the defense. Inez, her nerves rubbed raw from alcohol and drugs, did not seem capable of winding a watch. Using facsimilies, Bessinger demonstrated that, at one point, Inez would have to lift her husband's body to get him over the high railing. It was here that the case for the prosecution evaporated. Junius Crane was a large man weighing well over two hundred pounds. His wife did not even weigh a hundred. Inez Crane was acquitted."

"What a triumph for Hugo Bessinger."

"A triumph which did not satisfy him," elaborated Holmes. "The American investigator had worked up a complete case to convict Charles Storm of the murder of Junius Crane. He tried desperately to bring this out in the trial of Inez Crane. However, in this matter, he was at cross purposes with Attorney Crawford. The latter was intent on the acquittal of his client. The arrest and conviction of the true culprit was of secondary importance. He directed all his questions to Bessinger in such a manner as to suppress the detective's crusade against the surviving partner. This procedure resulted in bad blood between Bessinger and Crawford. It is said that they didn't speak to each other after the trial."

"You seem inordinately well informed about these doings, Holmes."

No more than anyone else with an interest," replied the detective. "I do have an associate in New York with whom I correspond on occasion."

"So far," said Watson, "you have informed me about the Crane case. Are you not investigating the disappearance of the lawyer?"

Holmes' eyes had a gleam of interest as they rested on his friend for a silent moment.

"An excellent observation, Watson. But there is an obvious association."

He then resumed his story.

"Bessinger made no secret of his theory. He accused Storm openly, after the trial, via the press. As a headline hunter his success was without equal. 'Is Storm Guilty? Is Bessinger Right?' 'Will the State Move Against Charles Storm?' These were the leadlines of stories of the day. Some answers were provided by the suicide of Charles Storm."

"Good heavens," said Watson. "This affair becomes stranger by the moment."

"Let me hasten to present all the facts I have," answered Holmes. "Though I don't wish to rush over an interesting indication of mass psychology. Storm's suicide had all the appearance of a 'way out' chosen by a guilty man. Bessinger's theory was vindicated and yet . . . . it smacked of the tool that had driven a man to his death. The investigator was never as popular from that day on."

"But how about James Crawford?" persisted Watson.

"His business improved after the Crane trial. About a year following, he also took a sea voyage. Upon his return he made a dinner date with Hugo Bessinger. The two men dined at Bessinger's home in the fashionable Chelsea district of New York. The detective's butler served the two men their meal which, according to him, was a quiet one. They retired to Bessinger's study for several hours of discussion. Bessinger then took his guest to the door. The butler heard them. Shortly afterwards, Bessinger asked his butler to check the front door and see if the lawyer had secured a hansom. The servant said that he did see a figure approximately a block away hail a hansom and get into it. That was the last report on James Crawford. He disappeared into thin air."

"I say, Holmes, now it is all beginning to fall together."

"As I knew it would, my dear Watson. And now you know as much about this interlocking affair as I do."

"But what shall we do, Holmes?" Watson was very concerned. "I mean, we can't let those other three chaps get the jump on us."

"We shall pause, my dear Watson, before our play at the first trick. As is obvious, this is a most complex case. Our main problem is not what shall we do but where shall we do it?"

There was a discreet knocking on the door at this point and Holmes rose with alacrity to answer it. As the door was opened, Watson saw Billy the page boy who handed a small package to the detective.

"I found one, Mr. 'Olmes, just like you said I might."

"Excellent, Billy! You have been of much assistance," replied Holmes. As he closed the door, Billy's face broke into a large grin. Billy fancied himself as an important cog in the detective machinery of 221B Baker Street. Perhaps he was.

Watson's fears were not allayed. Prestige was involved. "But, Holmes, we can't just sit here. I'll wager that Wolfie has a telegrapher pounding the key at this very moment."

"Quite possibly," said Holmes. He indicated the package as he crossed towards the door to his bedroom. "But I'm for bed to read a book. Goodnight, my dear Watson."

As Watson sat gazing into the dying embers of the fire, his mind went back over the strange events which Holmes had related to him. Had Holmes detected a revealing fact in the tangled skein? Was the sleuth "on to something?" Watson searched for a clue. His mental prophet of despair told him that this was fruitless but was drowned out by the thought that one can but try.

When Watson awoke the following morning, he found Holmes already gone. "Ah-ha!" he thought. "He's on to something for sure."

The Doctor ate a hurried breakfast, drank too much tea and stood by for action. It never came. Holmes, when he returned before eleven, was infuriatingly languid. He did state that he had been to Scotland Yard to go over their files. He did sit down and write out a number of telegrams which he dispatched via Billy. He did refer to the book he had secured the night before. Watson perceived that its title was: "The World's Greatest Detective, by Hugo Bessinger." Other than that, Holmes did nothing. When goaded by Watson, the Baker Street sleuth had one of his general answers: "When one depends on others, one spends a great deal of time waiting."

Watson was shocked to hear that Holmes had not called off the Challenge Match on press of business. It was an exasperated Doctor who accompanied his friend to the Grosvenor Square Bridge Club for the afternoon play

The Four Detectives.

121

THE PRESSURE PLAY

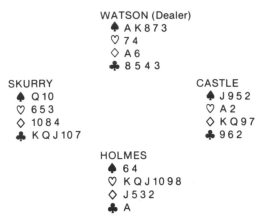

WATSON (Dealer)
♠ A K 8 7 3
♡ 7 4
◇ A 6
♣ 8 5 4 3

SKURRY
♠ Q 10
♡ 6 5 3
◇ 10 8 4
♣ K Q J 10 7

CASTLE
♠ J 9 5 2
♡ A 2
◇ K Q 9 7
♣ 9 6 2

HOLMES
♠ 6 4
♡ K Q J 10 9 8
◇ J 5 3 2
♣ A

CHALLENGE MATCH BIDDING: (Skurry and Castle vulnerable)

Watson	Castle	Holmes	Skurry
1S	pass	2H	pass
2S	pass	4H	pass
pass	pass		

Watson's values were minimum but sufficient for an opening bid. Holmes had ample values for his two level response and could even envision a slam if his partner had diamond cards. Watson's simple rebid of his good suit was obvious and Holmes then contracted for game since his hearts were self-sustaining. Harry Skurry led the club king.

PLAN YOUR PLAY and see if you can bring home this difficult contract.

Sherlock Holmes, like all good players, counted his losers. Obviously, the black suits presented no problems and his trump loser was inevitable. The contract hinged on the diamond suit. It took but a moment for the detective to plot a first line of play. He had little hope of success against a player of Betty Castle's calibre but if there is the possibility of the opponents making an error, it only seems reasonable to give them the chance. Holmes took the opening club lead and promptly led a diamond which he ducked in dummy. As Holmes had anticipated, Betty Castle realized that her opponent was fishing for a diamond ruff in dummy. She took the diamond trick and immediately led the heart ace and then another heart effectively preventing any ruffs by dummy.

Holmes now played a third round of hearts clearing the suit and led a small spade from his hand. When Harry followed with the spade 10, Holmes ducked the trick in dummy, Harry returned a low diamond to dummy's lone ace on the theory that the detective would win this trick anyway. Holmes now led a club from dummy which he ruffed. He cashed one more heart leaving this position.

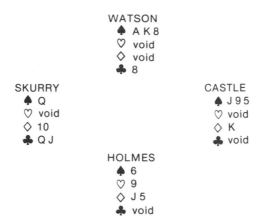

```
                    WATSON
                    ♠ A K 8
                    ♡ void
                    ◇ void
                    ♣ 8

   SKURRY                          CASTLE
   ♠ Q                             ♠ J 9 5
   ♡ void                          ♡ void
   ◇ 10                            ◇ K
   ♣ Q J                           ♣ void

                    HOLMES
                    ♠ 6
                    ♡ 9
                    ◇ J 5
                    ♣ void
```

Now Holmes played his last heart card discarding the club-8 from dummy. The pressure was on Betty. If she let go her diamond king, Holmes' diamonds would be winners so she dropped the spade-5 on the trick. Now the great sleuth played his low spade and cashed dummy's three cards in the suit.

Betty looked at Holmes in resignation. "Mr. Holmes, you have squeezed me more than any man I've ever known. Except my late husband," she added. Evidently, this just slipped out since Betty blushed beet red and hastily started to deal the next hand.

It is curious that on this same day of play, another hand of the same variety was dealt.

Cable from New York.

LEMONADE

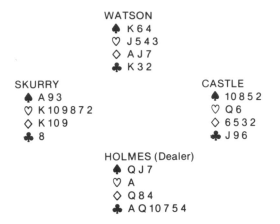

WATSON
♠ K 6 4
♡ J 5 4 3
◇ A J 7
♣ K 3 2

SKURRY
♠ A 9 3
♡ K 10 9 8 7 2
◇ K 10 9
♣ 8

CASTLE
♠ 10 8 5 2
♡ Q 6
◇ 6 5 3 2
♣ J 9 6

HOLMES (Dealer)
♠ Q J 7
♡ A
◇ Q 8 4
♣ A Q 10 7 5 4

CHALLENGE MATCH BIDDING: (Holmes and Watson vulnerable)

Holmes	Skurry	Watson	Castle
1C	pass	1H	pass
3C	pass	4C	pass
6C	pass	pass	pass

The first three bids were obvious and in the style that Holmes and Watson were using, the Doctor's raise to four clubs showed good values since he had gone beyond three no-trump. Holmes treated this bid as forcing and realizing that if his partner held the spade king and diamond ace or the spade ace and diamond king, he had an excellent chance to make slam. He bid six clubs.

Harry Skurry chose to lead the heart-10. With a sure spade loser, the contract was a touchy one. Can you arrive at a winning line of play?

THE PLAY

Holmes took the opening heart lead and with a square dummy played three rounds of trump. Harry discarded the heart-2 and the spade-3 on the second and third club leads. Now Holmes played a low diamond from his hand and successfully finessed dummy's diamond jack. A low spade was now led to Holmes' jack and taken by Harry's ace. Skurry returned a spade taken by dummy's king. A low heart from dummy drew Betty's queen and Holmes ruffed the trick. Watson detected a gleam in the detective's eye. Now Holmes cashed his good spade queen with Skurry pitching a heart. Sherlock Holmes now played his club-10 with Skurry dropping another heart and dummy the heart-5. The remaining cards were as follows:

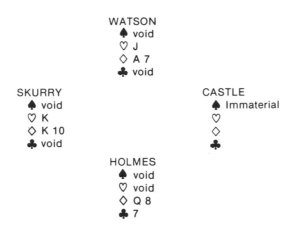

```
                    WATSON
                    ♠ void
                    ♡ J
                    ◊ A 7
                    ♣ void

SKURRY                              CASTLE
♠ void                              ♠ Immaterial
♡ K                                 ♡
◊ K 10                              ◊
♣ void                              ♣

                    HOLMES
                    ♠ void
                    ♡ void
                    ◊ Q 8
                    ♣ 7
```

Holmes' club-7 was the *coup de grace*. It was Harry's turn to shake his head in resignation as he discarded the diamond-10 making the detective's ace and queen of diamonds winners. A heart discard would have done him no good as can easily be seen.

"Holmes," said Skurry, "I felt like a lemon in a lemonade."

"You just had too many good cards," said Holmes with a twinkle in his eyes. "Is it not peculiar that if I had the diamond-10 instead of the diamond-8, the hand would have been extremely simple?"

"Providing that I held the diamond king," said Skurry.

"Without that card in your hand, I was doomed," admitted Holmes.

This was the final hand of the day and back in Baker Street Watson waxed enthusiastic.

"Your play of those two squeeze hands was superlative, Holmes."

"It is a fascinating play," conceded the detective. "I suppose most players would consider it difficult, nay exotic. And yet, it merely involves an elementary principle of physics."

"Good heavens, Holmes," interjected Watson. "What has physics to do with the way you played those two hands?"

"Two things cannot occupy the same space at the same time." Noting his friend's rather blank look, Holmes continued: "If one opponent holds three vital cards and you are able to play down to the eleventh trick, he must let go of one of them. It is singular that two such hands should come up in the same day and it is of additional interest that in both cases, the trump suit was used as the pressure card to force first Betty and then Harry to surrender a potential winner. In Harry's case, he was forced to discard before dummy which made the squeeze effective. In Betty's case, dummy had a useless card and this was not a factor in the operation of the squeeze."

"I shall certainly make careful note of those two hands in my diary," stated Watson. Suddenly, he paused as another thought registered. "Look here, Holmes, it is all very well to be discussing bridge hands but how about the Crawford mystery? After all, we have your reputation as a detective to consider."

125

Holmes smiled through a cloud of smoke from his pipe. "Our Challenge match efforts have not been without some reward, Watson. So often bridge duplicates life. Does it not occur to you that in our attempt to excel in this challenge of deduction, we are in something of a squeeze? I refer to a time squeeze. Of course, our adversaries face the same problem but these two hands today reinforce my thought that they possess the ability as well as the resources to learn as much as I can and possibly more. Therefore, my dear Watson, it behooves us to look in corners which they might not consider.

Holmes would not elaborate on this thought and seemed indisposed to discuss the case at hand any further.

The following day was a replica of the previous one. Holmes busied himself sending and receiving telegrams and made several short jaunts during the morning, but he continued his scheduled bridge play later in the day. In the evening, lengthy replies to Holmes' cables began arriving. The detective kept busy with these and Watson had the chance to skim through the book which seemed to interest Holmes. Beyond the fact that it was written by Bessinger himself in a pontifical manner and was heavily larded with the personal pronoun, he learned nothing. Billy remained on duty late and made several more trips to the cable office.

The third day, Doctor Watson noted in his Diary of The Challenge Match: "Holmes has said nothing. I have learned nothing. Nothing."

This notation is not strictly accurate. That evening Holmes received a long cablegram which he studied for some time. Feeling Watson's eyes upon him, he looked up saying: "Hugo Bessinger was buried today." Why this fact was of such interest to the sleuth, Watson could not fathom.

The morning of the fourth day found Holmes, again, the early riser. Upon his return he mentioned being at Scotland Yard and added that he had also been to the Foreign Office. Watson was muttering something which brought a query from the detective.

"What was that again, ol' boy?"

"I simply mentioned," said Watson, striving to emulate Holmes' frustrating calm, "that the gauntlet has been cast and no one seems prepared to pick it up."

"How now!" cried Holmes. "A challenge is a challenge." He regarded his old friend keenly. "Surely, you realize, Watson, that we can't be off to Brighton to view the scene of the crime. Brighton, in this case, is three thousand miles away. So we think. Questions suggest themselves and we try to secure answers. Then we think some more."

Watson was somewhat reassured as they left for the afternoon session of the Challenge Match.

It is curious that on this particular day's play two hands came up together which involved a standard bid but demonstrated it in its two forms.

THE DOUBLE TO BID

```
                    HOLMES
                    ♠ 2
                    ♡ K J 10 5 3
                    ◇ A Q 10 8
                    ♣ A Q 2
SKURRY (Dealer)                      CASTLE
♠ A K J 10 9 6 3                     ♠ Q 4
♡ A                                  ♡ 9 7 6
◇ void                               ◇ J 9 6 5 3
♣ J 10 9 5 4                         ♣ 8 7 3
                    WATSON
                    ♠ 8 7 5
                    ♡ Q 8 4 2
                    ◇ K 7 4 2
                    ♣ K 6
```

CHALLENGE MATCH BIDDING: (both sides vulnerable)

Skurry	Holmes	Castle	Watson
1S	double	pass	3H
4S	5H	pass	pass
pass			

OPENING LEAD: Spade King.

Opposite a passing partner, Harry Skurry would have bid four spades, but, as the opener, he felt much too strong for such action. A club fit with his partner and slam was very possible. Holmes doubled with the intention of bidding hearts if his partner responded in clubs or even diamonds. According to the system employed by Holmes and Watson, a double followed by a bid of a suit by the doubler promised 16 high card points plus a respectable suit of five cards at least. Holmes felt he was too strong for an overcall, even at the two level, and a jump-overcall would have been a weakness bid. Watson read his partner's action as the normal request for a bid but, also in accord with their system, a responding hand of nine to eleven points justified a jump response, not forcing. With the enemy strength on his left, Watson was a little hesitant but bravely came out with three hearts. Now Skurry went to four spades. Holmes, with the knowledge that Watson had real values and not just a token response drove to five hearts which ended the auction. After the play of the hand, Skurry apologized to Betty Castle for not saving at five spades, a contract which would have only gone down one trick.

Watson had no trouble with the hand. Skurry opened his spade king and shifted to the club jack. Watson took the trick in the closed hand and led a trump. On lead again, Harry led his spade ace in desperation but Watson could well afford to trump high in dummy as a precaution which proved unnecessary. He now drew the out-standing trumps and cashed out dummy's clubs discarding a diamond from his hand. It was all over.

Three hands later, the double appeared again but this time in its more common form.

STANDARD BID

HOLMES
♠ J 7
♡ J 7
◇ A 10 9 6 4 2
♣ 8 6 3

SKURRY
♠ 10
♡ K 10 9 5
◇ K J 8 5
♣ A Q 9 5

CASTLE
♠ K 9 6 4 2
♡ A Q 8 4 2
◇ 7 3
♣ 7

WATSON (Dealer)
♠ A Q 8 5 3
♡ 6 3
◇ Q
♣ K J 10 4 2

CHALLENGING MATCH BIDDING: (Skurry-Castle vulnerable)

Watson	Skurry	Holmes	Castle
1S	double	3D	4H
pass	pass	pass	

OPENING LEAD: Diamond Queen.

Watson was not comfortable about opening the bidding. With two black five-card suits, the majority of experts of the day advocated opening the club suit with the intention of bidding spades over partner's anticipated red suit response. However, this idea was by no means universal and a school of experts led by the great Spanish player, Eduardo Capplona, preferred the spade opening. (Note: It was the same Senor Capplona who later partnered with Septimus Sheingold and co-authored, with the English journalist-player, the Capplona-Sheingold System.)

Watson, because of his very minimum values, chose to open one spade.

Actually a club opening would have been bothersome to Skurry as the cards lay. However, he had a clear-cut action over one spade and promptly doubled. Holmes bid three diamonds knowing Watson would read this as weak and pre-emptive. Betty had some doubts about the value of her spade king but chose to go directly to four hearts which became the final contract.

THE PLAY

Betty Castle covered Watson's queen with dummy's king and Holmes took the trick with his ace and returned a diamond for Watson to ruff. The Doctor now led his club jack to give Betty a guess but she bravely finessed dummy's club queen which held. It was this play which secured the contract for her. Two rounds of trump cleared the suit. Betty now discarded a spade on dummy's diamond jack and another on the club ace. She then cross-ruffed conceding one spade trick. The rubber belonged to Skurry and Castle.

It was at this point that a cablegram was brought to Holmes. A faint gleam of satisfaction entered his eyes as he read it. He then folded the message, placed it in his pocket and reached for his cards. He might have reached slowly had he known what was in store.

THE FATAL DEUCE

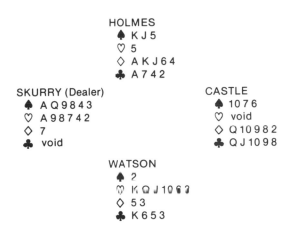

HOLMES
♠ K J 5
♡ 5
◇ A K J 6 4
♣ A 7 4 2

SKURRY (Dealer)
♠ A Q 9 8 4 3
♡ A 9 8 7 4 2
◇ 7
♣ void

CASTLE
♠ 10 7 6
♡ void
◇ Q 10 9 8 2
♣ Q J 10 9 8

WATSON
♠ 2
♡ K Q J 10 6 3
◇ 5 3
♣ K 6 5 3

Actually, everyone was in trouble before the first bid but they didn't know it yet. Holmes and Watson might have arrived at 3 notrump which could make on a spade lead by Betty Castle and a return of the suit. Holmes and Watson might also have ended up in four clubs or four diamonds which would suffer a sad fate. Undoubtedly, either minor suit contract would have been doubled. However, that was not the way the ball bounced.

CHALLENGE MATCH BIDDING: (Neither side vulnerable)

Skurry	Holmes	Castle	Watson
1S	2D	2S	pass
3H	pass	3S	pass
4S	double	pass	pass
pass			

Some of this bidding may seem strange indeed, but consider the problems. Skurry's opening bid requires no comment. Holmes had an immediate problem. Had Harry opened a heart, his action would have been simple. While lacking a fourth spade, his hand would certainly have warranted a takeout double. The detective had the high card strength to double and then bid his respectable diamond suit if allowed to at a reasonable level. However, Holmes could almost be certain that Watson would bid hearts and, as the cards actually lay, at a high level. Holmes satisfied himself with an overcall of two diamonds and wished he was vulnerable since the bid would then indicate the type of strength he held. Betty was now in the trouble seat. An immediate double of diamonds might not gain enough points and there was the danger that her opponents would uncover a playable heart suit. She chose to raise Harry's spades hoping to tempt Holmes-Watson to the three level in diamonds. Now Watson was really in difficulties. Holmes had often said it paid to believe one's partner. Watson knew the sleuth had opening bid strength for his overcall. Holmes was very cautious about minor suit overcalls regardless of vulnerability. Skurry had an opening bid; Holmes had an opening bid. Betty had a raise and poor Watson was looking at eleven high card and distributional points. Obviously, something was amiss and with rigid discipline, the good Doctor passed. Now Skurry showed his second suit, making Watson feel much better immediately. After Holmes passed, Betty returned to her partner's first bid suit and Skurry went to game. Actually, he was somewhat disappointed since three to the king in spades and a doubleton king-queen in hearts would have given him a splendid play for slam. At this point, Holmes could not resist a double and who can blame him?

THE PLAY

Holmes opened the diamond king and dummy's spade holding promised him two natural trump tricks. The diamond queen in dummy's hand caused him to shift to the club ace which Skurry trumped. Now Harry led the heart ace and continued a low heart. If Holmes trumped, he would lose a spade trick later so he discarded a low club. Skurry ruffed with dummy's spade six as Watson glumly followed suit. Now Skurry led dummy's club queen which Watson covered with the king and Harry ruffed the suit again. Now Harry led another heart and Holmes played his last club as dummy ruffed. Leading a diamond from dummy, Harry trumped in the closed hand and led another heart. Holmes, tenaciously holding on to his spades, discarded a small diamond and dummy trumped with its last spade. Harry led dummy's club jack and when Watson followed suit, he discarded a losing heart. Holmes trumped with his low spade and got off lead with his diamond jack. Dummy covered with the queen and Watson played his singleton trump deuce. This forced Harry to over-ruff. At the eleventh trick, Skurry finally led trumps coming out with his spade ace which dropped Holmes' jack. But Holmes was in control and could take the last two tricks to set the contract one.

As the detective was quick to point out, it was Watson's spade-2 which actually set the contract.

At the Archery Tavern that evening no one was late. The dinner was dispensed with rather rapidly. It seemed to Watson that there was a general feeling of satisfaction.

"Everybody can't be right," he thought. "Someone is due for a rude awakening." Mycroft had a suggestion which exhibited his eye for detail.

"It must be a family trait," thought Watson.

Holmes' older brother proposed that the four detectives draw straws to decide who would speak first. Arséne Pupin won the honor to be followed by Chow Lee Chan and Wolfgang Von Shalloway. Holmes mentioned that if the drama was to be in three acts, he was obviously the epilogue. He borrowed Wolfie's beer tankard and, using it as a gavel, called the crimefighters to order. The Frenchman, his eyes darting in a dozen different directions at once, took center stage.

ARSÉNE'S STORY

"*Mes amis,* zis is, according to Arséne, ze way ze case she 'appen. We 'ave decide to investigate ze disappearance of James Crawford. But, as I say to myself, is zis not intertwined wiz ze diappearance of Junius Crane? Are not ze two cases one large mural razzer zan two complete pictures? So we look at zis mural. What 'ave we? Junius Crane killed at sea. Charles Storm, an apparent suicide. Zis I do not believe, for ze obvious reason."

Amid a general nodding of heads, Watson's stare of disbelief stood out and the Frenchman noted it.

"M'sieu," he said by way of explanation, "ze man shoot himself in ze 'ead, *n'est ce pas?* But ze medical report show no powder burns. Why? Because ze man no shoot 'imself but 'e is shot! You are thinking, how about ze police in New York?"

Watson found himself nodding vigorously.

"Zey notice, 'ave no fear. But ze apparent suicide, she do one zing. She tie up ze case in nice, tidy *pacquet* wiz red ribbon. So . . . nobody want to undo ze *pacquet pour le moment.*

"In addition, we 'ave James Crawford 'oo disappear and, finally, Hugo Bessinger dead of natural causes. "Oo is left but *la femme* Ze Motive? Hah, ze old one — J'urgent! Ze monnaia! Onrnful invootigation ohow mo aat Julius Crane 'ave large insurance policy wiz Lloyds of London of a leetle-known type of coverage. It is called 'Key-Man Insurance.' Junius Crane is indispensable to Crane-Storm Brokerage House. 'E was ze driving force be'ind ze firm. Furzermore, I learn zat ze brokerage 'ouse is in very bad shape, indeed. It take ze *monnaie* from Lloyds, ze insurance *monnaie,* to — 'ow you say — bail out ze business. Zis 'appon boforo zo trial of Inez Crane. But I am a'ead of myself.

"Ze gray cells, ze tell me to use Inez Crane as my point of departure in attacking zis case. So . . . Inez and Storm conspire to do away with Junius on the 'Satanic'.

"Eet was Storm, in accordance with ze theory of Hugo Bessinger, 'oo do ze deed. But, ze cabin steward, 'e is not an unanticipated factor. No, no, no! I say zey wait for someone to come out on ze upper deck. When 'e' appear, zen zey 'ave wheel chair come out on passenger deck. Ze body, she not go over ze side until zey have ze witness. Why? Because zey need ze insurance *monnaie* now. Lloyds mus' be convinced zat Junius Crane is dead. True, the steward, 'e is certain zat ze figure pushing ze wheel chair is a woman. So, possibly Storm wear some woman's clothes secured from Inez. Zose Italians, zet zink zey know women. If ze steward 'ad been French . . . . . but zat is anuzzer story.

"Wiz Junius Crane disposed of, Storm and Inez 'ave control of business and ze

131

benefit of ze insurance *monnaie* to enable ze business to survive. Now, ze removal of Storm would place all ze eggs in Inez's pretty yellow basket. It will be noted zat after Storm's supposed suicide, Inez sold ze business for a very substantial sum indeed and went to live in Majorca. Zere, she is attempting to drink 'erself to death at zis very moment. *Voila!* My gray cells are most active. But *attendez,* per'aps zey are too active. After years of dissipation via drugs, alcohol and — 'ow you say — ze 'igh life', is Inez capable of all zis? It was prove' in court that she lacked ze strength to catapult her 'usband's body overboard. So I pause and inquire and search. No. Inez could not 'ave killed Storm eezer. The supposed suicide was committed wiz a 'eavy calibre Smith Webley *revolvaire* firing a .455 cartridge. It is doubtful if Inez could 'ave even pull ze trigger much less fire ze gun wiz any accuracy. Besides, ze character which I picture as Inez was not ze type of flower suited to ze frosts of raw violence. An *agent provocateur?* Yes, zat she undoubtedly was. But not ze actual 'and be'ind ze gun. Am I wrong? Impossible! But wait, Inez 'as already used one man. Why not two? Per'aps ze second man was 'er idea all along. From ze start, one zing has bozzered ze gray cells. Inez Crane, on trial for 'er life, selects to represent 'er a relatively unknown *avocat.* Why? So now ze gray cells are directed to our missing gentleman but now we see, in ze mind's eye, Inez and Crawford. So — what about zis missing lawyer? We find zat 'e is involved in an unsuccessful marriage. It would seem zat 'is wife 'ad a small estate which 'elped establish 'is law practice. Following 'is successful defense of Inez Crane, 'is business 'ad a flourishing period but nothing spectacular. Remember that 'is defense of Inez was based primarily on ze conclusions of Hugo Bessinger. So . . . it is Crawford, ze missing man, who kills Storm. Inez sells ze business and goes to Majorca. After a suitable period of time to wind zings up and let ze case die in ze minds of ze police, Mr. James Crawford conveniently disappears. 'E leaves very little be'ind 'im, zis I learn. And I also learn zat Inez Crane is living in Majorca wiz a man. Alas, ze time, she does not permit me to learn 'oo ze man is but I submit, *messieurs,* zat ze man is James Crawford. Disappear 'e did but of 'is own volition. I shall recommend zat ze police investigate ze possibility zat James Crawford and Inez Crane conspire' to kill Charles Storm and zat zey are boz, as of zis moment, living in Majorca on ze ample proceeds of ze sale of Crane-Storm brokerage concern. Zat is my zeory!

THE TALE OF CHOW LEE CHAN

The oriental detective looked at his French compatriot with a half-smile tinged with regret.

"Ah me, it might be better if my French friend and I were not working together. For I must stick a dagger in his theory and he has performed the same regrettable act to mine. My story of these strange doings has suddenly become a sad one. Just as M'sieu Pupin's gray cells turned to the woman, Inez Crane, did mine center on the end of the story, James Crawford. He was the object of our search. But I did feel, as did the pride of the Sûreté Francaise, that Crawford's disappearance was woven in with the Crane case. I learned that Crawford was a compulsive traveler. His friends joked that he must have had bags packed at all times. Immediately, the question came to me: Could he have been aboard the 'Satanic' when Junius Crane disappeared? I find that he could not. He was involved in an inheritance case in the city of Syracuse, New York, at the time of the incident aboard the 'Satanic.'

"But, in pursuing this line of investigation I find that James Crawford was also on a trip at the time of the Charles Storm suicide, or, as we all suspect, murder."

Chow Lee looked at the French detective again, apologetically.

"I fear that as a conspirator in the death of Charles Storm, the lawyer cannot be considered. But neither can my idea for another reason. I pictured the entire case in a different manner. The night that James Crawford dines with Hugo Bessinger and subsequently disappears, he had just returned from another trip. He certainly did a lot of traveling but this case does cover a span of some years.

"On this voyage, Crawford stopped at the island of Majorca. What is more natural than for him to see Inez Crane, his former client? Suddenly, there is a crystallization. Upon his return, he beats a hasty path to the door of Hugo Bessenger. Why? The only thing they have in common is the Crane case. So I pictured the following: In Majorca, Inez Crane sees James Crawford. She has stood trial for the murder of her husband and been acquitted. She cannot be tried again as that would involve, in American law, double jeopardy. Suicide has been accepted as the cause of the death of Charles Storm. Inez feels safe, secure; perhaps, in a drunken moment, she reveals to her former lawyer that it was she who conspired to kill her husband and then later did away with her co-conspirator. His mind in a whirl, Crawford leaves Majorca and, upon his arrival in New York, rushes to tell the true story to Hugo Bessinger. Would he go to the police? Would the police act with the case effectively closed? These things we shall never know. But Inez Crane, in a more sober light, could not know either. She rushes to New York in deathly fear that she has loosened an instrument which can destroy her. Somehow she manages to waylay Crawford and disposes of him. My theory grows thin here."

"The time was very short," stated Wolfgang Von Shalloway.

There was a general chorus of agreement from the others.

"Now," continued the oriental, "because of the acuteness of my French compatriot, I find my story dissolving like sand sifting through a screen. While the gun is not a natural weapon for we of the east, even though we did discover gunpowder, still, in our line of work, one must be familiar with them. Our perceptive French friend was very clever in discovering the calibre of the revolver that killed Charles Storm. I pictured a derringer-type weapon, the type a woman could use. This was a grievous error, the mistake of a beginner. I assumed an unproven fact. I have, I fear, lost much face."

"M'sieu, M'sieu, do not grieve. None of us 'ave been able to conduct ze detailed investigation we would normally do. If you fault yourself, picture my plight. If word of zis gets back to ze Sûreté, I am a doomed man. True, I find out about ze gun. I cancel out Inez Crane as ze dealer in death. But I assume that 'er assistant or partner is Crawford, simply because 'e is ze only one left. One sentence from you and my zeory goes poof! We 'ave, — 'ow you say — placed each uzzer in checkmate. We 'ave fail."

Arséne Pupin sank back into his chair, his head between his hands.

"You haf not failed." The words came from Wolfgang Von Shalloway and all eyes gravitated towards him.

"While the findings of my fellow investigators cancel each other out, they reinforce my diagnosis and, in fact, prove it. Their discoveries were excellent police vork and they supply the missing pieces to the puzzle vich I now place before you."

"Mon Dieu!" said Pupin. "Wolfie, how could this be?"

Chow Lee regarded the German impassively.

THE STORY OF WOLFGANG

Wolfie paused for a moment, as if to marshall his thoughts, then continued: "I, too, felt that the disappearance of James Crawford vas the final act of the play vich began aboard the 'Satanic'. Therefore, I started at the very beginning vith Junius Crane. I concentrated on his career and soon realized that there vas something out of focus. Here vas a man, supposedly constantly drunk, on a lengthy ocean woyage. But here vas also a man who used his partner's money to buy a small brokerage house and rapidly built it into a large one. I discovered, as did M'sieu Pupin, that Junius Crane vas the brains of Crane and Storm. Is this the same man who falls down a companionvay stairs and suffers vat is diagnozed as a hair-line fracture? Vith this thought in mind, I checked into the fortunes of the brokerage house after Junius Crane vas lost aboard the 'Satanic'. A moth of an idea vas beginning to circle the spark of a theory in my mind. Reinforced by Crane's insurance money, Crane and Storm flourished. But who made this possible? Certainly not Storm who, I found, vas really a figurehead. Could his vife haf learned enough from her husband to successfully guide the destiny of the business? Impossible! Inez appeared a very frail reed indeed. No Hetty Green vas she."

Holmes whispered a word of explanation into Watson's ear. "A famous woman financier of America." Watson thanked him with his eyes.

"Then," continued the German, "like a trumpet from Vagner, a thought struck me. The spark became a flame. The one fact vich seems to haf eluded my learned colleagues, just as many of their findings eluded me," he added somewhat hastily. "Inez Crane vas no tool forged for murder. Ve all agree on that. And yet, this sybarite from some unknown source found the strength to face a court and jury with her life in their hands. Vould the Inez Crane that we all picture haf been capable of that? I say no — unless . . ."

There was not a sound. It was as though the background noise of the Archery Tavern had come to a sudden halt and the very waiters had frozen in their tracks.

"Unless," continued Wolfie, "she knew that her life was really not threatened. Unless she knew that if the verdict vas guilty, if the theory of Hugo Bessinger did not stand up in court, that her husband vould suddenly appear vith some story about falling overboard but fortunately being able to svim to shore. Unless Junius Crane had never died at all."

Pupin and Chow Lee exchanged a quick glance, then their heads nodded as if in agreement.

"Now," said Wolfie," some clarity vas coming to the scene and many questions suddenly had an answer. The entire cruise, the continuous party life, the fall down the companionvay stairs — it vas all a charade. The scheme, from the start, vas the insurance money needed by the brokerage house to stay alive. So it had to appear that Junius Crane vas dead. Inez was part of the plot and, undoubtedly, Charles Storm vas as vell. A business sinking and the senior partners on a pleasure trip? Nein, gentlemen, it never did ring true. The cast on the leg vas part of it, of course. A hair-line fracture is difficult to diagnose, especially vith limited shipboard facilities. Inez Crane did propel the veel chair to the rail. But vot she threw overboard vas a carefully-constructed dummy. The testimony of the steward vas accurate as far as it vent. But Junius Crane vas carefully hidden elsevere. Ven the ship docked the following day, if anyone vas looking for him, they vere looking for a non-existent cripple. Undoubtedly, he suffered no injury at all."

The German paused to take another swig of dark lager, then brought his analysis to a close.

"You see, of course, how it all fits together. It was the supposedly dead Junius Crane who guided the destiny of Crane and Storm after the 'Satanic' incident. It vas the supposedly dead Junius Crane who disposed of his partner, Storm. And it is the supposedly dead Junius Crane who is now living with Inez in Majorca. My confreres have proven that neither Crawford nor Inez could haf been the murderer of Charles Storm and my theory concurs with their findings in every respect. That, gentlemen, is my case. It is complete."

"In every respect, save one." The voice was Sherlock Holmes' and each eye in the room swiveled in his direction.

"How and why did James Crawford disappear?"

"I am grateful to Chow Lee and M'sieu Pupin for the answer to that," replied the great German bloodhound.

"Since Crawford was in Majorca, could he not have seen Junius Crane and recognized him? Unfortunately, Crane also saw him. It was Junius Crane, completely capable of murder, who rushed to the United States to dispose of the lawyer. But he was not in time to prevent Crawford from visiting Hugo Bessinger. If he learned of the meeting, he could have . . . "

"But," interrupted Holmes, "is a word none of us likes, and 'if' makes me equally uncomfortable." As Wolfie bristled, Holmes continued rapidly. "Do not misunderstand me, for I am in agreement. I do think that the lawyer saw the supposedly dead Junius Crane in Majorca. However, I doubt if Crane saw him. At least, let us hope not, for then Crane might get the wind up and not be on the island when the authorities try to apprehend him and his wife."

The words of the Baker Street sleuth were greeted with complete silence. Watson could see the minds of the others trying to grasp what Holmes was driving at.

THE HOLMESIAN LINE

"Here is the line of investigation which I chose to follow, gentlemen, and the results. How fortunate I am to have an audience of experts to place it before." Holmes paused for the psychological moment as the faces of his listeners relaxed into smiles of appreciation. Then he plunged into his story.

"Chow Lee stated that his mind was directed towards the end of the story, James Crawford. I also started at the end, but, as a working hypothesis, I assumed that the lawyer was either dead or had disappeared for some reason. To me, the end of the story was Hugo Bessinger, the last person to have seen the missing man and to tell about it. I must admit there was another reason that I chose this point to begin my investigations. In bridge, a game in which Doctor Watson and I have become much involved, there is an expression: 'To go against the field.' I knew or felt that each of you would center on the Junius Crane case as the solution to the disappearance of James Crawford. What detective worthy of the name would not be intrigued with this bizarre series of events? All the elements were there. The disappearance at sea, the erring wife, the partner who possibly was her lover, the insurance money, the death of the partner . . . it all smacks of melodrama."

Holmes sighed for a moment, in retrospect, then proceeded:

"Believe me, it was most reluctantly that I decided to go against the field. But I knew that glued to the Crane case were three of the finest criminological minds in the world. What could I learn that you could not?"

It crossed Watson's mind at this point that Holmes was displaying a singular amount of gentle diplomacy. "He's got them," he thought, in a quick flash.

"Therefore," continued Holmes, "I directed my thoughts towards the American investigator. There was some mention at one time that, were he still alive, he might be with us now and no one would have been more ready to agree than Hugo Bessinger himself. In studying his career and his cases it was readily apparent that Bessinger had a colossal ego."

"He's not alone in that," thought Watson and then, mentally, rebuked himself for the thought.

"Bessinger," continued Holmes, "always proclaimed himself the world's greatest detective. The man who had never missed on a case. That was the trumpet of Wagner for me." Holmes shot a quick smile at Von Shalloway. "It beat on my gray cells." Another smile at Arséne Pupin. "I have made mistakes, gentlemen, as I'm sure you have. In the field of criminology, as in the game of bridge, is it not the disasters from which we learn?

"In any case, though Bessinger had no family and few, if any, friends, through an associate in New York I did receive information about the American investigator via his butler and his lawyer. I also secured a copy of the book on Bessinger's career which he wrote. The book was dull, but it did present one point that intrigued me. There were references, mainly relative to the successful criminal, which were never resolved. It was as though a chapter of the book was missing. Then I learned from the butler that Bessinger had a peculiarity which amounted to an obsession. He had to have the last word. He flew into towering rages if denied it and became quite incoherent. Also, he was not on good terms with James Crawford. Not since the trial of Inez Crane. It was he who openly accused Charles Storm of the murder of Junius Crane in the press. He wanted the accusation to come out in the trial. Crawford refused and confined himself to securing his client's acquittal. This produced a break between the two and the butler was surprised to learn that Crawford was dining with the investigator on that last night.

"The recent funeral of Hugo Bessinger was only attended by his butler, lawyer, and an unknown mourner . . . my associate in New York. Just before the lowering of the casket, his lawyer, acting on instructions in his will, placed an envelope sealed with wax in the inside pocket of the corpse. Thus Hugo Bessinger went to his final resting place. When I learned of this, light dawned. Like Chow Lee, I knew that Crawford had been on a trip which included Majorca, the present home of Inez Crane. And, like my Chinese friend, I thought it strange that the lawyer should immediately upon his return, arrange an appointment with the investigator. He would only do this if he had learned something in Majorca, something that proved Bessinger wrong. I can see what happened when Crawford made his revelation to the investigator. In a mind so preoccupied with his own reputation, Bessinger must have pictured screaming headlines like: 'World's Greatest Detective A Dupe!' Or 'Super Sleuth Falls For Insurance Fraud!' The world of Hugo Bessinger was crumbling around him and he killed Crawford. He then hid the body in a trunk and, supposedly, escorted his guest to the door. Remember, the butler wasn't present when Crawford departed. It was only a short time later, at his employer's suggestion, that he went to the front door to see if the recent guest had secured a hansom. He saw, or thought he saw, someone down the block entering a hansom. But we know it wasn't Crawford."

"How?" interjected Von Shalloway.

"A moment," replied Holmes. "Now the report of the funeral gave me the final clue. What was it the lawyer put in the pocket of the corpse? According to him, it was simply a sealed envelope and he was following Bessinger's specific instructions. Via my good friends at Scotland Yard, the New York police were persuaded to open the coffin and secure the sealed envelope. As you may have already guessed, it contained the missing chapter of Bessinger's book. In it, Bessinger tells the whole story. In it, he reveals that the perfect murder is the one where no murder is suspected and he had pulled it off. Bessinger had to have the last word, even in the grave."

This brought to a conclusion the conclave of crimefighters and their interesting experiment in the fine art of deduction. Holmes insisted that his confreres' work on the case had been just as important as his and thus the mystery of Junius Crane, Charles Storm, and James Crawford was finally untangled to everyone's satisfaction. The Cranes were apprehended on Majorca and returned to the United States for trial and conviction. It is presumed that the three great foreign detectives returned to their homelands satisfied that their contribution had been vital and that the great experiment had resolved itself into a draw between the four participants. But I wonder!

There were several other points of interest. At least to those who are great followers of the exploits of Mr. Sherlock Holmes. it is rumored that immediately prior to his departure for France, Arséne Pupin went to 221B Baker Street. It is strange that he should do so when he had good cause to know that both Holmes and Watson were not there at the time. The great French detective and amateur chef presented his card to Mrs. Hudson and entered the premises where he talked with Holmes' landlady for an hour. What this discussion was about we shall never know, but it is odd that on an average of twice a month thereafter, Holmes and Watson dined on *Coq au vin, Rouge et Noir.* The preparation of this sumptuous dish takes the better part of a day but Mrs. Hudson did not seem to mind. One thing, she would never tell anyone the recipe or how she came by it.

If you were invited to dinner by Holmes or Watson, and they entertained at very rare intervals indeed, you could have, if you wished, some of the finest bavarian beer known to man. Holmes never mentioned where he secured this brew but he seemed to have an inexhaustible supply.

It was several months after the solution of the disappearance of James Crawford that Holmes abandoned the dressing gown he had worn for so long. In its place, appeared a new one. Its muted but rich colors were known to have made women gasp and its shaping and design showed the obvious marks of master craftsmen. It was made, of course, of the very finest Chinese silk!

Note: "It will be recalled that in "The Adventure of the Noble Bachelor," Holmes and Watson did have Lord St. Simon and Mr & Mrs. Francis Hay Moulton for a cold supper. It was a catered affair and Lord St. Simon did not stay to enjoy the woodcock, pheasant, and *pate de foie gras* pie.

Sherlock Holmes explains.

138

CHOOSE YOUR LOSERS

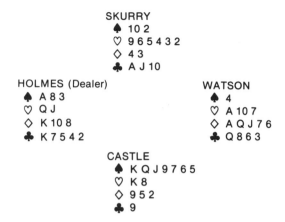

SKURRY
♠ 10 2
♡ 9 6 5 4 3 2
◇ 4 3
♣ A J 10

HOLMES (Dealer)
♠ A 8 3
♡ Q J
◇ K 10 8
♣ K 7 5 4 2

WATSON
♠ 4
♡ A 10 7
◇ A Q J 7 6
♣ Q 8 6 3

CASTLE
♠ K Q J 9 7 6 5
♡ K 8
◇ 9 5 2
♣ 9

CHALLENGE MATCH BIDDING: (Holmes-Watson vulnerable)

Holmes	Skurry	Watson	Castle
1C	pass	1D	3S
pass	pass	4C	pass
5C	pass	pass	pass

Harry Skurry led the spade ten. Let's suppose you were playing this hand instead of the great detective. What is your plan? Remember, all eyes are upon you.

When the dummy was exposed, Holmes realized that he had two potential losers plus a possible heart. He decided, for good reason, to plan to lose two trumps and avoid the heart loser. His line of play will indicate his thinking on this hand.

Holmes captured the spade lead with his ace and immediately led a low club. If Skurry took the trick, it would have to be with the ace, thus limiting the detective's trump losers to one so that he could afford to lose a heart. If Betty captured the trump lead, she was in no position to attack hearts. Skurry realized that the play of his club ace would just simplify things for Holmes so he played the ten. Dummy's queen of clubs took the trick. Holmes now abandoned trumps and played a low diamond from dummy to his king. He then played the diamond ten and a low diamond.

Skurry trumped the diamond lead with his jack and shifted to hearts but to no avail. Holmes rose with dummy's ace and then continued with dummy's diamond ace discarding his losing heart. Harry could trump when he wanted to but the rugby game was over for the defense.

THE DECISION

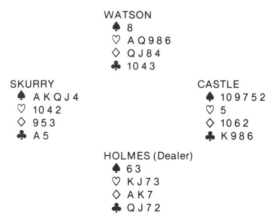

WATSON
♠ 8
♡ A Q 9 8 6
◇ Q J 8 4
♣ 10 4 3

SKURRY
♠ A K Q J 4
♡ 10 4 2
◇ 9 5 3
♣ A 5

CASTLE
♠ 10 9 7 5 2
♡ 5
◇ 10 6 2
♣ K 9 8 6

HOLMES (Dealer)
♠ 6 3
♡ K J 7 3
◇ A K 7
♣ Q J 7 2

CHALLENGE MATCH BIDDING: (Holmes-Watson vulnerable)

Holmes	Skurry	Watson	Castle
1H	1S	3H	4S
double	Pass	Pass	Pass

Holmes' opening bid and Skurry's overcall were reasonable. Watson had a problem and decided that his fifth heart card provided just enough extra value for a jump raise. By the book, he was a point short but the doctor felt his jump was the best bid available. Betty's hand was very weak but she decided to put pressure on her opponents by leaping to the spade game. It took Holmes but a moment to double. On defense, Watson's five heart cards looked bad but he did have values in the unbid diamond suit and respected his partner's double by passing.

The play of the hand was automatic. Watson opened his heart ace and upon viewing dummy, shifted to a small diamond. Holmes and Watson rapidly cashed three tricks in the suit and the contract was already down one before Skurry could take a trick.

Skurry had noted Watson's pause before his final pass.

"I do wish you had gone on," he commented. "Despite Betty's weak hand we should have done rather well against you. I would have led the spade king and then shifted to the ace and a small club. A club ruff nets us four tricks."

"Holmes and I were discussing a situation like this the other night," replied Watson. "It was my partner's feeling that a pass by him following Betty's four spade bid would have indicated a willingness to play in five hearts. It would then have been my duty to either go on or double."

"Quite right, my dear Watson," said Holmes. "With the balanced hand which I just held, defending seemed the best policy."

"One moment," said Betty. "Do I understand that had you passed, Mr. Holmes, your partner would have been forced to take some action?" As Holmes nodded, Betty continued, thoughtfully. "What an interesting concept. A forcing pass."

Strangely enough, Betty's term has remained in the lexicon of bridge to this day and another hand relative to the idea was dealt on the same session of play in The Challenge Match.

THE FORCING PASS

WATSON (Dealer)
♠ 4
♡ 8 5 4
◇ K̃ 8 5 3
♣ A K Q 7 4

SKURRY
♠ A J 10 9 8
♡ J 10 6
◇ A 9 4
♣ 6 3

CASTLE
♠ K Q 6 3
♡ A K Q 7 2
◇ Q 7 6
♣ 9

HOLMES
♠ 7 5 2
♡ 9 3
◇ J 10 2
♣ J 10 8 5 2

CHALLENGE MATCH BIDDING: Castle-Skurry vulnerable)

Skurry	Watson	Castle	Holmes
-	1C	double	4C
4S	5C	5S	pass
pass	6C	pass	pass
6S	pass	pass	pass

The auction started innocently enough but after Betty Castle's take-out double, Holmes, holding a hand devoid of any defensive values, went to four clubs. Skurry was delighted to bid four spades opposite his partner's known opening bid and implied fit in his good suit. Watson competed with five clubs. With Holmes holding five cards in his suit, suddenly Watson was also lacking in defensive values. Considering the vulnerability, Betty felt her bid of five spades showed her very good hand. Skurry, with an opening bid on his left, chose to pass. Now, Doctor Watson went to six clubs, a bid which he bitterly berated himself for later. Recalling the forcing pass conversation earlier, Betty passed, indicating that she was not averse to a slam contract. Harry Skurry divined his partner's thought and went to the spade slam counting on Betty for only one club loser, an assumption strongly supported by the bidding.

Watson led his club king on which Holmes played his eight. A shift was not desirable to him. Watson continued with his club ace and it was all over. Skurry trumped with dummy's spade king, a precaution which he could well afford. After drawing trumps, Harry cashed out the heart suit discarding his two losing diamond cards.

"Splendid example of that forcing pass situation and my thanks to you, Betty, for using it." The politician was beaming.

"And my thanks to you, partner, for reading my intent," responded Betty.

Watson's face was downcast. "I do believe you both should be thanking me," was his dry remark. "If I had just kept quiet, you would have been playing in five spades and Holmes and I wouldn't be having a vulnerable small slam scored against us."

ONE MORE TIME

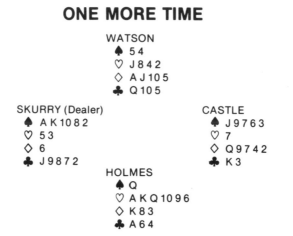

WATSON
♠ 5 4
♡ J 8 4 2
◇ A J 10 5
♣ Q 10 5

SKURRY (Dealer)
♠ A K 10 8 2
♡ 5 3
◇ 6
♣ J 9 8 7 2

CASTLE
♠ J 9 7 6 3
♡ 7
◇ Q 9 7 4 2
♣ K 3

HOLMES
♠ Q
♡ A K Q 10 9 6
◇ K 8 3
♣ A 6 4

CHALLENGE MATCH BIDDING: (both sides vulnerable)

Skurry	Watson	Castle		Holmes
pass	pass	pass	ɢ	1 H
1 S	2 H	2 S		4 H
4 S	pass	pass		5 H
pass	pass	pass		

With three original passes, the forcing pass was not involved in this auction. However, as regards competitive bidding sequences, Holmes expressed particular interest in this hand. He certainly had more than ample values for his fourth hand opening bid. Skurry now showed his fine suit. Watson raised the heart suit and, having passed originally, would have jumped to three hearts with two more points in his hand. Betty, with an eye on the vulnerability, gave her partner a simple raise. Holmes now bid the heart game but Skurry, holding the senior suit, bid four spades. Watson's pass simply indicated that he could not make a penalty double. After Betty passed, the bridge-playing detective was faced with a problem. Point-wise, his hand was, to use a modern expression: "loaded". However, Watson had freely raised his splendid heart suit. On the bidding, his heart cards might not even produce one defensive trick. For all Holmes knew, Skurry might be able to make four spades. Consider the West-East cards and you will see that Harry would go down only one at four spades. Not wishing to double with an offensively-oriented hand, and not being sure that five hearts would make, Holmes followed a philosophy which he advocated in situations like this and which Watson referred to as "One More Time" in his Challenge Match Diary. He bid five hearts. These days, the principle, which is followed by leading players, is called "Taking Out Insurance."

THE PLAY

Harry Skurry led his spade king and continued with the spade ace which Holmes trumped. Two rounds of hearts drew the opposing trumps.

Having already lost one trick, the minor suits presented a problem. But Holmes did some thinking. Harry had at least a five-card spade suit and had shown the ace and king already. With the club king also in his hand, an opening bid might well have come from Harry who was no shrinking violet. Holmes played his club ace and then a low club. When Harry played low, the sleuth inserted dummy's club ten. Betty Castle took the trick but she was hopelessly end played. A diamond return spelled disaster but her spade return was equally fatal since it allowed Holmes to discard his losing diamond while trumping in dummy. Holmes' daring contract was assured. Betty was fretful. "I think I should have bid four spades immediately, Harry. Perhaps I could have talked Mr. Holmes out of his contract."

"Competitive auctions based on distributional hands can be very treacherous," said Holmes. "But I do believe I would have gone to five hearts anyway for the same reason that I chose to make that bid over Harry's four spade call."

Betty dimpled. "You do make a girl feel better, Mr. Holmes."

The word "girl" might be considered a hopeful term but we should not blame Betty for making it since she did lose with good grace.

THE WILD ONE

The concept of the forcing pass continued to intrigue Betty and Holmes' words regarding the frequently amazing results from highly distributional hands defy argument. Both ideas were involved in the following hand played much later in the Challenge Match.

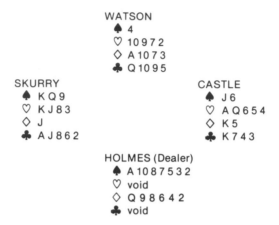

WATSON
♠ 4
♡ 10 9 7 2
◇ A 10 7 3
♣ Q 10 9 5

SKURRY
♠ K Q 9
♡ K J 8 3
◇ J
♣ A J 8 6 2

CASTLE
♠ J 6
♡ A Q 6 5 4
◇ K 5
♣ K 7 4 3

HOLMES (Dealer)
♠ A 10 8 7 5 3 2
♡ void
◇ Q 9 8 6 4 2
♣ void

CHALLENGE MATCH BIDDING: (both sides vulnerable)

Holmes	Skurry	Watson	Castle
pass	1C	pass	1H
2NT	3H	4D	4H
5D	5H	pass	pass
6D	pass	pass	dbl. all pass

Holmes' unrevealing demeanor never faced a sterner test than when he picked up this hand. He did not feel it advisable to take preemptive action immediately. With but six high card points in his possession, the sleuth knew someone would get the bidding ball rolling. He therefore passed and waited for the fireworks. Skurry's opening bid of one club and Watson's pass were automatic. Now Betty, with an opening bid of her own, smelled game for sure. She bid her heart suit and the next move was up to the detective. Holmes, at this point, could have doubled requesting Watson to bid spades or diamonds. Having passed originally, his bid could not be read as strength-showing but as a competitive measure. However, he felt that his holding required a shout rather than a whisper. Depending on Watson's well developed deductive powers at the bridge table, Holmes bid two notrump. Skurry had ample values to go to three hearts. Watson's thinking now followed a line which he and Holmes had found most effective if the bidding had taken a strange turn. Namely, that partner's intent can

144

most often be deciphered by what they had not done. Holmes had not opened. He had not made a take-out double of the two suiter variety. Therefore, he must be showing a wild, spade-diamond, two suited hand. He was not requesting a bid from Watson but demanding it. The good doctor, with a distinct preference between the unbid suits, bid four diamonds. Betty went to four hearts and Holmes to five diamonds. Skurry drove to five hearts and after two passes Holmes bid the diamond small slam. Feeling that six hearts might very well be in the cards but not being sure, Skurry passed. This was definitely a forcing pass since both opponents had originally passed and were now at the twelve trick level. With two possible spade losers and other problems, Betty doubled to end the free-wheeling auction.

Harry Skurry led the heart three and Holmes trumped Betty's ace. A low diamond to dummy's ace drew all but one of the outstanding trumps. A low spade from the board was taken by the sleuth's ace and he now returned the suit, trumping in dummy. Holmes led a heart from dummy, trumping in his hand. Another low spade fetched Harry's king and dummy trumped. Betty overtrumped with her diamond king and desperately led a small club. Holmes trumped the trick and exposed his hand. Six diamonds, doubled, and made.

There was a scattering of cheers from the usually staid onlookers at the Grosvenor Square Bridge Club. Betty Castle looked dazed and Harry Skurry was shaking his head in disbelief. "I just don't believe it," he said. "Twelve high card points between you and you brought it off."

"Bridge can be a strange game indeed," said Holmes. "To me the most unusual aspect of this unusual deal are your cards, Harry, in conjunction with Betty's. You have nine heart cards around thirty-one points and yet you can't make four hearts. Against this contract I would have little difficulty finding the spade ace lead. A continuation of the suit gives Watson a ruff. His diamond ace provides the defense with a third trick and you must lose a club trick eventually. But," said Holmes cutting the cards toward Skurry, "it is unusual situations like this that add to the game's fascination."

THE ARSENIC TRICK

It was mid-morning on a week day and Holmes and Watson were just finishing a late breakfast. Outside, it was clear but cold as a north wind drove over England pushing cirrus clouds from horizon to horizon. The rays of a winter sun limped earthward bringing light but little heat. Passers-by on Baker Street were buried in coat collars and barricaded behind mufflers. Those without gloves had their hands dug deeply into pockets.

Doctor Watson was diligently applying some of Mrs. Hudson's homemade marmalade to a last popover with glances at the "Morning Banner" as he did so. Holmes, between sips of coffee, was reconstructing hands from the previous day's play on some foolscap. Watson had long since divined that the bridge-playing detective was working on an idea relative to the world's greatest game. Evidently, he was not satisfied as yet since he had revealed nothing to his trusted comrade and biographer.

The tranquil atmosphere was intruded upon by a rap on the door. At a word from Holmes, Mrs. Hudson appeared in the outer portal of the famous suite of rooms shared by the sleuth and Watson.

"A Doctor Digbody to see you, sir," she said, directing her words to the great detective.

"Fancy that," said Holmes. "Do show him up, Mrs. Hudson, and my thanks." As their landlady vanished, Holmes turned toward his fellow lodger. "You remember Digbody?"

Doctor Watson's expression indicated that he was not sure that he did.

"Oh, perhaps your paths have not crossed. General practice, relatively successful, but the good man has a genius for analysis. He has been helpful to me on several occasions. I did once suggest that he change his name. Digbody . . . hmmm . . . hardly appropriate for one in medicine, would you say, Watson?"

Doctor Watson's thoughts on the subject were suppressed as the subject of their discussion arrived.

As Holmes assisted their visitor out of his coat, Watson noted that Digbody was fairly tall and very neat and tidy in appearance, though his ample shock of hair was somewhat windblown. His long hands, while carefully tended, revealed chemical stains much in the same manner that Holmes' did. As Digbody unwound a white silk muffler, introductions were made and Watson shook hands with his fellow member of the medical profession.

Holmes had an observation. "You are the early bird, Digbody, on this most inclement day. I see that you are but recently from the suburbs but took the time to drop by your flat before your arrival here."

Digbody's eyes widened into that surprised look, so common to visitors of Sherlock Holmes, as was the expression of puzzlement which replaced it.

146

"I have just come from Kensington," he stated, "and did drop by my digs for a moment, though I'm blessed if I know how you figured that."

"Your clogs," said Holmes, indicating the doctor's serviceable galoshes, "have been in recent contact with the snow. I rather imagine that some has fallen in the outskirts. And those unopened envelopes in your suit coat pocket, they must have come by late post. Simple observation indicates that you came from the suburbs but went to your lodgings for your mail. Of course, deduction reinforces the later proposition."

"How?" asked Digbody. He was no waster of words.

"Your scarf, my dear chap. Much more suited to formal evening wear. I imagine the north wind prompted you to grab the first one at hand, probably on your way out of your flat."

As Digbody shook his head in wonderment, Watson joined the conversation. "Holmes has an extraordinary genius for minutiae," he remarked.

"As I well know," agreed Digbody. "Actually, that's why I'm here." His eyes centered on Holmes apologetically. "This problem arose in connection with my practice and I could only think of you. I do hope my visit is not inopportune."

"Of course not," replied Holmes with gusto. "Since Watson and I have no intention of braving the elements, what better thing than a problem to consider and solve. Do tell us all," concluded the detective as Watson nodded with eager anticipation.

"I may be sitting on top of an attempted murder," was Digbody's melodramatic response. "That's the nuts and bolts of it."

Once started, his words tumbled forth.

"I was called in on a case at the insistence of the patient, one Montgomery Vail. The chap recently retired from the foreign service and lives in a gloomy, barn-like house out in Kensington. Mrs. Vail is a rather quiet woman, sort of fades into the surroundings, you know."

"Self-effacing," commented Holmes. "Frequently an asset in the diplomatic corps." Noting Watson's escalating eyebrows, he added, by way of explanation: Other wives are not jealous of her, you see."

"To be sure," continued Digbody, as Watson nodded in understanding. "I was a bit bothered about medical ethics but the Vail's family doctor seemed happy to wash his hands of the whole thing. He had diagnosed Vail as suffering from influenza. With complications," he added, with a quick half-smile at Watson.

"The addition," commented Doctor Watson, "meaning 'I don't know.'"

"Exactly," said Digbody. "After a superficial examination, I saw no reason to disagree. There is an epidemic of influenza in France now and quite a few cases on this side of the channel as well. I was writing out a prescription for the poor fellow and at that moment we were alone in his bedroom. Vail seemed to rouse himself from a semi-coma. 'Doctor Digbody,' he said, 'you have a considerable reputation as an analyst. I want you to know that I am being poisoned.'

"I was thunderstruck, naturally. My patient's words seemed to exhaust him and he sank back into his pillow and a restless sleep. I really didn't know quite what to do."

"A most uncomfortable situation," murmured Watson in sympathy.

"My first thought," continued Digbody, "was the obvious and easy one. Vail was in delirium which might explain his remarkable statement. Then it occurred to me that his symptoms could indicate poisoning. Mrs. Vail was still downstairs securing the

147

milk toast I had suggested, so I popped into Vail's bathroom and found his comb and brush. It took but a moment to get several strands of his hair into an envelope. I was sitting by the patient when Mrs. Vail returned."

"Capital!" said Holmes, with enthusiasm. "You might try the field of detection if you ever weary of medicine."

Digbody's face flushed with pleasure. "I'll leave that in your capable hands, Holmes."

"Of course, you analyzed the hair samples?"

Digbody nodded. "Arsenic. And it was present in the hair ends." He addressed Watson. "Don't you agree, Doctor, that the poison must have been introduced some time ago to have gotten that far?"

Watson's reply was somewhat tentative. "Yes, I would think so."

"About a month," stated Holmes. "The whole thing bears a resemblance to a case in Venice a decade ago. A wife introduced, at intervals, arsenic into her husband's food. In very small amounts at first. Since her husband's resultant illness was gradual, poison was not suspected."

"Was she successful? The wife, I mean?" Watson had to know.

"In part," responded Holmes. "The husband died. However, he was a chemist and, unknown to his wife, had donated his body to science. A doctor detected the arsenic in the liver and intestines of the corpse. A very ingenious murder was thus exposed."

"Do you think, Holmes, that this case could be similar?" Digbody's face was stern.

"Possibly. The more so if one of Vail's tours of duty took the husband and wife to Italy. But let us not jump to conclusions."

Holmes rose to his feet and began pacing the room with that quick, nervous stride that Watson knew so well.

"How many servants in the Vail household?" he asked.

Three. Before I left I made sure that Mrs. Vail and the servants understood that the master of the house was to have nothing to eat until I returned."

"Very good thinking, Digbody."

"Indeed," echoed Watson. "With a new doctor on the case, the murderer might want to hurry the job."

"I believe Vail is safe enough for the moment. He is very weak, of course, but there probably isn't more than a grain of arsenic in his body now. Not a fatal amount, but . . . ." Digbody's words dwindled to a halt.

"But," said Sherlock Holmes, "the stage is set. The *coup d'etat* is a near thing. It would seem to me gentlemen that some haste on all our parts is required."

It was arranged that Doctor Digbody would return to Kensington immediately. Holmes assured him that he and Watson would be on his heels.

Following his departure, Holmes and Watson dressed warmly and did brave the elements after all.

Upon their arrival in the London suburb, Holmes showed no interest in the Vail mansion but directed his footsteps towards the local pharmacy. As they entered the establishment, Holmes broke his thoughtful silence.

"You know, Watson, poison is a subtle weapon, but it does narrow the field."

"You mean the culprit must be in regular contact with the victim."

"Exactly," said Holmes, with a pleased expression. "I think we can concentrate on the actual members of the Vail household. For the time being, at least."

"It can't be. Yes, it is. Mr. Sherlock Holmes!"

The pharmacy appeared deserted and momentarily Holmes and Watson could not locate the source of the loud voice that rang out. As they exchanged startled glances, there was the sound of movement from the rear of the establishment. Holmes spied a youngish man rushing from behind the drug counter towards them.

"And surely this is the good Doctor Watson," continued the sandy-haired man as he descended upon them and energetically pumped Holmes' hand. Turning to Watson he performed the same exercise on a startled doctor. "Just wait until my dear mater hears of this."

Watson sputtered an uncomfortable: "Awfully sorry, can't seem . . . ." but got no further.

"Oh dear, you don't know me. Probably never would without chance bringing you here." He peered into Holmes' hawk-like face with a half-amazed, half-reverent expression.

"I'm Cooldock, gentlemen, Horace Cooldock. Chief pharmacist here. Only one, in fact. When I studied for the trade, my good old professor was a great admirer of your medico-legal discoveries, Mr. Holmes. Especially your hemoglobin precipitate re-agent for the testing of blood stains.* No doubt, Doctor Watson was of some help in that discovery?"

"Actually, no," said Holmes, recovering somewhat from the enthusiastic greeting. "I chanced upon that process at the time that Watson and I were originally introduced."

"Well, it certainly made the guaiacum test old hat," continued the pharmacist. He turned to Watson and insisted on shaking his hand again. "How indebted I am to you, sir, for your recounting of Mr. Holmes' adventures. Needless to say, I have read and re-read every one."

Holmes directed a frosty glance towards Watson. Ever since his brother, Mycroft Holmes, had said to Watson in Holmes' presence: "I hear of Sherlock everywhere since you became his chronicler,"* the great detective had blamed his author for making him a figure of sensationalism. This bothered Watson not a whit since he knew that Holmes secretly was delighted by the aura of infallibility which surrounded his name.

Horace Cooldock bubbled on. "You gentlemen are not here without a reason. How can I be of help?" He directed a conspiratorial glance towards the Baker Street twosome. "Mum's the word and all that."

Seldom had Holmes been blessed with such an eager witness.

"I do have a small interest," stated the detective, "in the household of Montgomery Vail. Are you familiar with anyone there?"

"Indeed I am. New to the area, you see. Bound to notice them."

"Have they made any purchases here?" inquired the detective.

Cooldock was on familiar ground. "Indeed they have, sir. I've filled a number of prescriptions for the gentleman who, I understand, has been a bit under the weather since they arrived."

*See "Study in Scarlet"

*See "The Greek Interpreter"

149

Holmes' keen glance sparked an answer to an unspoken question.

"No, sir, I haven't ever seen Mr. Vail. The butler has been in several times. Mrs. Vail, also, for household supplies. Quite a gardener, Mrs. Vail."

"How do you know that?" queried Watson.

"Bought some arsenic, she did. Fairly large amount. Uses it for a spray on the flowers to kill mealy worms. The mater is keen on that sort of thing. Mentioned it to her and she said it would work."

Holmes had learned what he wanted but he asked several more general questions to divert their eager ally. Then he and Watson departed but not before Horace Cooldock had given the doctor his name and address and extracted a promise that Watson would write him as soon as he had another case history ready for publication.

On the quiet street outside, it was Watson who waxed enthusiastic. "I say, Holmes, we struck a rich vein there."

"So rich," said the sleuth, "that I believe we are now ready to visit the actual scene of these strange doings."

Following directions received from Doctor Digbody, Holmes set a brisk pace for the Vail mansion.

In the gloomy Tudor mansion set well back from the road, Digbody introduced Holmes and Watson to Mrs. Vail. Digbody's patient was upstairs in a fitful sleep. The servants were all in the rear of the house. The three men and Mrs. Vail were in the sizeable drawing room. A look of alarm crossed the face of the lady when she heard the name of Sherlock Holmes.

"But, Mr. Holmes, you are a detective. What brings you to these parts?"

"An unofficial consulting detective," replied Holmes, automatically. He was always didactic about titles. "However, I do dabble in forensic medicine, Mrs. Vail. Poisons in particular and it was on this subject that Doctor Digbody consulted with me."

"Poisons?" Mrs. Vail's hand adjusted a strand of her dark hair. She was younger than Watson had pictured. Her pale face, though drawn and worn from worry, had a firm bone structure.

After a long look into Holmes' eyes, Mrs. Vail continued: "Would you please explain?"

"You are evidently a dedicated gardener, Mrs. Vail," said Holmes. "I deduced that from the state of the flower beds outside."

An expression of pleasure flitted across Lenore Vail's face.

"The place was rather overgrown when we first came."

"A situation which you have obviously remedied. Now, Mrs. Vail, do you by any chance use an arsenic spray on your flowers?"

"Yes," she responded.

"And most effective it is, too," continued Holmes. "Do not be alarmed, but there is little doubt that your husband is suffering from arsenic poisoning." Holmes rode over the gasp of dismay from the lady. "It is quite possible that your husband has a very low tolerance for this poison. An errant breeze, some of the spray wafted through an open window, might cause your husband to react in a most unusual manner."

"Good heavens!" said Mrs. Vail. "I have done a lot of spraying. But I never dreamed it could be the cause of Montgomery's illness."

Both Watson and Digbody had a problem concealing their amazement. Holmes' words had no basis in fact, whatsoever. "He is laying a false scent," thought Watson.

"Obviously, the lady knows nothing of poisons or, if she does, she must consider Holmes a fool."

"Mrs. Vail, perhaps we can dispense with the flower spray for a while." Lenore's voice was vehement. "I'll never use the terrible stuff again."

Holmes' raised palm stemmed further words.

"At the moment, this thought is just a working hypothesis." He directed his eyes to Digbody. "Perhaps, Doctor Watson and I could see your patient. With the permission of Mrs. Vail, naturally."

The lady rose. "Of course, Mr. Holmes. Anything to have Montgomery well again."

She led the way for the three men towards the great stairway in the entrance hall. At the foot of the stairs, Holmes paused to gaze admiringly at a life-size oil on the wall. It depicted Lenore Vail in her late teens in a formal gown. Her high cheekbones and the shadow they cast were strongly defined by the artist.

"The infant prodigy," said Holmes cryptically.

"Millais," added Digbody.

"My uncle commissioned the painting," said Mrs. Vail simply.

It was Watson's thought that the years had been kind to the lady. One could never doubt that the painting was of her or that, in more exciting and colorful surroundings, she would be extraordinarily pleasing in appearance.

As they mounted the stairs, Watson wondered what a painting of the renowned John Everett Millais was doing in the home of a government employee of scant fame. His works certainly fetch a fine fee, nowadays, he thought. (Note: It is interesting to consider that Watson's comment could indicate that Millais was alive at the time of this happening. This would place the date of the adventure no later than 1896.)

The bedroom of the patient was dark. A single gas jet threw a feeble light on the scene and permitted obscure shadows in the corners of the large room. One wall had a recessed area of about eight feet which, at one time, might have been the haven for a breakfront or armoire. In it now was an old-fashioned bed hung with silk-lined tapestry. Directly opposite the bed which seemed to protrude from the wall was a row of windows which were heavily curtained. As Mrs. Vail entered and indicated for the others to follow, a figure in the bed stirred. Montgomery Vail was a corpulent man, if the outline of his blankets was to be believed. Drawing closer, Watson noted that his face was obese and flaccid with a pasty hue. As Lenore Vail arrived at the side of the bed available for traffic, a loose floorboard squeaked loudly and suddenly. The sound reached the man in the bed and one eye fluttered open, then the other. His mouth opened several times and then he managed words in a voice hoarse with weakness.

"I seem to have attracted a delegation." As his eyes rested on Holmes, his thin lips parted in a humorless smile. "Surely this gentleman is a mortician."

A thin cackle forced its way up from his chest with a chilling sound. For one of the very few times in Watson's memory, Holmes seemed non-plussed. He had frequently been referred to, usually by the lawless, as a figure of doom but never as the attendant after death.

As Mrs. Vail placed a cool hand on her husband's forehead, Digbody reassured his patient. "Dr. Watson and an associate were in the neighborhood. I asked them to have a look at you."

As Watson automatically took Vail's wrist, feeling for the pulse, it occurred to him that the sick man bore a resemblance to a buddha though there was no oriental cast to his face. An apparently unrelated thought crossed his mind, as he realized suddenly that Mrs. Vail did have a semi-oriental quality in her features. The pulse under his fingers was stronger than he had anticipated.

"It's a bad sign when doctors congregate," muttered Vail.

"Now, now . . ." Digbody's tone was brisk. "Additional opinions can sometimes be most helpful." He glanced towards Watson. "However, I am sure that Dr. Watson concurs with me. Despite what you think, I'm sure this is nothing more than a serious case of influenza."

The Millais Painting.

152

Watson nodded. It seemed the thing to do. Holmes had remained in the background, studying the figure in the large bed. After fluffing her husband's pillows, Mrs. Vail joined Holmes. The two doctors exchanged a few comments more noteworthy for their technical sound than any information they contained.

"I believe I'll have some beef bouillon prepared for you, said Digbody as he crossed towards the door. When Watson vacated the bedside to join him, he heard the floor squeak again.

Downstairs, Mrs. Vail went to the kitchen to prepare the bouillon. Holmes accompanied her to have a few words with the servants. When he reappeared with Lenore Vail, it was the detective who was carrying the tray with the bowl of clear broth and a plate of plain biscuits.

"Excellent beef broth," he stated, with a knowing glance at the two doctors standing in the hall. "I had a spoonful myself. Now I'll take this up to your husband, Mrs. Vail. Perhaps there is something which Watson or Digbody wish to say to you."

Without waiting for a reply, the detective went up the stairs quickly.

Lenore Vail watched his retreating figure for a moment and then turned to Digbody. "Doctor, upstairs you mentioned influenza again. But Mr. Holmes said that Montgomery was suffering from arsenic poisoning."

"Poison is an alarming word," was his reply. "In your husband's present condition let us try and keep him from any worries."

Watson was surprised to hear the bedroom floorboard creak and automatically placed Holmes at the patient's bedside. "It is an old house," he thought. "Evidently sound travels in it."

"I don't want you fretting either, Mrs. Vail," continued Digbody. "We shall pull your husband through. Meanwhile, I am a trifle concerned about you."

A single sounding of the door chimes interrupted him. The butler appeared quickly from the rear of the house, opened the door and picked up the evening paper from the veranda.

"No matter how ill he is, Montgomery insists on looking at the journals morning and night. When he was still active, we traveled a great deal. A newspaper from home was a thing to treasure."

Digbody recaptured his interrupted thought as the butler mounted the stairs, paper in hand.

"You have been under a considerable strain, Mrs. Vail. My prescription for you is some overdue sleep." As the lady began to form an objection, he continued: "I will arrange this evening for a nurse to be here bright and early tomorrow morning. She need stay for only a few days and her presence is as much for your sake as your husband's." Digbody's manner was firm. "I shall wait for a little while and then check your husband's condition before departure. The butler can let me out. Now I see no reason why you should not retire immediately, Mrs. Vail. You can be of scant use to your ailing husband if you are not in good health yourself."

Lenore Vail had no answer to this statement and curbed her hostess manner in the face of it. Holmes and the butler appeared on the upper landing as she was saying her goodnights. After a pleasant word or two with Holmes and some instructions to the butler, she disappeared into her own room on the opposite side of the stairwell from her husband's.

Alone in the great hall, the three men stared at each other.

"Have you learned anything, Holmes?" queried Watson.

"Quite a lot," stated Holmes. "And none of it helpful to the devoted wife. I want to have just a word with the gardener and then we'd better be back to Baker Street." As Holmes retired to the servant's quarters, Digbody went upstairs to check his patient's condition. The two men returned at the same time. Digbody reporting that Montgomery Vail seemed somewhat improved. Holmes had little to say until they were on their way back to the metropolitan center.

"There are many times that I recoil at what seems overly obvious," he confided, "but one cannot deny the existence of facts. Fact: Montgomery Vail is suffering from chronic arsenic poisoning. Fact: Lenore Vail purchased a large amount of arsenic from the local pharmacy. Fact: Mrs. Vail does all the cooking. The servants consist of the butler, a housemaid and a gardener. Evidently, Vail approves of his wife's activities in the kitchen since he did not choose to secure a cook. Fact: The gardener, when I questioned him, did admit that Mrs. Vail used more arsenic in her spray than he would have considered necessary. Fact: Lenore Vail prepared the spray herself."

"The net seems to be tightening around the lady. But how about the motive?" Watson had not been with Holmes for so long without developing some instincts regarding detection.

"I can give you one," replied Holmes, "though it does not charm me. Lenore Vail is considerably younger than her husband though she does little for her appearance. In fact, the pains she takes to appear plain are unusual and therefore suspicious. Vail, on the other hand, has slipped badly. His appearance is hardly appealing and I rather imagine his career with the foreign office was disappointing. What has Lenore to look forward to but a dull life with a retired and rapidly aging husband?"

"But what are we to do?" asked Digbody.

"If we accept Lenore Vail as the guilty party the fact that we know her husband is suffering from arsenic poisoning plus my appearance on the scene will prevent her from continuing with the scheme. She did not strike me as being a foolish woman."

And so the matter stood until the following morning.

Sleep came hard to Doctor Watson that night. The cold aggravated his old wound received in the fatal battle of Maiwand. The pain subsided in the early morning hours allowing him to fall into an exhausted sleep. As a consequence, he was late in rising and found Holmes missing.

Watson was consoling himself with a second large kipper when Holmes returned to their lodgings. The detective seemed especially alert and his eyes held, again, the sparkle of the chase. Watson, somewhat grumpily, registered a complaint.

"Really, Holmes, you allow me to remain abed while you are out having all the fun."

"The fun," said the detective with a chuckle, "consisted in going over dusty files at the Yard. I had exhausted my own clippings by eight a.m."

"What were you looking into, Holmes?"

"The past — which is so often the key to the future. I also dropped by the foreign office and completed my morning jaunt in Harley Street."

"Oh?" said Watson, hoping for more news.

"One Harriet Ness, a practical nurse and a policewoman as well, is now down in Kensington tending to Montgomery Vail. It is Miss Ness who will prepare the food for the ailing man at the doctor's orders."

"That should spike any poisoning attempts."

"One would think so," responded Holmes. "We will drop by after the day's play and see what fate has dealt us in this affair." A faraway look came to the detective's eyes. "I have a most uncomfortable feeling. This case could end in a stalemate like that cursed Windibank affair."*

At the Grosvenor Square Bridge Club, Watson could only admire silently the manner in which Holmes, obviously, sponged his mind clear of the poisoning of Montgomery Vail and directed the total power of his great intellect to the game at hand. During the afternoon play, several hands of interest came up, two of which Holmes referred to later. The following is one of them:

LOSE A LITTLE, SAVE A LOT

```
                    SKURRY
                    ♠ A J 7
                    ♡ A J 8 7 5
                    ◇ K
                    ♣ Q 8 3 2
    HOLMES                          WATSON
    ♠ 10 9 8                        ♠ K 6 5 4 3
    ♡ K Q 10 9 4 3                  ♡ 2
    ◇ J 6                           ◇ 8 7 4 3
    ♣ 6 5                           ♣ 9 7 4
                    CASTLE (Dealer)
                    ♠ Q 2
                    ♡ 6
                    ◇ A Q 10 9 5 2
                    ♣ A K J 10
```

CHALLENGE MATCH BIDDING: (Castle-Skurry vulnerable)

Castle	Holmes	Skurry	Watson
1D	2H	double	pass
pass	pass		

---

*See "A Case of Identity." It is interesting to note that this adventure, in which James Windibank never paid the piper for his cruel deceit, remained a cockleburr under Holmes' saddle blanket for many years.

Though Harry Skurry's double was delivered in an even tone, there were faint overtones of gloating. The results would seem to justify his concealed glee. Harry led his singleton diamond king which Betty Castle allowed to hold. Skurry then shifted to his lowest club taken by Betty's king. The slaughter was under way and Holmes ended up taking only four tricks for a resounding 700 point loss. Though Skurry now had a hearty respect for his opponents, he could not resist a small comment.

"It would seem that your pre-emptive jump overcall backfired on this hand — to the tune of a whopping penalty."

"One's feelings are governed by one's views," stated Holmes. The kibitzers cocked their ears. This had the ingredients for another Holmes coup.

"You feel, Skurry, that Watson and I lost 700 points. My view indicates that we saved 1440 points."

Harry's jaw sagged as a terrible suspicion forced itself upon him. Holmes unerringly dealt the deck face up, reconstructing the four hands.

"Let us assume," continued Holmes, "that we were sitting north-south and Watson opened with one diamond. Would you bid with the west hand?"

Skurry surveyed the cards. "The hand is weak but the suit isn't. I would overcall one heart."

"At this point, I would have several options if sitting north," said Holmes. "A bid of two hearts is conceivable but I think I would try two notrump. Watson would, naturally, show his second suit and bid three clubs which I would raise to four. Having taken us past three notrump and shown four card support for clubs, my sequence would be not only forcing but strongly slam invitational. Watson would temporize with a four diamond bid at which point I would bid hearts showing my control. Looking at two potential spade losers, Watson would surely settle for five clubs. I could now place the contract at six clubs but a better bid would be five spades."

"Using that cue bid♣ of yours, again," said Skurry, nodding.

Betty Castle, whose eyes were darting from hand to hand, was shaking her head in a discouraged manner.

Holmes continued his analysis. "Realizing that I had control of spades, Watson would now bid seven clubs which makes with trumps behaving and the diamond jack dropping on the second play of the suit."

"Wait," said Skurry. Disappointment had slowed down his thinking. "Against seven clubs by South, I would open the heart king, taken by the ace in dummy."

Betty Castle picked up the replay. "Unblock the diamond king in dummy. Then draw trumps in three rounds ending in the closed hand. The diamond ace drops the jack and the diamond suit is run with dummy discarding two spades along with hearts. A spade to the ace and a heart ruff in the declarer's hand. Then a spade ruff in dummy. Thirteen tricks."

As Holmes began dealing the next hand, Skurry sighed. "My moment of triumph was short-lived."

It was the very next hand which prompted some thoughts by Holmes which were not relative to the game of bridge.

♣See The Red Aces Hand. "Sherlock Holmes, Bridge Detective."

THE SLIM CHANCE
SKURRY

HOLMES (Dealer)	WATSON
♠ Q J 10 7 2	♠ K 8 5 3
♡ A J 8	♡ K 9 4
◇ 5 3	◇ 10 6 2
♣ A J 6	♣ K Q 7

CASTLE

Try bidding these hands. Skurry overcalls with two diamonds at his first opportunity. Then check your auction against that in the Challenge Match.

CHALLENGE MATCH BIDDING: (Skurry and Castle vulnerable)

Holmes	Skurry	Watson	Castle
1S	2D	2S	pass
4S	pass	pass	pass

The bidding might have progressed differently though the final contract would have been the same. At his second opportunity, Holmes could have bid an invitational three-spades which Watson would have accepted. However, Holmes, having just lost 700 points, was anxious to square the vulnerability and possibly recoup by winning the rubber. He drove to game.

PLAN YOUR PLAY

Harry opened with the diamond king on which Betty played the four. Skurry continued with the diamond ace and then queen which Holmes ruffed. Locate the problem. It is obvious and you should see it immediately. You have spotted it? Good! Now think like a bridge player.

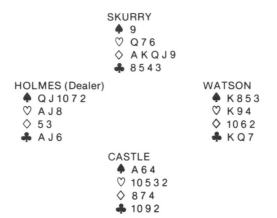

THE COMPLETE HAND

SKURRY
♠ 9
♡ Q 7 6
◇ A K Q J 9
♣ 8 5 4 3

HOLMES (Dealer)
♠ Q J 10 7 2
♡ A J 8
◇ 5 3
♣ A J 6

WATSON
♠ K 8 5 3
♡ K 9 4
◇ 10 6 2
♣ K Q 7

CASTLE
♠ A 6 4
♡ 10 5 3 2
◇ 8 7 4
♣ 10 9 2

Clue: In his play plan, Holmes took the only action with a chance of success. All other avenues were closed to him by information which he secured.

THE SLIM CHANCE

Having lost two diamond tricks and facing an inevitable trump loser, Holmes had to bring in the rest of the tricks. Clubs presented no problem and the great bridge-playing detective automatically realized that the whole hand depended on the location of the heart queen. Having trumped the third diamond lead, Holmes led his spade jack. Betty Castle took the trick and shrewdly led a club. If partner held the ace, doubtful on the bidding, the contract would be down. If declarer held it, her switch would give nothing away.

Holmes realized that the heart queen had to be with Skurry. Harry had made a risky two level overcall in a minor suit and was a sound bidder. True, he had the four top diamond honors but had to have a little more for his bid. The only additional card he could hold was the red major queen. Holmes shifted his attention to another key card. Do you know which one he was thinking of?

Holmes took the club return in hand and drew the remaining trump in two leads. He now played the heart jack. Harry covered with his queen and the trick was won with dummy's king. Holmes now played Watson's heart four. Betty played low and Holmes finessed the heart eight. The play brought a gasp from the kibitzers but when the eight spot held the trick there was a round of applause. Holmes played his heart ace and then spread his hand, claiming.

"Good Heavens, Holmes," said Watson. "A finesse of an eight is certainly tempting providence."

"When all else is impossible, the seemingly impossible must be true," replied Holmes. "The expression is not quite relative to this hand but 'twill do. When I realized by bidding and play that Harry must hold the heart queen, the ten of hearts became the key card. It was not impossible for Betty to hold that card and fortunately she did. The important point is that I had no other choice but to attempt a . . . a . . ."

". . . A backward finesse," suggested Watson.

"What a fine name for it, Watson."

A buzz of conversation from the kibitzers indicated that they agreed and Doctor Watson knew that his spur of the moment title would be much discussed. Actually, "The Backward Finesse" is mathematically an inferior play except in conditions like this hand where it presents the only possible solution.

Before another hand could be played, the doorman of the Grosvenor Square Bridge Club made his way through the large group of onlookers and handed Holmes a note. As he read it, Holmes' lips tightened and his penetrating eyes swiveled towards Watson briefly. He then requested that the day's play be terminated at this point pleading personal business. There were no objections and Holmes hurried from the club with Watson in tow.

Outside, Holmes handed the message to a puzzled Watson. It read: "Montgomery Vail just died from a cause you might anticipate. Digbody."

"I say, Holmes," said Watson excitedly, "what strange farrago is this?"

Holmes' eyes were thoughtful. "When everything else proves impossible, what seems impossible must be true."

Having repeated a pet idea, the great bridge-playing detective lapsed into silence as they made their way to Kensington.

Inside the gloomy suburban mansion of the late Montgomery Vail, Holmes and Watson found Doctor Digbody awaiting their arrival. With him was a most capable-looking woman with a "no nonsense" air about her. Holmes evidently knew her, addressing her as Miss Ness.

"The policewoman," thought Watson.

Digbody briefed them rapidly. "I checked the patient when I arrived. The bed-clothes were in a considerable disarray as though he had suffered a seizure. He was dead. I can tell you now what the autopsy will prove. Death by arsenic poisoning."

"That is impossible, Doctor," said Harriet Ness. Her voice was calm but did not lack in authority.

"One moment," interrupted Holmes. "Where is Mrs. Vail?"

"In her room," replied Digbody. "She took the terrible news quite well but was obviously close to hysteria. I felt it wise to give her a sedative and insist that she lie down. The drug has taken effect so it won't be possible to question her now."

"Nor is it necessary," said Holmes. His eyes returned to the policewoman. "What was your point, Miss Ness?"

"When I arrived this morning, the patient was in relatively good condition. I prepared the breakfast according to Dr. Digbody's instructions. I was present when the patient ate it. Since that time, no one else was in the room until Dr. Digbody arrived."

"When was the last time you saw Vail?" asked Holmes.

"When I took the paper to him. It was delivered late today." Her brows knitted for a moment. "I also filled his water carafe from the tap in his bedroom. When I left, he was reading the paper with great interest."

Watson could not restrain himself. "But this is impossible. What could have happened?"

"I know what happened," stated Holmes, "and I believe I know why."

He rose from a large armchair and crossed the hall to gaze at the Millais painting which seemed to interest him so much. Suddenly, he turned to Harriet Ness. "Would you get me the newspaper you took to the deceased?"

"Of course, Mr. Holmes." She went rapidly up the stairs.

"I don't mean to keep you in suspense, gentlemen," continued Holmes. "While Miss Ness secures what I suspect will be the final clue in what Watson referred to as 'a strange farrago', let us consider our facts. There is no doubt that Vail was being slowly poisoned by arsenic. It is obvious that his wife had the means and opportunity to administer the poison. It is also apparent that she alone was a suspect. The servants had no reasons whatsoever and any enemies that Vail might have had could not have reached him. Now let me introduce what may seem to be an unrelated fact though I believe it had much to do with what occurred."

Holmes crossed to the painting again, indicating it to Digbody and Watson.

"Here we have a life-size oil by Millais, a painter of international repute. So famous, in fact, that he was made baronet by the queen. Surely, this painting must have been costly. Far too costly for a man in Vail's financial state. His wife explained this simply by mentioning that her uncle had commissioned the painting. I made little note of the remark at the time but it came back to haunt me. As did the subject of the painting. Consider the face, gentlemen, and especially the high cheekbones."

"Like a cossack," muttered Watson.

"You are close, Watson. The Magyars. Another race of horsemen who invaded and settled in Austria-Hungary. The Magyar cheekbone is as distinctive a feature as the Hapsburg lip, so evident in any painting of Anne of Austria."

Harriet Ness descended the stairs with the newspaper which Holmes had requested. The detective's eyes devoured the front page and a smile of satisfaction altered his stern features.

"Let me read this to you: 'Earl of Broom dies in family castle after long illness'." He placed the paper on an occasional table.

Digbody was puzzled. "Is that headline revealing?"

Holmes nodded. "It is, when you remember that the house of Broom is a very famous one. The males of the family were invariably in the military. As was often the case in olden times, England was frequently ruled by enemies of this ancient family. On such occasions, the Broom men sought employment in foreign armies. Two of them were hired by the Hapsburgs and achieved great prominence in the Austrian Army. They married in the land of their employment and brought foreign wives back to England when the political climate was more suitable for their presence. Thus the Magyar strain was introduced into this old Saxon blood line."

A realization came to Doctor Watson. "You feel then that Mrs. Vail is a Broom?"

"Indeed I do, Watson. I imagine that the now departed Earl of Broom was responsible for this Millais painting. And that Mrs. Vail will now come into a considerable sum of money, having survived her uncle."

Watson shook his head in a discouraged fashion. "Your analysis is masterful and fascinating, Holmes, but how does it tie in with Vail's death?"

"In the original plot, Montgomery Vail was not supposed to die. You will note that the Earl of Broom was in the throes of a long illness. Being very old, indeed, it was just a matter of time. Vail, anticipating that his wife would become an heiress of note, used the time to his advantage. He poisoned himself."

"Oh come now, Holmes." Doctor Digbody was not convinced.

"Wait," said the detective. "Vail took small doses of arsenic for two reasons. First, his sickness had to cast strong suspicion upon his wife. Second, after a month's time, Vail's body would have a semi-immunity to the poison. A dosage which would kill a normal person would only render him severely ill because of this induced tolerance. The time table of the plot was based on the Earl of Broom's death. Following this, Vail intended to apparently recover. At a suitable time, he would dine with Mrs. Vail making sure the dishes they both ate were poisoned. She would die and he would recover. The entire incident would be passed off as a miscalculation on the part of Mrs. Vail."

Digbody was convinced now. "How macabre!" he said, with a shudder.

"But Holmes," questioned Watson, "what alerted you to this most intricate scheme? And why did Vail die?"

"The first question is so obvious that I shall answer the second one first. Vail was playing a dangerous game with a weapon he did not understand. The newspaper gave him the information he had been waiting for. He was ready to progress to the final act of his carefully-planned drama. He took a last dosage of arsenic to increase his tolerance and overdid it. He died by his own hand. As to my unmasking Montgomery Vail as the true culprit, we have Miss Ness to thank for that. She was the last one to see Vail alive. She kept a constant vigil on his room and until you, Digbody, arrived, no one went into that room. No one else had the opportunity to poison Vail so the seemingly impossible had to be true. Vail was poisoning himself. Once I arrived at this conclusion, the other threads quickly wove the fabric we call motive."

"It's tight," admitted Digbody. "I just hope you can prove it."

"Of course," said Holmes, as he directed his attention to Miss Ness. "While you kept watch on the victim's door, did you hear anything?"

"You mean that squeaky floorboard right by the bed?"

"She's sharp," thought Watson as Holmes nodded.

"No, Mr. Holmes. I didn't hear a sound."

"Good," said Holmes. "That means that Vail did not leave his bed. Therefore the arsenic which he used must have been secreted in the bed itself."

It was. An ornament on a bedpost was loose. In the cavity under it was a packet of arsenic crystals, the weapon used by the murderer. How fortunate that his victim was himself.

Thus ended what Doctor Watson called, in his diary of the Challenge Match, one of the strangest cases in Holmes' long career. There was nothing to be gained by exposing the villainy of Montgomery Vail so the whole matter was suppressed. Were it not for Watson's recently discovered diary, the case would never have come to light. Holmes had no objections to Watson's recounting of the case in the diary since he admitted that a remark at the bridge table had certainly helped in his solution.

Footnotes of Watson reveal that there was one other result from what he chose to call "The Arsenic Trick." Doctor Digbody was most grateful to Holmes for extricating him from a very touchy situation. To prove it, he agreed to a request of the great detective and had his solicitor apply for a change of name. After a suitable period of time, Hubert "Goodbody," M.D. had to move into much larger quarters on Harley Street to accommodate his rapidly-growing practice.

THE TRUMP REQUEST BID

As is frequently the case in a long match, some most unusual hands did come up in the Challenge Match. The following is one of them. It should be mentioned that the Challenge Match not only provided the newspapers with much copy but was greatly appreciated by other lines of activity. The betting fraternity did a rousing business booking wagers on the day's result, the winner of the week, and, of course, the winner of the match. Odds fluctuated constantly and a common question in London at the time was: "What's the morning line on the The Challenge Match?"

The bridge columnists of the day fared very well also. Any time that ideas were sparse, they would drop by the Grosvenor Square Bridge Club and pick up a couple of hands. Watson, in his diary, makes special note that on the day that this hand was played, Vincent Gollo of the "Morning Banner" was in evidence. Also, Septimus Sheingold of the "Morning Star" and Star Features Syndicate. Sheingold's column was syndicated as far as Afghanistan. A late arrival was Ezra Maize of Ace News Syndicate. The kibitzers on this day included a bridge knowledgeable group indeed.

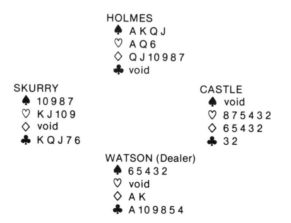

```
                        HOLMES
                        ♠ A K Q J
                        ♡ A Q 6
                        ◇ Q J 10 9 8 7
                        ♣ void
   SKURRY                                    CASTLE
   ♠ 10 9 8 7                                ♠ void
   ♡ K J 10 9                                ♡ 8 7 5 4 3 2
   ◇ void                                    ◇ 6 5 4 3 2
   ♣ K Q J 7 6                               ♣ 3 2
                        WATSON (Dealer)
                        ♠ 6 5 4 3 2
                        ♡ void
                        ◇ A K
                        ♣ A 10 9 8 5 4
```

Look at the North-South hands and see how you would bid them. It is quite possible that your auction will be superior to the one evolved by Holmes and Watson. Skurry and Castle were silent throughout.

CHALLENGE MATCH BIDDING: (Castle-Skurry vulnerable)

Watson	Skurry	Holmes	Castle
1C	pass	2D	pass
2S	pass	4S	pass
5S	pass	7S	pass
pass	pass		

Watson, with three quick tricks and distributional values opened a club. Holmes promptly jump-shifted to show his huge hand. Watson mentioned his second suit and Holmes jumped again in spades. Watson, his bridge acumen honed by constant play with the great bridge-playing detective, sensed something unusual. Holmes' 2-diamond bid was absolutely forcing to game and strongly slam invitational. Why had Holmes chosen to jump bid in spades? A simple raise would have shown 4-card trump support and would be absolutely forcing inasmuch as game had not been reached. Watson deduced, quite correctly, that Holmes was trying to show him superior spade support. Watson's hand looked very good with three first round controls and a big fit with Holmes' bid suit. Lacking bidding tools, the doctor bid five spades with the hope that Holmes would go on if he held the top cards in the suit. The great detective was doing a lot of guessing but, with his partner going beyond game missing the four top honors in his suit, Sherlock Holmes decided that Watson must have useful values in diamonds. He went to the grand slam in spades.

You may have bid the hand better but let us see if you can play it as well as Watson. Clue: The good doctor outshone himself.

Harry Skurry led the club king against Watson's seven spade contract.

When dummy came down, Watson was much relieved. But he suddenly remembered Holmes' cautionary words: "When a hand looks easy, ask yourself what can go wrong." The doctor's brow knitted as he considered the danger possibilities. There could be a bad trump break. Also, a void in dummy and in his hand spelled unusual distribution around the table. Watson took that thoughtful pause before playing to the first trick, a precaution which so often delivers the winning line. Dummy's magnificent diamonds could not provide enough discards to solve the club problem. Watson recalled the dummy-reversal hand that Holmes had played in Bath which had been so instrumental in the solution of the singular adventure of "The Panamanian Girls."* He decided to make dummy the master hand and realized that the diamond ace and king were bothersome cards. Now his plan was clear and, as the first step, he made what seemed like an unusual play. On Skurry's club king he discarded dummy's diamond seven, a winner, Taking the trick with his own ace, Watson led a low spade to dummy. Betty Castle showed out revealing the bad trump break. Watson now played dummy's heart ace, discarding his own diamond ace. He ruffed a heart in his hand and returned to dummy with another spade. Dummy's last heart was trumped by Watson and another spade, his last, was played to dummy. Now Watson played dummy's last spade, drawing Skurry's final trump. On this trick, he discarded his own diamond king. Dummy's hand was now high and the grand slam was an accomplished thing.

Holmes displayed a degree of enthusiasm which was most unusual for him. "My dear Watson," he said, "your play was superb. As the cards lay, the hand was fraught with peril, but you eluded it like a mongoose befuddling a cobra. The necessity for a dummy reversal was obvious but your unblocking of your diamond honors was brilliant. And your preservation of two losing hearts in dummy for ruffing purposes to absorb your trumps was dummy play of the very highest standard."

As Watson grew quite pink with pleasure, Skurry cut in. With his lengthy trump holding plus his diamond void, Harry had been waiting his moment like a hungry

*See: "Sherlock Holmes, Bridge Detective." Also "Popular Bridge," Oct. 1974. Also "Grand Slam, Thirteen Great Short Stories About Bridge."

vulture gliding in lazy circles above a mortally-wounded deer. To have the deer suddenly bound to its feet and out of harm's way made him quite testy.

"I've never seen such unusual play. Discarding the diamond ace and king. Really . . ." He had to subside, since he was scoring the grand slam and realizing, as he did so, that Watson's play was the only way it could be made.

"The two top diamonds were worth no more than the seven and eight spot in my hand," replied Holmes. "From the ace through the seven, they were all equals. It is obvious, when we note it in a *post mortem,* but it takes a shrewd player to see it at the table."

"Well, the bidding was singularly strange," stated Skurry trying to get in the last word.

"Agreed," said Holmes. "I have a few thoughts about that."

But the great bridge-playing detective did not reveal them until he and a delighted Watson were back in their suite of rooms on Baker Street.

"That seven spade hand gave me an idea regarding our bidding, Watson," he said thoughtfully, filling his pipe. "Actually our final contract depended on how many top honors I held in the trump suit."

"What do you have in mind, Holmes?" Watson was certain that his friend was coming up with another brilliant bridge innovation.

"The use of an otherwise worthless bid. Suppose the bidding went as follows: You open a club. I jump-shift to two diamonds and you mention your second suit, as we did at the table today. At this point, I bid three spades. According to our methods I will very seldom raise your second suit without four cards in it. Suddenly, your hand, with its controls, looks strong. You now bid five notrump."

"Five notrump? What could I possibly mean by that?"

"In its natural sense, nothing. It would be a ridiculous bid. But, if we give it a conventional meaning, it could solve many problems. Suppose the bid means: 'Partner, if you have one of the three top honors in our agreed trump suit, bid six clubs. With two, bid six of the suit and with three please go to seven.' " The great detective thought for a moment, then continued: "Look here, Watson. I can alter my hand by injecting one card and it provides a nice demonstration of what I am driving at."

He jotted down the following:

♠ A K Q J
♡ A K Q
◇ Q J 10 9 8 7
♣ void

"Let us assume that your hand is as it was. I open 2 diamonds with this monster and you respond 3 clubs, showing good values. I temporize with 3 diamonds and you raise to 4 diamonds. I now bid 5 notrump and you bid six diamonds showing two of the top three honors in diamonds. I then bid seven. Think it over, my dear Watson. I believe we can well incorporate this idea in our bidding structure."

"What shall we call it, Holmes?"

"Why not 'The Trump Request Bid'? "

"Excellent, Holmes." Watson was delighted. "I shall write up the hand immediately along with your newest idea."

And he did.

Mention was made that this day's play was well-attended by the leading bridge columnists of the time. The grand slam hand was so colorful that they all used it. And, as a follow-up, used Holmes' "Trump Request Bid" as well. It gained immediate public acceptance and became quite a subject for bridge conversation. However, since the bid only found use on rare occasions, it gradually faded from the public mind.

Singularly enough, that bridge genius and supersalesman of the game, Ely Culbertson, came up with the same general idea many years later. He called it "The Grand Slam Force," the name by which this conventional asking bid is known to crack players of our time.

The Foreign Office.
Somewhere within . . . The Mahler Safe.

TIGHTENING THE SCREW

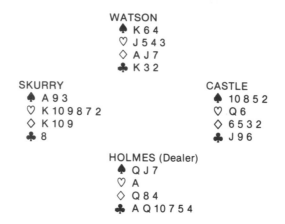

WATSON
♠ K 6 4
♡ J 5 4 3
◊ A J 7
♣ K 3 2

SKURRY
♠ A 9 3
♡ K 10 9 8 7 2
◊ K 10 9
♣ 8

CASTLE
♠ 10 8 5 2
♡ Q 6
◊ 6 5 3 2
♣ J 9 6

HOLMES (Dealer)
♠ Q J 7
♡ A
◊ Q 8 4
♣ A Q 10 7 5 4

Much later in the match, this interesting hand came up. Again Harry Skurry developed that "lemon" feeling.

CHALLENGE MATCH BIDDING: (Skurry-Castle vulnerable)

Holmes	Skurry	Watson	Castle
1C	pass	1H	pass
3C	pass	4C	pass
6C	pass	pass	pass

Holmes had ample values to jump in his club suit after Watson's one heart response. Watson's four club bid, which took the pair past the haven of three notrump, was definitely forward-going. With clubs as trumps, Holmes knew that Blackwood was of little value since he would undoubtedly end up in six. Therefore he "blasted" to the small slam.

Harry Skurry led the heart ten. Look at the Holmes-Watson hands and plan your play.

THE PLAY

Holmes immediately realized that, with a sure spade loser, the diamond king had to be with Skurry. Therefore he mentally placed it there. Harry's lead could indicate a heart honor as well. An idea began to form in the sleuth's mind. Holmes played a low heart from dummy winning the trick with his singleton ace. He now led a low club to dummy's king, returning the suit to cash his ace and queen. Harry discarded the heart deuce and the spade three. Now Holmes played a low diamond. When Harry followed low, he finessed dummy's diamond jack which held the trick. A low spade was played from dummy to Holmes' jack and Harry's ace. The politician promptly returned a spade to dummy's king. Holmes led a small heart from the board fetching Betty's queen which Holmes gratefully trumped. The appearance of the heart queen firmed up his original idea. He cashed the spade queen with Harry dropping a heart. Holmes now played the club ten pitching dummy's heart five. Skurry played another heart on this trick.

At this point the cards were as follows:

```
                    WATSON
                    ♠ void
                    ♡ J
                    ◊ A 7
                    ♣ void

     SKURRY                          CASTLE
     ♠ void                          Immaterial
     ♡ K
     ◊ K 10
     ♣ void

                    HOLMES
                    ♠ void
                    ♡ void
                    ◊ Q 8
                    ♣ 7
```

Holmes played the club seven. Skurry's pudgy features sagged into a look of resignation. If he dropped the heart king, Holmes could discard dummy's diamond seven, cross to dummy via the diamond ace and cash the now good heart jack. On the other hand if Harry let go a diamond, Holmes could get rid of dummy's heart jack and play to the diamond ace and back to his diamond queen. Harry looked at his partner, shaking his head. "He's done it to me again, Betty," he said.

Betty shrugged. "Well, at least Mr. Holmes squeezed you instead of me. A lady does have to keep her dignity, you know." Betty's words were very Victorian but there was a twinkle in her eye. Secretly she despised "that brazen Irene Adler" whom Holmes always considered "the woman."

SO ELEMENTARY

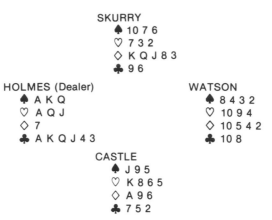

```
                    SKURRY
                    ♠ 10 7 6
                    ♡ 7 3 2
                    ◇ K Q J 8 3
                    ♣ 9 6
HOLMES (Dealer)                      WATSON
♠ A K Q                              ♠ 8 4 3 2
♡ A Q J                              ♡ 10 9 4
◇ 7                                  ◇ 10 5 4 2
♣ A K Q J 4 3                        ♣ 10 8
                    CASTLE
                    ♠ J 9 5
                    ♡ K 8 6 5
                    ◇ A 9 6
                    ♣ 7 5 2
```

CHALLENGE MATCH BIDDING: (Holmes-Watson vulnerable)

Holmes	Skurry	Watson	Castle
2C	pass	2NT	pass
3C	pass	3NT	pass
6C	pass	pass	pass

OPENING LEAD: King of diamonds.

Another small slam in clubs demonstrated, according to Holmes, a very elementary point. Study the Holmes-Watson hands and consider the lead. What would be your game plan?

Holmes immediately realized, as do you, that his diamond loser was inevitable. Since it was the only trick he could afford to lose, two situations had to exist or the contract had no chance at all. Does your thinking coincide with that of the Baker Street bridge expert?

Skurry took the first trick with the diamond king and continued the suit with his queen. Holmes trumped with the club jack. He now played his club-three and when Skurry dropped his six, the detective finessed dummy's trump eight. The eyes of kibitzers widened but dummy's card held the trick. Holmes led a low heart and played his jack which also held. A small club to dummy's ten allowed Holmes to repeat his successful heart finesse. He now drew Betty's remaining club card and claimed the balance of the tricks.

"It was the only way to fly, my dear Watson," said the great bridge playing detective. "Quite elementary, really." And it is, when you think about it.

THE CASE OF THE MYSTERIOUS IMPRINT

As has been previously mentioned, there were frequent interruptions in the play of the "Challenge Match." The period to which I now refer via Watson's detailed "Diary" was one of them. Betty Castle was out of London, involved in a very social wedding. Harry Skurry was delivering speeches on behalf of his political party in the north of England and Holmes had just concluded a most sensitive case shrouded in secrecy because of its association with the King of Scandinavia. Watson makes particular note of this, though, as we shall later see, there seems to be a confusion relative to dates.

As a medical man, Watson welcomed a respite from Holmes' constant activity, though, as a dear friend, he could never fathom which of the extremes of the detective's life was the most difficult.

Any student of the career of that most unusual of men knows that Holmes was involved in an amazing number of cases. He most frequently dealt with a variety of affairs simultaneously and drove himself unmercifully to arrive at successful conclusions. Yet, when a breathing spell occurred as it had to on occasion, Holmes sank into such a deep despondency that Watson welcomed a return to activity when the detective's thinking-machine mechanism made sleep impossible and food unwanted.

Following the Scandinavian adventure, Holmes was exhibiting those first signs of depression and it was almost with a feeling of relief that Watson opened the outer door of that famous suite of rooms at 221B Baker Street and found an unannounced visitor. Billy, the page boy, was present, of course, but close on his heels was the somewhat sinister and certainly mysterious Mr. Wakefield Orloff.

Orloff, because of a previous association with Holmes (See "The Adventure of the Soft Fingers") was one of the very select group afforded immediate entry to Holmes' and Watson's domicile. With them as with the world, Wakefield Orloff preserved the facade of a simple employee of the Foreign Trade Department. Holmes knew differently. Orloff knew that he knew. Holmes knew that Orloff knew that he knew. In discussing this unusual gentleman with Watson, Holmes had once said:

"It is a dog trying to catch his tail, my dear Watson. That walking arsenal is certainly a creature of Mycroft though I suspect his activities are even more widespread. One thing is certain: we shall never allude to his profession. To a man in Orloff's line of work, that would constitute an unforgivable breach of etiquette."

I mention this statement from another section of Watson's "Diary" since never once, during this visit did Orloff mention Sherlock Holmes' older brother, confirming, it would seem, Holmes' thoughts about the scope of his activities.

As soon as the door was closed behind him, Orloff's movements followed their familiar and unvarying pattern. The lethal bowler hat, with its steel-lined brim, was placed within easy reaching distance. He sat in the visitors' chair with his weight balanced on the balls of his small shoes, the toes of which Watson knew were steel-shod. His attitude was completely relaxed but his position erect. Holmes had once hazarded the guess that Orloff had a knife concealed between his shoulder blades which possibly explained why he never leaned back. He regarded the Baker Street duo with his usual bland smile. His green eyes were fathomless.

"Well, gentlemen," he said, "as usual, it is a spot of trouble that brings me your way."

"Home-grown?" queried Holmes from the mantlepiece where he was filling his pipe from the famous Persian slipper, "or of a foreign variety?"

"The locale of the problem is France — Paris, to be specific."

"Oh, dear!" said Holmes through a cloud of smoke. "Not some more government papers! Those diplomatic chaps do seem unusually careless."

Orloff's lips tightened as he shook his head negatively. He was a security agent and Holmes' remark had struck a tender area.

"No, Mr. Holmes, it is a national treasure. You haven't read anything of it in the journals because our French friends are very sensitive about anything stolen from the Louvre."

Watson's eyes widened. "Whatever it is must be of great value." A sudden thought struck him. "I don't recall of ever hearing of a robbery in the Louvre."

"You haven't," said Orloff. "Considering that it contains close to a quarter of a million articles of inestimable value, it is unusual that the great museum hasn't been the target of culprits. In fact, it is this aura of security that the Sûreté is most anxious to preserve. For that reason, it is not known that the crown of Theodora, Empress of the Byzantines, has been taken."

Holmes' breath came out in a low whistle. "The thief or thieves were not playing for small stakes. I imagine the Sûreté is a ferment of activity."

Orloff's smile of agreement was grim. "But the Paris police are under a temporary handicap. The chief of the Sûreté, Marie-Francois Garon, is in Lyons on that Millery case. (Note: This would place the year of this adventure as 1889 and I make this point now for reasons that will be revealed later.) With Garon is Dr. Alexandre Lacassagne, their best forensic medicine man and Arséne Pupin. The case has captured the headlines of every newspaper in France. To uphold his reputation, Garon must solve it." (Note: Solve it he did in 1890. Known as the "Gouffé Case" finally, it was the high point of Garon's career. This great detective died in 1933 but, fortunately, wrote his memoirs which make excellent reading for those interested in the Sûreté Francaise.)

Holmes' keen mind had captured Orloff's train of thought completely.

"So the French police are faced with a major crime but denied the use of their best men."

"Exactly," said the Security Agent. "Hence, Arséne Pupin made a telephone call from Lyons to Paris yesterday." (Note: This further confirms the date of the adventure since the telephone was but newly-developed and probably not in use between Lyons and Paris prior to 1889.)

"Pupin's instructions were brief," continued Orloff. "Get Sherlock Holmes!"

Now it was Holmes' turn to look grim.

"Ouch!" he said. "My friend Arséne's command must have gotten a cool reception in Paris."

"Undoubtedly, it did," agreed Orloff. "However, that can't be helped. At the moment, we — the Foreign Trade Department that is — are in desperate need of some help from the French regarding a certain matter. Therefore — " Orloff allowed his words to dwindle to a halt.

" — Therefore, 'we' would like to have a certain consulting detective go to Paris immediately," said Holmes, with a twinkle in his eyes. He shot a quick glance of inquiry at Watson.

The good doctor nodded with enthusiasm.

"I can have someone handle my cases of the moment," he said. "Possibly Goodbody," he added, as an afterthought.

"Excellent," said Orloff. "I have already made the necessary travel arrangements and hotel accommodations." He looked as though he were about to rise.

"A moment," said Holmes. "Let us have what background there is at your disposal so we won't arrive in Paris in a complete vacuum."

Orloff's weight shifted slightly backward. Watson was struck again by his complete lack of unnecessary movement. "Nerves of steel!" was his mental diagnosis. The security agent's eyes narrowed as he selected his words.

"The famous sixth century mosaic of Empress Theodora and her court, in the church of San Vitale in Ravenna, Italy, shows the crown. The Byzantines were renowned for their rare gems and their jewelry designs influence the styles of this day. The potential value of her crown rather staggers the imagination, especially since it can be broken up and the stones sold singly.

"For what it is worth, Theodora herself is not without considerable interest. She was a dancer, actress, and then courtesan, and, finally, the mistress of the Emperor Justinian for five years before she married him and became Empress. Rumor has it that she was the iron of the combination. Under Justinian, the Byzantines certainly flourished. With his capital at Constantinople, Justinian was able to recapture much of Italy from the Goths. He established the Empire of the East as the dominant force in the Mediterranean world. As is almost always the case with the conqueror, the wealth of the Byzantines was fantastic. His construction of Hagia Sophia, one of the most impressive buildings in the world, was proof of that!"

Holmes indulged in a dry chuckle. "The Louvre, itself, did not exactly suffer from the far-flung triumphs of Napoleon."

"Enough of history," said Orloff. "The crown was on display under a glass case mounted on a pedestal with the usual rectangle of a strand of chain to keep viewers from actually touching the case. Since the glass enclosure contained only one object, it was considerably smaller than the one surrounding our own crown jewels in the Tower."

"Was there any construction or repair work going on in the Louvre at the time of the theft?" asked Holmes.

"How did you know that?" responded Orloff.

"I didn't. It seemed the easiest explanation for the presence of additional and possibly unknown personnel. I presume the possibility of a visitor to the Louvre being the guilty party has been ruled out?"

"Absolutely," stated Orloff. "As is customary, the paintings, sculptures, works of art, were carefully checked after the Louvre was closed. The crown was there after the closing. It was not, when the Louvre was opened to the public the following morning."

"A thief in the night," said Holmes, thoughtfully. "One more question, which is certain to draw a negative answer but must be asked: Have any of the precious gems from the crown of the Empress appeared?"

Orloff shook his head. "The theft was but two days ago. The thieves are almost certain to lie low for a period. Then the gems will start to appear in rings, necklaces, and other forms of adornment. To dispose of them to the best financial advantage will be time-consuming, but certainly well worth the effort. In fact, if the job is handled skillfully, I seriously doubt if the jewels will even be recognized in their new settings."

Holmes was nodding through Orloff's words. "The necessity of haste on our part is obvious. Once they break up the crown, any recovery will be virtually impossible."

And it was with haste that Holmes and Watson departed for the French capital. Orloff had secured lodgings for them in the "Étrangère", an inconspicuous hotel. The reservations were in Watson's name. Holmes approved Orloff's foresight feeling that there was no advantage in advertising their presence in Paris. It will be recalled that it was the great English detective who had tracked down Huret, the boulevard assassin, an exploit which won for Holmes an autographed letter of thanks from the French president, and the Order of the Legion of Honor. He was well-known in Paris. While Watson registered for them and a bellboy collected their limited luggage, they were approached by a small man with a black moustache and eyes that shone like shoe buttons. The stranger mentioned that they had mutual friends in London and took the liberty of accompanying Holmes and Watson to their suite of rooms. After the bellboy departed, he presented his credentials identifying himself as Inspector Achille Martine of the Sûreté. The Englishmen, anticipating some coolness, nay possible hostility, were pleasantly surprised.

"This is indeed an honor for me, Mr. Holmes," said Inspector Martine. "I have long been a great admirer of both you and your compatriot, Doctor Watson, not only in the field of criminology where I ply my trade, but also at the bridge table. Your exploits in the 'Challenge Match' are the talk of Paris."

As Holmes and Watson expressed their appreciation of his welcome, the Frenchman made an appeal.

"Gentlemen, I well know the serious matter which brings you both to our shores. But — I am a member of 'La Société de Bridge Aux Contracts. If it is possible, during your visit to arrange an evening of play at Le Club Bridgeur, It would be a wonderful thing. At the moment, Signorina Poluffo, the famous female player from Italy, is in Paris. I have arranged, if it is permitted by your schedule, for a match. Signorina Poluffo will play with our leading bridge expert, Henri Sarque, against your partnership."

Holmes, with Watson's agreement, stated that the match would be welcomed by them both but his manner indicated that the matter of the missing crown of the Empress Theodora had first claim on his interest. The French policeman immediately became all business.

"If I ever saw the impossible crime, this is it, gentlemen. For reasons which you may not, as yet, be aware of, this robbery could not have occurred." He shook his head sadly. "But it did. I trust I have not dampened your enthusiasm."

"Au contraire, you have heightened it," stated Holmes. "It has been my experience that the impossible crime has a way of pointing a finger at the perpetrator." Holmes shot a glance at Watson. "You will recall our experience with the Black Pearls?" (See "Sherlock Holmes, Bridge Detective.") As Watson nodded, the Baker Street sleuth continued. "It is the commonplace which is so often baffling. A man is run down on the street by a hansom cab and dies. His wife collects a large insurance policy. The hansom cannot be located. Was it an accident or was it murder? Nothing impossible nor even very unusual but a baffling problem to face."

"*C'est vrai*, said the Frenchman, stroking his moustache. "You indicate a line of reasoning which I had not considered, M'sieu Holmes."

"What", asked Holmes, "makes this particular robbery so baffling, or, as you expressed it — impossible?"

"The security measures. The Crown of Theodora is displayed in a small room, actually an ante-chamber. There is no possible way of entering this room save through the much larger one adjacent to it. And, gentlemen, displayed in that room is the greatest treasure of France — probably the most valuable painting in the world: Leonardo da Vinci's masterpiece, the Mona Lisa. There is not even a door between the *galerie* in which the Mona Lisa hangs and the room in which the crown was displayed. But, to get into the room containing the Da Vinci painting, the thieves would have had to open a door of steel secured by three huge padlocks of intricate design. Our locksmiths, the finest in Europe, assure us those padlocks were not tampered with."

"The hinges?" suggested Holmes.

Martine shook his head. "The door is hinged from within. In fact, I can assure you the door was not opened prior to its official unlocking on the morning the theft was discovered."

Watson had a thought. "The small chamber containing the crown. It has no windows?"

Again, the French detective registered a negative. "None. Architecturally, I can definitely state that it was impossible to reach the smaller chamber without passing through the *galerie* containing the Mona Lisa. To compound this impossibility, the walls were obviously untampered with." He shrugged his shoulders in a typical French manner. "The mentality of the thief or thieves also is mysterious. Obviously, to be able to remove the crown of Theodora, they had to have access to the picture *galerie*. The Byzantine jewels are of great value indeed, but . . . . "

"Why did they not take the Mona Lisa?" Watson concluded the Frenchman's sentence excitedly

Holmes preserved a discreet silence.

Achille Martine looked at them both keenly.

"It is a most baffling puzzle, *n'est-ce pas?*"

"It is indeed," said Holmes, who chose this moment to be diplomatic. "M'sieu Martine, I have no official standing in my own country and even less in yours. This case is a matter for the Sûreté, of course."

As he paused, the Frenchman waved his hands violently.

"M'sieu Holmes, Arséne Pupin is the Deputy Chief of the Sûreté. His instructions left no room for doubt. You are to be afforded complete freedom of action. *Le roi le vent.*" A small shudder accompanied his next sentence. "The Deputy Chief can become quite incensed if his orders are not followed to the smallest detail. The case is yours and, in effect, the army of the police of Paris is under your command." Again, his shoulders rose in a Gallic shrug. "However, this is not without historic precedence," he added philosophically. *"Le Grand Empereur* was a Corsican."

Holmes' smile had a tinge of defeat. He had been outmaneuvered in his diplomatic gesture.

"I would," he said, slowly, "like to request that the room in which the crown was displayed be completely untouched. I don't even want anyone to enter it."

Martine nodded in agreement. "It shall be so, M'sieu."

Holmes continued. "There is another matter which we have not touched upon. The repairs which were taking place in the Louvre. I assume they were in the picture gallery containing the Mona Lisa."

"That is so," replied Martine, attempting to conceal his surprise. "The roof of the *galerie* is supported by a row of pillars. They are partially for ornamentation but do have a structural function. Cracks appeared in two of the pillars. A crew of masons were hired for repairs. The picture *galerie* was closed to the public and, perforce, the ante-chamber as well. That is how we have been able to conceal the theft of Theodora's crown from the public. Ostensibly, the repair work is still going on."

"But, in actuality, it is completed?"

"Yes, M'sieu Holmes," said Martine. "The morning the theft was discovered, the masons completed their work. I might add," he said, hastily, "that at no time were the workmen in the picture *galerie,* or the Louvre itself for that matter, without the constant attendance of a group of police."

"That answers an obvious question," said Holmes, drily. He thought for a moment, and then continued: "M'sieu Martine, both Doctor Watson and I are most grateful for your cooperation and the detailed information which you have given us. Could we meet tomorrow morning at, say, eight and enter the Louvre?"

"Certainly, M'sieu Holmes. Yours to command."

As Inspector Martine rose to leave, Holmes had an afterthought.

"In the normal procedure — working procedure that is — of your great museum, is there not a cleaning force which operates after closing time?"

Martine nodded. "The Louvre is one of the great attractions of Paris and, indeed, of the world. Every night, the pictures are dusted, floors are cleaned or polished. Were I of the British Navy, I would say that the Louvre 'runs a tidy ship.' "

"And the glass case in which the crown of Theodora rests — is it cleaned?"

"*Oui,* M'sieu. The case is surrounded by a retaining strand of chain to prevent the viewers from attempting to touch the case, but the cleaning crew run a cloth over it nightly so that the crown may show to its best advantage. It is," added Martine somewhat wistfully, "a most beautiful thing. I have viewed it often." Suddenly, he smiled at Holmes. "The cleaning personnel is also under surveillance, M'sieu Holmes. And, as a standard procedure, are searched before leaving the museum."

With this last piece of information, the French detective took his leave and Holmes and Watson unpacked and prepared for a night's rest. One point of the conversation continued to bother Watson.

"I can't understand any of this as yet, Holmes," he said. "But one fact is especially puzzling. Why, since they had an equal opportunity, did the thieves not take the Mona Lisa? Why settle for, by far, the lesser treasure?"

"That is simple, indeed. Rubies, pearls, emeralds, have no names — unless, of course, they are very famous gems — like the Carstair Pearls, the Hope, the Kohinoor, the Regent, the Sancy diamonds, or the Midas Emerald and the Rajah Ruby. But suppose you had purloined the Mona Lisa. May I inquire as to where you would go to sell it?"

Watson gazed at his famous friend in resignation. "It is all so terribly simple, Holmes, after you have explained it."

The following morning found Holmes and Watson on the Rue de Rivoli at the entrance to the Louvre where they were met by Achille Martine. The French inspector took them to the room which had housed the missing crown of Theodora. In passing through the picture gallery, they both took a long look at that most famous lady with the enigmatic smile. A brief glance by Holmes at the entrance door to the gallery confirmed the words of Martine the night before. The picture gallery was spotless — a fact which drew a comment from the English detective.

"But yes," replied Martine. "The masons were most careful. They even used a special receptacle to mix the mortar necessary for the repairs."

Inside the ante-chamber, Holmes' attention centered on the glass case in the center of the small room. The famous Byzantine crown evidently had been the only display item since no other *objets d'art* were in evidence. The English sleuth raised the surrounding chain and stooped to pass under it. Standing beside the pedestal, his ever-present magnifying glass appeared and, using it, he surveyed the now empty case closely. Evidently, his study was not without results as Watson detected a grunt of satisfaction from his friend who, straightening, turned to the French detective.

"M'sieu Martine, would it be possible for you to secure a camera?"

"Of course," replied Martine. "It will not take me long. Is there anything else you require?"

"A camera will do nicely," said Holmes, walking around the case and surveying it. "I am sorry to inconvenience you."

"Ce n'est rien," said the Frenchman as he left the room.

Holmes now took a small can of talcum powder, which he had bought, much to Watson's mystification, on their way to the museum.

Watson could contain himself no longer. "Have you chanced upon something, Holmes?"

"Indeed, Watson. A very clear thumb print unless I'm mistaken and some other prints, though they appear smudged. I'll know better in a moment."

Holmes carefully shook some of the powder into the palm of one hand and then, leaning close to the case, he gently blew the powder onto the glass surface. He then viewed the area again with his magnifying glass.

"Oh yes, Watson, I do believe we are in luck."

He resumed studying the case with his glass, and every so often, repeated his actions with the talcum powder.

"Something tells me I'm being dense, Holmes, but you did say 'print'?"

"Finger prints, Watson. Some from an over-zealous detective, perhaps, but some might very well be from the thief."

"I've never heard you refer to fingerprints, Holmes. What use are they?"

Holmes looked up from his work with a smile. "I am surprised at you. The whole idea originated in India, ol' boy, where you did spend some time." Holmes did not choose to explain his somewhat cryptic remark.

Martine returned in short order with an efficient-looking camera. Holmes had all the lights in the room turned on and proceeded to take a series of shots of the glass case. Watson noted that he concentrated his efforts on those areas where he had applied the talcum powder. Finally, satisfied, Holmes returned the camera to Martine.

"If these pictures could be developed as soon as possible, I believe it will be of great assistance. In the meantime, Inspector, can you continue to keep everyone out of this room? That includes members of the police as well."

"It shall be done, M'sieu Holmes," said Martine. "And now, of what further service can I be?"

"I would like to go over some ground which you have already tilled," replied Holmes.

Holmes inspecting the display case of The Crown of Theodora.

"*Naturellement,*" replied the Frenchman pleasantly. "The masons who were at work in the *galerie.* It was a firm owned by Pierre Dancoeux. Here — I shall write down his address." He did so, then added: "Or, per'aps you wish me to accompany you?"

"That will not be necessary," said Holmes, "though you might give the gentleman a phone call. Some veiled reference to international complications and the fact that your office is using me in a consulting capacity."

Warmth flooded the Frenchman's eyes. "You are most considerate, M'sieu Holmes. You should 'ave been a Frenchman."

"My grandmother was of the Vernet line, "stated Holmes,

"*Mon Dieu,* the family of the famous artist *Militaire*?"

"His sister," said Holmes with some pride. The Frenchman embraced Holmes like a long lost brother. "M'sieu, your brilliance and diplomacy are now completely explained."

Watson had other thoughts. "Brilliance, yes," he said to himself. "As for diplomacy, I could have a few surprises for our French detective." The good doctor was no doubt recalling Holmes' brusque treatment of Lord St. Simon and others of his ilk.

"After Doctor Watson and I meet with Dancoeux, possibly we could have á talk with the man in charge of the guard in the picture gallery? During the period that the workmen were present, I mean."

"He shall be here awaiting your return, M'sieu Holmes," said Martine, as he rather effusively escorted the great sleuth and Watson from the Louvre.

In the mind of Inspector Martine, he was now dealing with a fellow countryman, a subliminal deception heightened by the Legion of Honor earned by Holmes.

Holmes and Watson had no problem locating the establishment of Pierre Dancoeux near the Boulevard Richard-Lenoir. The master mason was fat. His face was big and jowled, and his skin glistened. Fierce eyebrows were set above small penetrating eyes. He wore a greasy, black beret, and his manner would have been brusque save for the phone call he had obviously received from the Sûreté. He ushered Holmes and Watson into his office as if into the grand ballroom of Versailles. Actually, it was a dingy room smelling of cement, sweat, and the Mexican cigar that Dancoeux was chewing on. His teeth were large and a dirty yellow. His manner was civil enough as he responded to Holmes' questions.

"The job, M'sieurs, took but two days. The main problem was to assure ourselves that the structural strength of the two pillars with cracks had not been impaired. They had not. Once certain of this, we mixed the cement and filled the cracks." He removed his beret and mopped a sweaty brow. "This took a little doing since we had to match the original mixture of the pillars, but the job — she came out *très bon!*"

"Must have been somewhat difficult mixing the filler within the Louvre," said Holmes casually. "Or did you do that outside on the street?"

The fat man laughed. "*Mais non*, M'sieu! This type of work is not unusual. I have piece of equipment — 'ow you say . . . ?" He paused for a moment, his brow knitted. "In your language — it is mos' like small coffin."

This seemed to strike Dancoeux as humorous and he laughed again. "The box is watertight. We take it close to the job with the ingredients within. Then we add water and work the mixture with the trowels until it is ready."

"The tools required — did you leave them overnight in the Louvre?" asked Holmes.

"*Certainment*, M'sieu," the hirsute Frenchman nodded. "There were two large ladders plus the box for the mixture." He thought for a moment. "My workmen may have taken their tool boxes with them from habit. I don't actually recall."

Holmes glanced around. "I assume your workmen are on another job now."

The mason's large lips tightened. "They are at this moment in the nearest wine shop swilling *vin ordinaire*. I 'ave jus' given them their weekly wages. *Mon Dieu*, they complain about pay but they spend it quickly enough." He indicated a wastebasket next to his battered desk. Holmes picked it up, extracting four envelopes which had been hastily ripped open. A tinge of excitement was apparent in his manner. "I see that a man's name is written on each of these. You have, then, four men in your employ?"

Dancoeux nodded. "I total what they have coming and place the money in the envelopes. On the job, they are slow, indeed, but when I give them the money — hah! Then one sees how fast they can move. Poof! The envelopes are open — the francs are removed, and off they go. I will get no more work out of those *canards* today. And in three, four days, they will be asking for an advance on next week's pay." He spat in a corner. Evidently, he did not hold his workmen in high esteem.

"May I take these?" asked Holmes, indicating the envelopes.

"But of a certainty, M'sieu. They are of no use to me." The Frenchman's small eyes regarded Holmes inquiringly and his voice had a tinge of cunning. "The job —

177

she was approved. We take our tools and leave everything in good order. But I have reason to know there has been a theft. The police are asking questions and the picture *galerie* is not open to the public. Has the mystery been solved?"

Holmes did not consider it expedient for him to reveal information.

"There is a matter of allocation of funds. My friend and I appreciate your time, M'sieu Dancoeux."

Cued by Holmes' words, Watson made for the door. The mason's manner indicated that he did not believe Holmes' pat explanation at all but he did not pursue the matter as he ushered the two Englishmen out of his establishment.

On their way back to the Louvre, Holmes carefully swathed the empty pay envelopes, secured from the mason, in a large handkerchief. He then borrowed a handkerchief from Watson in which he placed what appeared to be a miniature cavalry sabre. Folding the handkerchief around it, he placed it in his inside coat pocket with the envelopes.

"What in the world is that, Holmes?" asked Watson.

"A letter-opener which I seem to have acquired from Dancoeux's desk. I trust you will not mention this to Inspector Martine since I am guilty of petty theft." As his friend gazed at him in amazement, Holmes continued: "I am more than a little interested in the fingerprints of our fat master mason."

At the Louvre, Holmes and Watson found Achille Martine awaiting their return. With him was a uniformed policeman whom he introduced as Sergeant Boney.

"The sergeant, along with two gendarmes, were present all the time that the repair group were inside the Louvre," he explained. "Oh," continued the inspector, "your pictures will be delivered shortly, M'sieu Holmes." Turning to his fellow policeman, his tone became stern. "M'sieu Holmes has important thoughts to contribute to this great mystery. You are to answer all of his questions to the very best of your ability."

The sergeant simply nodded. He was a dark-complexioned, fairly tall young man with a rangey grace of movement. " 'Gascogne', I'll wager," thought Doctor Watson.

Holmes offered Boney a cigarette from the gold case with the great amethyst embedded in its cover, which had been a gift from the King of Bohemia. As the sergeant lit both their cigarettes with a wooden match, Holmes began his questioning.

"There were four workmen employed on the job?"

"Plus their boss, Dancoeux."

"And it took two days?"

"In time, M'sieu Holmes, but not consecutively."

"Perhaps you had best tell me what occurred from the beginning."

Boney drew deeply on his cigarette, then related his information in short, carefully-chosen sentences.

"Well-trained," thought Watson, "but then, he has told this story before."

"When the cracks in the pillars were first noticed, the *galerie* was immediately closed to the public. That afternoon, I was summoned with two men to — 'ow you say — augment the regular guards. Dancoeux arrived in the afternoon. With him was the manager of the Louvre. They studied the pillars for some time. What they discussed, I did not consider my business."

"No workman came with Dancoeux?"

"Not until the following morning, M'sieu."

"How did they come?" asked Holmes.

"By wagon. Dancoeux drove and one of his men sat beside him. The other three were in the back with their equipment."

"Continue, please," said Holmes, pleasantly.

"Dancoeux and his men brought two large ladders into the Louvre. I was present when the door to the *galeries* was unlocked to admit them. Also present was the manager and an architect." The policeman began to reach for his notebook. "His name was . . ."

". . . No matter," said Holmes quickly. "What happened then?"

"The ladders were placed beside the two pillars in question. The architect and Dancoeux took turns mounting them. They then conferred for a considerable period of time with the manager. Evidently, they were in agreement since Dancoeux chipped a small piece from one of the pillars. He took this outside to his wagon. Using a mason hammer, he reduced the sample to dust."

"Analyzing the composition of the cement, I suppose," said Holmes.

"I assumed so, M'sieu. Then he took a mixing box in which he placed cement and sand. Not a large amount. He then returned to the *galerie,* two of his men carrying the box and the other two bringing buckets of water."

"You got a good look at this box, I'm sure. What was its size?"

"In your English measurement, M'sieu, four feet long, and approximately the same depth."

"And the width?" asked Holmes.

"No more than two feet."

"Continue, please," said Holmes.

"Dancoeux mixed the cement and sand with some water. After sufficient time for the mixture to reach the desired consistency, Dancoeux applied some of it to one of the cracks. Evidently, he was not satisfied. He had his men take the mixing box back to the wagon. This time he put a considerable amount of ingredients into the box. It was carried back into the *galerie."*

"Somewhat heavier than before," suggested Watson.

"*Oui,* M'sieu. There was a handle on each end of the box and the men carrying it had to work."

"Somewhat like a coffin, indeed," mused Holmes. "Then what happened?"

"Evidently, Dancoeux had secured the blend he wished. He and his masons added water, troweled the mixture and began to apply it to the cracks in the pillars. That occupied them for the rest of the day."

Holmes gazed at Sergeant Boney intently. "They were never out of your sight?"

The policeman's answer was firm. "Not once during the entire time."

"And when the gallery door was closed and locked, you are certain that they all left? Dancoeux and all four workmen?" As Sergeant Boney began to bristle, Holmes answered himself. "But, of course, you are. You are a trained professional. Did they leave the ladders? And how about the mortar box which they used?"

"All left within the *galerie,* M'sieu. I was informed that they would return the following morning to check on how the mortar had hardened and to do any final patchwork necessary."

"Reasonable," said Holmes. He turned towards Watson as if ready to leave and then whirled back to the sergeant. "And the toolboxes, Boney? Did they take them or leave them in the gallery?"

The policeman's face was impassive. "Dancoeux did not have one, M'sieu

Holmes. He carried a trowel in his pocket. The four workmen each had a small tool box." A faint glint of triumph appeared in his deepset eyes. "And I inspected the contents of each toolbox as they left the *galerie.*"

"Touché," said Holmes. "You are most efficient, Sergeant. Not only in your duties to the Republic of France, but also in giving a clear account of what occurred. By the way, what happened the following morning?"

Boney's manner was friendlier. "I was here with my men before Dancoeux and the workmen arrived as was the manager. We unlocked the *galerie* and Dancoeux inspected the work done the previous day. Some rough edges were chiseled smooth. The mortar box was taken to the wagon and some ingredients placed within. It was returned, some more concrete was mixed, and the final touches added to the job. All of the men were there when the manager, M'sieu Larrileux, went into the adjacent room. There was a shout that could have been heard in Calais, or so it seemed. I was standing by the door when I heard him screaming that the Byzantine Crown was gone. I immediately shut the door. No one left the room. Within fifteen minutes there were twenty men from the Sûreté here. Everybody, including M'sieu Larrileux himself, was searched to the skin. Every piece of equipment was searched. The *galerie* itself was gone over — 'ow you say? — like a fine-tooth comb. Not so much as a pin could have been hidden there."

"And the adjacent room?"

"The same, M'sieu." The sergeant sighed. "I trust this is what you wished to know."

"You have given me a very complete picture," said Holmes, with approval.

"I am glad someone has something." For the first time a faint hint of a smile appeared on his gloomy features. "All I have, M'sieu, is a nightmare. A crime which could not happen."

At this moment, Achille Martine reappeared with a package which he handed to Holmes. A wave of his hand dismissed Sergeant Boney who retreated out of earshot.

"Here are the photographs you requested, M'sieu Holmes," said the inspector.

"My thanks," said the Baker Street sleuth. "Boney has been very helpful. He is extremely efficient."

"My thought also, M'sieu," replied Martine with alacrity. "As he undoubtedly told you, the manager, Larrileux, discovered the crime. Boney acted with great presence of mind. He shut the *galerie* door and ordered everyone to remain exactly where they were until I arrived with the first squad of men."

"About Larrileux," asked Holmes, "what were his actions when he discovered that the crown of Theodora was missing?"

"Evidently, he was in shock. He came running into the *galerie* shouting that it was gone — disappeared."

"Then he did not search for it?"

"Boney would not let him. He had one of his gendarmes telephone headquarters and refused to let anyone move until our arrival, as I just said."

"Then Larrileux did not touch the glass case," persisted Holmes.

"Only I touched the case," replied Martine. "I removed it so that I could inspect the pedestal on which the crown formerly rested. At the time I had some wild thought that the crown could have been taken and secreted within the pedestal. My search was fruitless, naturally. How could this have possibly been done?"

"It wasn't a bad idea," said Holmes.

Martine was reticent as he advanced another thought. "M'sieu Holmes, I have great respect for your talents, as has the Republic of France. But, perhaps, I can save you valuable time. You know as well as I that Alphonse Bertillon of the Sûreté evolved the most brilliant invention of this century in the field of criminology when he developed Bertillonage. As Director of the Police Identification Service, he has made the identification of criminals an exact science. Naturally, in this case, our first suspects were Dancoeux and his workmen. The mason may or may not have told you but he and his men were all measured and photographed by specialists in Bertillonage. They do not have criminal records. Anthropometry is infallible."

"We all have our own methods, Inspector," replied Holmes. "However, what I have in mind will certainly not require a night's work. If you are still of a mind to have that bridge match, Doctor Watson and I are at your disposal."

The Frenchman's face was immediately wreathed in a broad smile.

"*Magnifique!* I shall phone Le Club Bridgeur immediately. I happen to know that Signorina Poluffo and Henri Sarque are available. Would eight o'clock be convenient? That would give us time for a number of rubbers."

When Holmes and Watson found themselves back in their rooms at the Hotel Étrangère, they were not only facing a baffling criminal case but a bridge match as well. While in modern times such conflicts are commonplace, there is every reason to believe that the Holmes-Watson contest against Poluffo-Sarque was the first International Bridge Match.

However, Holmes seemed little disposed to discuss the upcoming game. Instead, he busied himself with various items which he had collected during the day. The letter-opener of master mason Dancoeux was placed on the desk of the hotel room along with the pay envelopes of Dancoeux's employees. Next the package of pictures taken by Holmes and developed by the photographic department of the Sûreté joined them. Watson noted that Holmes undid the package with care, preserving it to place alongside the other items. Then, with a strong light on the desk, the detective went to work with his pocket glass, chatting with Watson as he studied his clues. Watson was bubbling with questions, naturally,

"I say, Holmes, what was that chap, Martine, referring to when he mentioned 'Anthropometry'? Surely, he wasn't mispronouncing 'anthropology'?"

Holmes lowered his magnifying glass for a moment to indulge in a hearty laugh.

"No, he wasn't, but your thought strikes close to truth. It was but a decade ago that Alphonse Bertillon first joined the Paris police." (This further confirms the date of this adventure as 1889 since Bertillon became an assistant clerk in the Prefecture of Police in Paris in March, 1879.) "He is the son of Dr. Louis Adolphe Bertillon, Vice-President of the Anthropological Society of Paris. The Bertillons are one of the most distinguished scientific families in the world. Anthropometry is but another word for Bertillonage, a system of criminal identification developed by young Bertillon and used by the Sûreté and the other leading criminal investigation departments of the world."

Holmes was peering closely at the package which had contained the photographs and now returned to several of the pictures. "I believe I've isolated Martine's prints, Watson. They show up quite clearly on the pictures of the glass case and correspond with prints on the package he gave me."

"Does this have anything to do with Bertillonage?" asked Watson.

"Not really," replied Holmes. "When Eugène Francois Vidocq organized the

Sûreté in 1810, he instigated a system of records of known criminals. But they were sketchy indeed — based on whether the individual was tall or short and listing various scars, characteristics, etc. This system of records continued until Bertillon arrived on the scene. He did come from surroundings where anthropology was the leading topic of conversation. It took a man of his background to realize that a culprit can change his hair color, expressions, appearance, but his skeletal measurements are a constant."

Holmes was now studying the pictures intently.

"Don't stop there, Holmes," pleaded Watson. "I find this fascinating."

"Alphonse Bertillon began measuring convicts. Their height, the circumference of their heads, the length of their arms, fingers, feet. Finally, he wrote a report which caused a sensation eventually. A hypothetical case might best explain his discovery. Say, the Paris police are searching for a known criminal. In Marseilles, there is a man who could be the criminal in question. Bertillon proved that if fourteen basic measurements of the man in Marseilles corresponded to those of the Parisian criminal, the odds were better than a quarter of a million to one that he was, indeed, the man. Prior to Bertillon's discoveries, identification of criminals had been a hit-and-miss affair. He brought science to the problem. He also instigated the practice of taking not only full face but profile pictures as well of suspects. To crown his triumphs, Bertillon developed a method of cataloging the measurements so that any individual file card can be found within minutes. Bertillonage has swept the world and is even used in such far off places as the United States and South America."

Sherlock lowered his magnifying glass for a moment, gazing into space.

"However, I feel that Alphonse Bertillon and his identification system are at their zenith now. Some changes are due and soon." (Holmes missed the mark slightly here. The height of Bertillon's popularity occurred in 1892 when he was able to solve the Ravachol Case. For this feat, he won the Legion of Honor and his name became a household word.)

The sleuth was now studying the pay envelopes.

Watson was capable of some deduction, too. "Holmes, if you think the Bertillon system is on its way out, I must assume that you feel that fingerprints will replace it."

"How right you are, my dear Watson. There is nothing new about fingerprints really. In 1857 a British administrative officer in Bengal, India, first came up with the idea of using fingerprints as a method of identification. One of his duties involved the payment of allowances and pensions to natives. Because of their similarity of coloration and clothing, one Indian looks pretty much like another to an Anglo-Saxon, and Sir William James Herschel was plagued with forgeries and false claimants. He evolved the idea of having the genuine claimant place his thumbprint on the payroll list. When an Indian came to collect the due money, Sir William would look at the thumbprint under a magnifying glass, as I am doing now. If the claimant was an imposter he was quickly detected, since his thumbprint did not coincide. The forgeries were eliminated from Bengal quickly. Sir William's idea worked so well that he did not continue investigations along this line. The natives of Bengal are highly superstitious and felt there was 'magic' associated with their thumbprints. However, an idea had been born and it captured the attention of Sir Frances Galton in the 1860's. One Edward Henry, also in service in India, became fascinated with the theory of fingerprints as well. They are both working on a method of classifying fingerprints, a problem that has not been solved as yet. But it will, Watson, it will be. Once the English bulldog gets its teeth implanted, it seldom lets go."

Holmes could be quite nationalistic on occasion. He leaned back from the desk as though finished with his work.

"This much is known. Everyone's fingerprints are different and they will not change in a lifetime. If your fingers, Watson, suffered a severe burn, your prints would grow back into the same telltale design."

"Truly fascinating," breathed Watson. He indicated the various items that Holmes had been studying. "The glass case which surrounded the crown of the Empress Theodora was cleaned nightly. I recall your establishing that fact. Holmes, I have reached a conclusion!"

"Please elucidate, my dear Watson."

"You have found Inspector Martine's prints on the glass case. He did say that he handled it after the robbery. And you have found other prints."

Holmes nodded. "Only one that was not smudged but it is an excellent thumb print."

"Therefore," continued Watson, pleased as punch, "you have been comparing that print with the finger prints of Dancoeux taken from his letter-opener and the finger-prints of his workmen which must have been on their pay envelopes. Which one matches, Holmes?"

"None of them does," responded the detective. "Our little conversation regarding identification methods has allowed me to conceal my immense surprise. From the size of the unidentified thumb print, Watson, I can only deduce that the unknown person, who we can reasonably assume to be the thief, happens to be a woman."

Watson was thunderstruck. "But Holmes, how could this woman have gotten into the Louvre?"

"I wish I knew, Watson," confessed Holmes, frankly. "If you should arrive at any further conclusions, please make me privy to them. For the moment, I am up the proverbial tree."

Frequently, Holmes, when baffled, chose to drop a case mentally and await the coming of inspiration. Such seemed his inclination at this time, so the mystifying affair of the Louvre robbery was abandoned conversationally. Watson and Holmes dressed formally, well knowing that the French were not only dedicated to bridge, but quite decorous. They dined in a small restaurant that Holmes knew of and arrived at the appointed time at Le Club Bridgeur. Their reception was of such enthusiasm that it even surprised as cool a hand as Holmes. Evidently, the fame of the Challenge Match was greater than he and Watson had considered possible. The club itself was furnished in a luxurious manner and crowded by bejeweled ladies and gentlemen resplendent with decorations from many lands. Of course, the fame of the British pair was the spark of the occasion but the reputations of their adversaries was no little thing. Vittoria Poluffo was a striking brunette in a low-cut gown of blue, a color which she always wore when playing bridge. The Signorina was acknowledged as the leading female player of the day and was the "Capitana" of the "Signorinas Azzurra," the all-female bridge team of Italy which had swept everything before it. Henri Sarque was known as France's iron man of bridge. Holmes and Watson were facing a real challenge. While the attitude of the crowd of onlookers was most cordial regarding the Englishmen, the general sentiment was, naturally, strongly with the Continental pair. Immediately prior to a short discussion of systems and the beginning of play, Holmes had a quick word in private with his partner.

"My dear Watson, we do have an advantage in that we have played together so consistently. I feel we should make all possible use of this fact and attempt to get off to a fast start. Both of our adversaries are at the peak of their games and the honor of England is at stake."

"Stout fellow," responded Watson warmly. "We shall attack!"

And attack they did.

THE LEGEND

HOLMES
♠ 10
♡ A Q J 4
♢ J 10 6 4
♣ A 8 7 5

SARQUE
♠ Q 7 5 4
♡ K 10 3
♢ 9 7
♣ Q 9 6 4

POLUFFO (Dealer)
♠ A K J 8 3
♡ 8 5
♢ A K
♣ K J 10 3

WATSON
♠ 9 6 2
♡ 9 7 6 2
♢ Q 8 5 3 2
♣ 2

Neither side vulnerable.

Sarque	Holmes	Poluffo	Watson
-	-	1S	pass
2S	pass	4S	pass
pass	pass		

The final contract appears automatic but it was not at the table. Signorina Poluffo was an aggressive player. Her hand was very strong and while her partner denied more than ten points with his simple raise, the thought of a slam attempt did cross her mind. With her five-card suit supported, she possessed 22 points. She had played and made 31 and 32 point slams before. However, it being the first hand, Vittoria decided to settle for an apparently safe game. Vulnerable, she and her partner would have the Englishmen under pressure. The famous female player's decision proved wise and her play at the first trick was brilliant.

On lead, Watson, with very scanty values indeed, was uncomfortable. He and Holmes were dedicated to short suit leads when the player on lead had trump control. However, the doctor remembered his final words to Holmes: "We shall attack!" He came out with the club-2. When Sarque exposed his hand, Vittoria was glad she had settled for game being off two aces. However, with 30 combined points, she felt assured of making her contract. This comfortable feeling did not dull her play technique, however. When Holmes played his club ace, the Italian lady smoothly played her club king. The play cost her nothing. With the club queen in dummy, her jack-ten of the suit were equal to the king but it was a tribute to her table presence that she made the play so effortlessly. There was a surreptitious exchange of wise looks between certain kibitzers.

As Holmes gathered in the trick, his mind was analyzing the situation. Watson might well have led from four clubs to the jack-ten and, considering dummy, a diamond shift looked appealing. But, thought the great detective, if the declarer held a singleton club, her hand must be highly distributional. Might she not have mentioned another suit on her way to game? Holmes chose to return the club suit and selected the club-8 to indicate that he could stand a return of the higher ranking of the two outside suits. Watson trumped the trick with the spade-6 beginning a trump echo to indicate three cards in the suit. Following his partner's signal, Watson played the heart-9. Signorina Poluffo was now feeling the chill wind of fate. She rose with dummy's heart king which Holmes captured with his ace. Back came a club which Watson trumped with the spade-2. Watson played the heart-7 and declarer helplessly watched Holmes capture the trick with his heart jack. Knowing Watson to hold three spade cards, Holmes did not attempt to cash his high heart but again played a club which Watson ruffed.

There was complete silence in the room. The Poluffo-Sarque cards had appeared invincible and yet this English team had defeated what, at first glance, had seemed like a cold game by three tricks. A legend was born at that moment about the infallibility of the Holmes-Watson team. Britain had gotten off to a very fast start indeed.

The tide of battle flowed at a fairly even rate for some time but Holmes was desirous of keeping the pressure on his opponents. His opportunity came in the following hand when the British lion struck again.

THE CONFIRMED FIT

HOLMES
♠ void
♡ A J 10 4 2
♢ A 8 7 2
♣ Q J 10 3

SARQUE (Dealer
♠ A J 9 5 4 2
♡ K 6
♢ K 10 4
♣ A 7

POLUFFO
♠ K 10 7 6 3
♡ 8
♢ Q J 6 3
♣ 8 6 2

WATSON
♠ Q 8
♡ Q 9 7 5 3
♢ 9 5
♣ K 9 5 4

Poluffo-Sarque vulnerable.

Sarque	Holmes	Poluffo	Watson
1S	dbl.	3S	pass
4S	dbl.	pass	5H
pass	pass	pass	

Henri Sarque's opening bid was made on a strong hand and Holmes' take-out double could boast the most perfect distribution for the bid possible. Vittoria Poluffo now jumped in her partner's suit. Her bid showed excellent support but denied strength since she might well have redoubled with more in high cards. Even though Henri Sarque knew his opponents' principal strength was on the wrong side for him, his partner's trump support had increased the value of his hand considerably. He went to four spades. Holmes doubled again on the theory that Sarque and Poluffo had an excellent fit in spades which made it a certainty that he and Watson had a fitting suit somewhere. The bid was co-operative in nature but the great sleuth was hoping his partner would bid. Watson, firmly dedicated to the attack theory, entered the bidding for the first time with a call of five hearts. Now the great French player showed his skill. His heart honor was badly placed and his spade ace was a dubious winner on the bidding. Rather than double in pique, he calmly passed as did his partner.

Sarque chose to lead his spade ace expecting it to be trumped but feeling that the lead would give nothing away.

When Holmes' hand came down, Watson promptly isolated his problem. A club he woud lose and a diamond as well. If the trump finesse succeeded, or if Sarque held a singleton king, the hand would make. Watson trumped in dummy and played Holmes' diamond ace. He then played a low diamond from dummy to force an entry into his hand. Vittoria Poluffo played her diamond jack and Watson his last diamond. Now Sarque was thinking. Things looked bad. But there was the possibility that his partner held the club king. Sarque overtook Vittoria's diamond jack with his king and played his club ace which won. He then led his last club but Watson captured the trick in the closed hand. Down came the heart queen. Sarque smoothly played low but Watson let his red lady ride. With the finesse succeeding, he drew the one outstanding trump and claimed.

"You are a daring bidder, Mr. Holmes," commented Vittoria Poluffo.

"Or a timid player," responded Holmes.

As any afficionado knows, Holmes' distrust of females dated back to the Irene Adler affair. However, he had a deft hand for diplomacy when he felt called upon to use it

"Against a player of M'sieu Sarque's calibre, or yours, Signorina, I was quite certain that four spades would make. And it would have," he added.

The Continental team must have felt disappointed at the turn of events. But they grimly fought back. It was five hands later that they became, as Sarque later stated, *"tres desolé"*.

THE DEADLY CONTROL

HOLMES (Dealer)
♠ 3
♡ A 4 2
♢ 9 8 6 4 2
♣ A 9 7 5

SARQUE
♠ A Q 6
♡ Q 8 3
♢ Q J 7 3
♣ J 10 6

POLUFFO
♠ 9 5 2
♡ K J 10 9 7 5
♢ A K
♣ 3 2

WATSON
♠ K J 10 8 7 4
♡ 6
♢ 10 5
♣ K Q 8 4

Poluffo-Sarque vulnerable.

Sarque	Holmes	Poluffo	Watson
-	pass	1H	2S
2NT	pass	3H	pass
4H	pass	pass	pass

Vittoria Poluffo's opening was minimum but her suit gave her comfort. Watson now unveiled the weak jump overcall used by the English partnership at this time. Sarque chose to best describe his hand and his spade stoppers by bidding two notrump. Vittoria rebid her long suit and Sarque went to game on his considerable values.

Doctor Watson chose the club king as his opening lead. Vittoria felt secure. Her two-club losers were inevitable and she would certainly lose the trump ace. However, the remainder of the tricks seemed to belong to her and she had two excellent diamonds in dummy for discards once trump was drawn. But Holmes, surveying dummy, had other ideas. Can you see what he was thinking of?

When Signorina Poluffo played dummy's club six on the opening lead, Holmes overtook his partner's king with his own club ace. It was at this moment that Bertram Jabot Beckerié, the great French bridge journalist of Le Roi Features Syndicate murmured *"magnifique"* to himself. Holmes now returned the spade three, a play which almost drew a gasp from the kibitzers surrounding the table. Suddenly, Vittoria's heart sank. Holmes was too good to voluntarily give her a free finesse in spades without some sinister idea involving her contract. She captured Watson's king of spades with dummy's ace and led a small trump from the board. Now Holmes unleashed his deadly defense. He rose with the trump ace and then played his club-9 to Watson's known club queen. The club-nine indicated no interest in the suit but Watson did not need this signal to perceive what his partner was doing. Taking the club lead, Watson returned the spade jack which Vittoria covered with dummy's queen only to see Holmes trump it for the setting trick. Another apparently secure contract had fallen before the Challenge Match team.

The spirit of the Continentals seemed destined to receive one crushing blow after another. They fought hard, they scored games but rubbers eluded them with frustrating consistency. As sometimes happens, a number of similar hands were dealt that night.

Holmes and Watson in Paris.

189

WATSON'S MOMENT

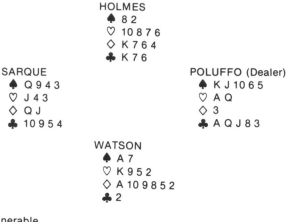

HOLMES
♠ 8 2
♡ 10 8 7 6
◇ K 7 6 4
♣ K 7 6

SARQUE
♠ Q 9 4 3
♡ J 4 3
◇ Q J
♣ 10 9 5 4

POLUFFO (Dealer)
♠ K J 10 6 5
♡ A Q
◇ 3
♣ A Q J 8 3

WATSON
♠ A 7
♡ K 9 5 2
◇ A 10 9 8 5 2
♣ 2

Poluffo-Sarque vulnerable.

Sarque	Holmes	Poluffo	Watson
-	-	1C	1D
pass	2D	2S	3D
3S	pass	4S	dbl.
pass	pass	pass	

Again the Continentals had scored a game and again Vittoria Poluffo had been dealt superior values. As she opened one club she wondered what could go wrong with this hand. Watson overcalled a diamond with his six-card-suit and good values. The moment Watson bid, the table-wise Sarque deducted the values of his doubleton queen-jack of diamonds. He passed and Holmes raised his partner's overcall. Now Vittoria came in with her spade suit. Watson competed with three diamonds and, having passed originally, Sarque now showed his support for his partner's second bid suit by bidding three spades. Holmes passed and Signorina Poluffo, knowing her partner promised four spades, drove to game. Watson, surveying his hand, could reasonably expect one diamond trick though that was not certain on the bidding. His spade ace was a certainty and the heart king looked like another winner. But he envisioned a setting trick and made a daring penalty double. Do you see what Watson had in mind?

The good doctor led the club two. Dummy's club nine forced Holmes' king which was captured by Vittoria's ace. The Italian star led her spade king which Watson took. He now underled his diamond ace counting on Holmes to hold the king which, fortunately, he did. Back came a club which Watson trumped. The good doctor got off lead with the diamond ace, trumped by declarer. Now Vittoria could dispose of one of dummy's hearts on her long clubs but not two. She was forced to try the heart finesse after drawing trumps and running the clubs. It failed, as she expected it would, and the contract was defeated. The female player shook her head in despair. It was her French partner who voiced what she was thinking.

"Ze trump control — c'est la mort!"

By now Holmes-Watson had built up an awesome lead but there was still a sting left in the Continental champions.

ROMAN REVENGE

HOLMES (Dealer)
♠ K J 7
♡ K 6 4
◇ A 9 8 3
♣ K Q J

SARQUE
♠ 8 6 5
♡ 2
◇ Q J 6 4
♣ 9 8 7 3 2

POLUFFO
♠ A 3
♡ A Q J 10 9 5
◇ 10 5 2
♣ A 6

WATSON
♠ Q 10 9 4 2
♡ 8 7 3
◇ K 7
♣ 10 5 4

Holmes-Watson vulnerable.

Sarque	Holmes	Poluffo	Watson
	1NT	dbl.	2S
pass	pass	pass	

After Holmes' opening notrump, Vittoria Poluffo could count seven tricks with an easily establishable suit and two prime entry cards. She had the contract down in her own hand and doubled. Watson promptly ran to two spades. Sarque passed. Holmes recognized his partner's bid as a rescue and passed. Now Vittoria did not dare double and wondered if she should have just passed originally. Watson later assured her he would have bid two spades in any case. The great Italian player wisely chose to let the contract stand. A three heart bid by her at this point could have proved somewhat costly.

Sarque led his singleton heart. Watson played low from dummy and Vittoria took the trick with her nine. Now she did some counting. Her heart ace followed by a heart ruff by Sarque would provide three tricks. Her black aces would run the total to five but that was not enough. Remembering, with agonizing clarity, the murderous defense she had faced all evening, Vittoria was now able to exact some Roman revenge! She played her club ace and then her second club, taken in dummy. When Watson led a spade off the board, Vittoria took her trump ace. Now she played her heart ace and then the heart five. Sarque trumped the trick and returned a club which Vittoria trumped. The contract was down and there was a round of applause

191

from the spectators and compliments from both Holmes and Watson. Triumph, alas, came too late for the Continental stars as their English opponents were far ahead and kept adding to the margin. It seemed that the Challenge Match Team could do no wrong on this particular evening.

The following hand was automatic in both bidding and play. Holmes had but one road to follow and he spied it promptly as will my good readers. It is only included because of its effect in fields other than bridge.

THE WEE ONE

```
                        HOLMES
                        ♠ Q 10 4
                        ♡ A 5
                        ◇ A 9 8 3
                        ♣ A Q J 10
      SARQUE (Dealer)                      POLUFFO
      ♠ K 7 6 2                            ♠ A 9 5
      ♡ K 7 4                              ♡ J 10 9 6 3 2
      ◇ 10 5                               ◇ J 7 6
      ♣ K 9 7 4                            ♣ 8
                        WATSON
                        ♠ J 8 3
                        ♡ Q 8
                        ◇ K Q 4 2
                        ♣ 6 5 3 2
```

Holmes-Watson vulnerable.

Sarque	Holmes	Poluffo	Watson
pass	1NT	pass	2NT
pass	3NT	pass	pass
pass			

Holmes' opening notrump was standard. Watson, with eight points, invited game and Holmes accepted. Vittoria Poluffo made the obvious lead of her heart jack.

Holmes figured it was now or never with dummy's queen which he played. Unfortunately, Sarque was able to top the fair lady with his king and Holmes did not even duck but took the trick with his ace. He realized that the contract depended on the club suit and the finesse, if it lost, would lose to Vittoria. The opponents had struck at his weakest spot so everything depended on bringing in the black minor. Holmes played his diamond ace at the second trick. He then carefully led his diamond nine to dummy's king. In dummy, he led a club playing the ten from his hand. When the trick held, he led his diamond eight to Watson's queen. Again a club was played from dummy. When Sarque played low, Holmes took the trick with his club jack. Now his carefully preserved diamond three was led to Watson's four. Another club lead was won by Holmes' queen and his club ace felled Sarque's king and provided the game going trick. Holmes had run home with the contract.

Vittoria Poluffo had a comment. "Actually, Signor Holmes, the diamond four in Doctor Watson's hand was the most important card."

"Exactly, Signorina," responded the great detective. "My diamond three, a small card, was vital."

Suddenly, his expression changed. His eyes grew opaque for a moment and then sharpened and transferred themselves to his partner.

"A small card, Watson, and a small man."

The match was over and it was a smashing victory for Britain. Holmes gracefully accepted the praise heaped upon him and his partner by the admiring onlookers but Watson, who could sense his mood so well, knew that the sleuth was suddenly impatient to leave.

Champagne was being served and the glittering gathering of bridge fanciers were striving to conceal their disappointment. The only kibitzer whose disposition had been sweetened by the English victory was Achille Martine. Since it was the Sûreté Inspector who had secured the Challenge Match Champions and made the entire affair possible, the Holmes-Watson victory added luster to his star in Le Club Bridgeur firmament. As Martine pressed glasses of champagne into Holmes' and Watson's hands, he was as effervescent as the wine. The *non sequitor* which came his way from the English detective must have seemed strange.

"M'sieu Martine, do you by chance have a circus performing in Paris at the moment?"

"Circus, M'sieu? But yes. There is a small one playing at the Arena Royale." The Frenchman indicated their surroundings. "Surely, M'sieu Holmes, the club does not remind — !"

Holmes allowed him to go no further. " — Not at all, my dear sir. Doctor Watson just happens to be a fancier of the tanbark rings, the equestrians and clowns."

Martine was mollified. "Anyone who can play bridge like your esteemed partner can amuse himself with toy trains as far as I'm concerned."

Watson, who had been regarding Holmes with an amazed expression beamed The Baker Street sleuth now made excuses for them both, promised to contact Martine on the morrow and, finally, he and Watson were able to effect an exit from Le Club Bridgeur.

As they returned to their hotel, Watson's puzzlement found expression.

"My dear Holmes, I have heard you come up with some strange statements through the years but you know jolly well that I haven't been to a circus since I was a small boy."

"An oversight which we shall remedy tomorrow, Watson," said Holmes, with a wise smile. "Unless, of course, you can suggest a better place to find a very small man."

It was early the following day when Watson found himself, along with his famous friend, at the Arena Royale. "The Raoul Brothers Circus" was lauded to the sky by posters festooned around the arena. These captured Holmes' attention and he found what he was looking for in a billboard advertising the side show. Watson had a clearer view of what his friend was after when he read the title of one of the attractions. "David and Goliath, the Amazing Opposites. The World's Smallest and Largest Man."

"Well, you are looking for a tiny man," he said.

Holmes nodded and then, noting an attendant entering the box office, sprinted away from Watson, his long legs covering ground rapidly. The detective engaged the stranger in a brief conversation and then strolled back to Watson. Evidently, he had received directions since he took the doctor by the arm and directed their progress to an adjacent lot which, at the moment, served as a parking place for a number of wagons of varied sizes. Apparently, the Raoul Brothers Circus travelled by horse rather than rail since the wagons were all plastered with circus posters.

A short time later, the Englishmen were standing beside one fairly small wagon which resembled a house on wheels. A rap at the entry door in the rear drew no response.

"Possibly out for breakfast or practicing their act in the arena," suggested Watson.

With a quick look around them, Holmes tried the door handle which turned easily. Opening the door, the detective hopped quickly into the wagon interior indicating for Watson to follow him. Closing the door behind Watson, Holmes located an oil lamp which he lit. The interior did resemble a small house or, at least, a room of one. There was a tiny bed in one corner. Against a wall, neatly rolled up, was a long bed roll. Evidently, bunks, sizeable enough to accommodate Goliath, were not available and the giant slept on the bedroll on the floor. One portion of the interior served as a kitchen and it was here that Holmes fastened his attention. Going over utensils with his magnifying glass, a cup finally drew a sound of approval from him.

"Here we have it, Watson," he said.

He crossed to the oil lamp and raised the flame for more light. Holding the cup close to the lamp, he surveyed one portion again with his glass for a considerable period of time. Finally, his keen features relaxed into a smile of satisfaction.

"I carefully memorized the central papillary ridges of the mysterious imprint we found in the Louvre. The print on this cup corresponds with it in every way. We've found our man, Watson."

The entrance door suddenly opened and there was a shrill cry.

" 'Ere now, and 'oo be you?"

Whirling around, Watson located the source of the irate voice standing just outside the wagon. It was a tiny man whose height was that of a pre-teen child but whose features were those of an adult.

"Well, now," said Holmes crossing to the door and jumping to the ground outside. "Haven't they got those posters wrong?"

As Watson joined his friend outside the wagon, Holmes continued, indicating the midget.

"Watson, let me present Wee Willie." Holmes had a grim look. "You are a bit of a distance from your old haunts, Willie, which last included Dartmoor, as I recall."

" 'Olmes!" breathed the midget, as recognition reluctantly forced itself into his eyes.

Suddenly, the tiny man seemed even smaller to Watson. Around the corner of the wagon came certainly the largest man the doctor had ever seen. He was a full eight feet in height. Watson immediately diagnosed his amazing size to excessive secretion of the pituitary gland but then had a second thought. The man's body was in complete proportion to his height. His shoulders were like the proverbial barn door. His hands, dangling from massive arms, resembled two hams. He was truly a giant.

Wee Willie

The arrival of his friend dispelled the fright which had infiltrated the midget's eyes.

"You're a bit off the 'ol path yerself, 'Olmes," he stated, "An' wotcha doin' nosin' round our wagon?" He didn't wait for an answer but turned to his co-worker. "Goliath, this 'ere's that bleedin' detective, Sherlock 'Olmes, wot I tol' yer about. Jus' maybe 'im and 'is friend, Watson, shouldn't be round 'ere."

There was a low semi-growl from the giant who started towards the Baker Street duo.

"A moment, said Holmes, sharply. His steely glance stopped even this man-mountain in his tracks. Holmes transferred his gaze to the midget and shook his head. "You are just whistling down the wind, Wee Willie. I know you pulled the Louvre robbery and I know how you did it. You made just one tiny mistake, but it was a fatal one."

"What him talk about?"

Watson could not identify the giant's dialect but guessed that it was probably of the Urals.

The midget was regarding Holmes keenly.

" 'E don't just talk fer the sound. I'll give 'im that. If 'Olmes says 'e's gotcha, you been 'ad."

Suddenly, Wee Willie reached a decision. Skipping nimbly around Holmes and Watson, he jumped into the interior of the wagon screaming: "Grab 'em! Goliath!"

195

As the giant surged towards Holmes and Watson, there was suddenly a fourth presence on the scene. It was the seemingly plump figure of Wakefield Orloff. There was a peculiar hissing sound and a black object flashed past Watson's head. It was Orloff's bowler hat spinning towards its mark. The rigid, steel-reinforced rim of the hat crashed into the forehead of the giant and brought him to a jarring halt. A glazed look appeared in Goliath's eyes and his figure reeled for a moment. Orloff flowed past Watson right behind his hat. The man's speed was unbelievable but each step seemed timed like a Rugby player approaching the ball. His right foot swung up and his steel-shod toe smashed into the knee-cap of the giant. The sound of crunching bone made Watson wince. Before a groan had time to climb from Goliath's slack mouth, Orloff's left leg swung in a vicious arc and his toe into the giant's other kneecap. The huge man started to crumble as Orloff seemed to float into the air with the supreme grace of a ballet master. Both heels of his deadly shoes drove into the falling giant's jaw in a *La Savate* move. The ground shook as the giant fell unconscious.

Like a cat, Orloff whirled around. Wee Willie's tiny figure appeared at the door to the wagon. In both hands he was holding a strange-looking gun which he tried to bring to bear on Holmes. Orloff's right hand flashed behind his head to the vicinity of his shoulder blades and then swung forward again. The sun glistened briefly on the polished blade of a Spanish throwing knife which thudded into the shoulder of the midget. With a strangled gasp, the tiny man dropped the gun and promptly fainted. Holmes caught his body, as it tumbled from the wagon, and gently laid it on the ground.

The whirl of events had been a matter of seconds and yet Watson's and Holmes' lives had been in danger twice and two assailants, now inert, lay helplessly on the ground.

Stunned by the sudden and breathless action, Watson gazed at the deceptively squat figure of the Security Agent.

"Orloff," he stammered, "where in the name of heaven did you come from?"

A thin smile creased Holmes' features. "He has been with us right along. On the Channel boat, Wakefield was an aged man with a snowy white beard and a cane. At the Hotel Étrangère he was most impressive as a buxom dowager duchess with a lorgnette. However," said Holmes with genuine admiration, "I do believe your impersonation of a Polish Count at Le Club Bridgeur was a high point. Did the monocle give you any trouble?"

"A little," responded Orloff. "So you knew that I was dogging your footsteps right along."

"My dear chap," responded the great detective, "I was counting on it."

It was at this moment that Holmes made a friend for life. The fact that he had walked into the proverbial lion's den in his search for Wee Willie with the complete confidence that the Security Agent would be available at the right place and time was a supreme compliment which could not go unnoticed by a mind as acute as Wakefield Orloff's. The agent's fathomless green eyes, for a brief moment, kindled with a warmth completely foreign to them.

The next half hour surged through Watson's mind in kaleidoscope fashion. Inspector Martine and a squad of Sûreté men were summoned. Goliath and Wee Willie were removed from the scene in a police ambulance. Suddenly, Watson found himself back in the suite of rooms in the Hotel Étrangère. Holmes was displaying the gun that

Wee Willie had attempted to use to Achille Martine and Wakefield Orloff. The Security Agent was regarding the weapon with a puzzled expression.

"Air gun, of course," he said. "I've never seen anything quite like it."

"I agree, M'sieu," echoed Inspector Martine.

"Small wonder," replied Holmes. "I know of only two men capable of creating such a gun: Von Herder, the blind German mechanic who worked for Professor Moriarty is one, but Von Herder is dead. The other man is Straubenzee." Holmes' eyes swiveled to Watson. "You will recall that he was the gunsmith associated with Count Negretto Sylvius." As Watson nodded, the great detective back-tracked.

"But I get ahead of myself, gentlemen. Regarding the theft of the crown of Theodora, here are my conclusions: First, cracks very conveniently appeared in two pillars of the picture gallery. Those cracks may have been caused by a Straubenzee-designed device. Air guns are soundless. But that is of little importance. What is important is that, from the first, I was certain that Pierre Dancoeux and his masons were involved in the theft."

Before Inspector Martine could interject a thought, Holmes continued:

"I know. All of the masons were checked against the Sûreté's Bertillonage files. None of them had records and this was the work of a criminal gang, without a doubt. All right, Pierre Dancoeux is a Frenchman with no previous criminal association. However, I strongly suspect that his workmen are not French at all. I first got this idea when Doctor Watson and I went to Dancoeux's place of business. He knew we were coming. When we arrived, he told us that he had just paid his men their weekly wages. During the week and at mid-day? . . . a strange time for payment. Unless his masons were English and Dancoeux feared I might recognize one of them. Now, as you know I found a fingerprint on the glass case which had contained the crown. It was not of Dancoeux or any of his workmen, nor of you, Inspector Martine. And it was a peculiar fingerprint in that it was quite small. Momentarily, I considered that it might have been made by a woman. It was not until the final bridge hand at Le Club Bridgeur last night that the truth dawned on me. The fingerprint was that of a midget. This suddenly provided other answers. Specifically, how the crown was stolen. The robbery did seem impossible. The workmen were searched and constantly watched, their tool boxes searched, the picture gallery burglar-proof. However, you will recall that Dancoeux and his men used a mortar box. It was inspected as well. They mixed the mortar in their wagon and then took the mortar box within the Louvre. They repeated this action a number of times. The mortar box became familiar, accepted. It was a piece of necessary equipment. Here is what Dancoeux did:

"Toward the end of the day's work, they took the mortar box to their wagon and effected a switch. The box that they brought back was a different one. There was mortar in it but only in a top shelf. Underneath was Wee Willie, the midget. They finished for the day and departed, leaving their ladders and box. Everthing was checked and the doors were locked securely but the thief was already inside.

"During the night, Willie got out of the box and took the crown. He returned to his hiding place with his prize. Under the alert eyes of Sergeant Boney, the doors were opened the following morning. The mortar box was taken to Dancoeux's wagon and the switch was repeated. Now the theft was discovered but the genuine mortar box was back in the picture gallery. Willie and the crown of Theodora were in Dancoeux's wagon. Now I don't think Dancoeux has the crown or that he planned the robbery. He was the front man enticed into the scheme by promises of wealth. His workmen were imported. Willie was hired. The air gun we were so fortunate to find in Willie's possession gives us the clue to the brains of the scheme. The gun is the work of Straubenzee, without a doubt. He was involved with Count Negretto Sylvius who, in turn, was part of a criminal group headed by old Baron Dowson. Another member of Dowson's ring is a Dutch gem expert, Van Seddar."

"Oh-ho!" interjected Inspector Martine. "We know of him."

"And I rather imagine that it is he who has the crown. If you get him fast enough, I think you will find the crown intact."

The French policeman rose. "M'sieu Holmes, I shall not sleep until Van Seddar and the crown are in my hands."

"A moment," said the great sleuth. "Willie will talk to lighten his sentence. So will Van Seddar. The recovery of the crown is vital but Baron Dowson is also a prime target." Holmes' eyes were resting on Wakefield Orloff and a faint smile touched his lips. "If Inspector Martine can put pressure on Wee Willie, Van Seddar and Dancoeux, possibly Mr. Orloff via the prestige of his — er — Foreign Trade Department can apprehend and convict Baron Dowson, who is in England. I have had my eye on him for a long time."

There was a grim look in the green eyes of Wakefield Orloff that boded no good for the infamous Baron and his associates.

As far as Watson and Holmes were concerned, this was the end of the strange adventure of "The Mysterious Imprint." It was another of the crimes where Holmes found his solution at the bridge table which explains its inclusion in Doctor Watson's detailed 'Diary of the Challenge Match."

The Crown of Theodora, Empress of the Byzantines, was recovered and rests in the Louvre now. The criminal ring of Baron Dowson was captured and convicted. In fact, Baron Dowson was later hanged on evidence secured by Sherlock Holmes. (See: "The Adventure of the Mazarin Stone.") The giant Goliath died, though not as a result of the punishment inflicted upon him by the deadly Wakefield Orloff. As Watson explained to Holmes, the man's size was the result of an over-active pituitary gland. While his body had grown in proportion to his height, his heart had not. In cases like Goliath, the life expectancy is seldom over forty-five and the giant died of heart failure.

Certain other events occurred in connection with this case which might be of interest to *aficionados* of the great bridge-playing detective. For one thing, Holmes' theory regarding fingerprints was certainly vindicated. In 1892, Juan Vucetich of the Police Department of la Plata, Argentina, solved a murder and secured a conviction on the basis of a thumbprint. In 1896, the aforementioned Edward Henry worked out a fingerprint classification system which is in use today. The Henry system was adopted in British India in 1897 and by Scotland Yard in 1901.

Now the most amazing event: In 1911, the Mona Lisa was stolen from the Louvre. If the French had followed the technique of Sherlock Holmes and installed a finger-print classification system, the thief would have been identified in a few hours. The culprit, one Vincenzo Perrugia, had a criminal record and left his fingerprints at the scene of the crime. As it was, Perrugia was not arrested and the famous painting recovered until twenty-eight months after the theft.

Now a theory by your author. It is without proof, and is offered only as a suggestion since it may explain certain incidents and contradictions which have plagued Sherlockians and Holmesians for years.

As previously noted on several occasions, there can be little doubt that "The case of the Mysterious Imprint" occurred in 1889. At the beginning of the case history, Watson states that Holmes had just concluded an adventure dealing with the King of Scandinavia. Yet, according to Watson, "The Adventure of the Noble Bachelor" occurred in 1887 and in it Holmes tells Lord St. Simon that he had already had the King of Scandinavia as a client.

In the "Mysterious Imprint," Watson mentions the fact that Holmes had received the Legion of Honor for the Huret case. Yet in "The Adventure of the Golden Pince-Nez" he states that the arrest of Huret took place in 1894.

Holmes made note of Straubenzee and his association with Count Sylvius yet in "The Adventure of the Mazarin Stone" Holmes refers to previous crimes of the Count in 1892, placing the Mazarin affair post-92. Van Seddar and Baron Dowson were also mentioned in the Mazarin Stone case. These puzzling cross references have prompted the following thought: When Watson made available to the reading public of the world the four novels and fifty-six short stories dealing with the exploits of Sherlock Holmes, there was the problem of protecting the identity of certain individuals involved. It will be recalled that Watson never recounted "The Adventure of the Second Stain" until Holmes had retired from London and become involved in bee-farming on the Sussex Downs.

But no such problem existed with Watson's "Diary of the Challenge Match" which was, according to the terms of his will, to remain unavailable for better than fifty years. This seeming eccentricity can be explained away by a number of reasons with "The Hoax" and "The Adventure of The Soft Fingers" leading the list.

Therefore, your author is of the feeling that the dates in "The Diary of the Challenge Match" are accurate since there is no reason for them not to be. I suggest that Watson may have altered dates in certain of the stories which were made available during his and Holmes' lifetime simply to obscure the identity of participants. This security measure had no effect on Watson's masterful writings since it was what Holmes did that mattered, not when he did it.

A thought for the consideration of those legions of followers of the exploits of the greatest bridge playing detective of them all: Mr. Sherlock Holmes.

DEVYN PRESS INC.

3600 Chamberlain Lane, Suite 230, Louisville, KY 40241

1-800-274-2221

CALL TOLL FREE IN THE U.S. & CANADA TO ORDER OR TO REQUEST
OUR 64 PAGE FULL COLOR CATALOG OF BRIDGE BOOKS,
SUPPLIES AND GIFTS.